# DRUM CIRCLES FOR SPECIFIC POPULATION GROUPS

An Introduction to Drum Circles for Therapeutic and Educational Outcomes

Edited by **Simon Faulkner**

Jessica Kingsley Publishers
London and Philadelphia

First published in Great Britain in 2021 by Jessica Kingsley Publishers
An Hachette Company

2

Copyright © Jessica Kingsley Publishers 2021

Activities on pp.176–178 adapted with kind permission of Dave Holland.

Front cover images source: Shutterstock®.

All rights reserved. No part of this publication may be reproduced, stored in a retrieval system, or transmitted, in any form or by any means without the prior written permission of the publisher, nor be otherwise circulated in any form of binding or cover other than that in which it is published and without a similar condition being imposed on the subsequent purchaser.

All pages marked with ★ can be photocopied and downloaded for personal use with this program, but may not be reproduced for any other purposes without the permission of the publisher.

A CIP catalogue record for this title is available from the British Library and the Library of Congress

ISBN 978 1 78775 524 6
eISBN 978 1 78775 525 3

Printed and bound in the United States by Integrated Books International

Jessica Kingsley Publishers' policy is to use papers that are natural, renewable and recyclable products and made from wood grown in sustainable forests. The logging and manufacturing processes are expected to conform to the environmental regulations of the country of origin.

Jessica Kingsley Publishers
Carmelite House
50 Victoria Embankment
London EC4Y 0DZ

www.jkp.com

*by the same author*

**Rhythm to Recovery**
*A Practical Guide to Using Rhythmic Music, Voice and Movement for Social and Emotional Development*
ISBN 978 1 78592 132 2
eISBN 978 1 78450 397 0

*of related interest*

**Self-Expression through Art and Drumming**
*A Facilitator's Guide to Using Art Therapy to Enhance Drum Circles*
Jen Mank
ISBN 978 1 78592 715 7
eISBN 978 1 78450 310 9

**Group Music Activities for Adults with Intellectual and Developmental Disabilities**
*Maria Ramey*
ISBN 978 1 78592 993 9
eISBN 978 0 85700 434 5

**Music Therapy for Multisensory and Body Awareness in Children and Adults with Severe to Profound Multiple Disabilities**
*The MuSense Manual*
*Roberta S. Adler and Olga V. Samsonova-Jellison*
ISBN 978 1 78592 736 2
eISBN 978 1 78450 447 2

'If you use music in your work with groups, any group of any age to assist members with life improving experiences, you should read this compendium of knowledge and strategies for leading therapeutic community drum circles. A solid but concise foundation of research supporting benefits of expressive therapies is described and in conjunction with cognitive approaches. The specific group work skills for each population discussed by experienced professionals are in a format including important attributes, positive outcomes, setting up for success, common challenges, practical applications and exercises. This will be a treasured and practical addition to your recourses.'

– *Sheldon Braaten, PhD, Executive Director of Behavioral Institute for Children and Adolescents*

'Simon Faulkner offers a multitude of ideas for drum circle facilitators (DCFs) to share with the groups they serve. By first providing a foundation of scientific research on the benefits of group drumming, he and DCFs from around the world offer their extensive knowledge on the application of strategies in serving populations with physical and mental challenges, differing age groups and trauma-impacted groups. This rich evidence-based compendium is a welcome addition to the growing body of research on drumming for healing, bonding and creating community, and will be especially appreciated by music and occupational therapists, mental health professionals and educators.'

– *Tanice G. Foltz, PhD, professor of Sociology and Director of Women's and Gender Studies, Indiana University Northwest*

'Congratulations to Simon Faulkner and the authors of this new drum circle compendium. As a long-time theatre educator, professional school counsellor and educational consultant in Canada, I believe strongly in the power of the circle and artistic expression, including drumming and social-emotional development. I appreciate working within the circle as it is a great equalizer and it is respectful to Indigenous traditions, which is of key relevance to our school populations. This comprehensive book demonstrates that you do not have to be a musician, or musically inclined, and that exercises implementing self-discovery can be done through drum circles. Rhythm is within our breath, heartbeat, walk and talk. Using the drum as an external object to connect with the self and others is powerful and challenging while positive, and an excellent addition to the toolbox for educators and mental health supports.'

– *Mary Frances Fitzgerald, BEd, MEd, education consultant: health, wellness, diversity, executive: ATA Council of School Counsellors, sessional: Concordia University*

This book is dedicated to all the therapeutic practitioners
and community helpers who gave of themselves to
support those in need during the COVID-19 crisis,
and into the ongoing recovery period.

*'Words can never reach far enough into music to touch her essence.'*

Carolyn Kenny[1]

---

1  Kenny, C. (2006) *Music and Life in the Field of Play: An Anthology.* Dallas, TX: Barcelona Publishers, p.70.

# Contents

1. Introduction ................................ 9
2. Deepening Awareness through Cognitive Reflection ...... 19
3. A Somatic Approach ......................... 21
4. Group Dynamics and Group Skills ............... 23
5. Duty of Care ................................ 26
6. Evaluating Your Programs .................... 28
7. Pricing Your Work ........................... 30
8. Managing Challenging Behaviours .............. 31
9. Early Childhood ............................. 33
   *Mary Knysh & Lulu Leathley*
10. Youth ..................................... 45
    *Lucas Coffey*
11. Autism .................................... 59
    *Nellie Hill*
12. Trauma .................................... 67
    *Simon Faulkner*
13. Mental Health ............................. 78
    *Dr Jane Bentley*
14. Drugs and Alcohol ......................... 86
    *Bek Wermut*
15. Refugees .................................. 98
    *Christine Stevens*

16. Neurodiverse Communities . . . . . . . . . . . . . . . . . . . . . . 109
    *Ray Watters*

17. Working with Physical and Intellectual Disabilities . . . . . . . 122
    *Jorge Ochoa and Jacqui Barrett*

18. Working with Seniors. . . . . . . . . . . . . . . . . . . . . . . . . . 133
    *Lulu Leathley*

19. Working with Dementia and Alzheimer's . . . . . . . . . . . 145
    *Jana Broder*

20. Grief and Loss . . . . . . . . . . . . . . . . . . . . . . . . . . . . . . . 152
    *Carolyn Koebel and Laura Pawuk*

21. Living with Cancer . . . . . . . . . . . . . . . . . . . . . . . . . . . 166
    *Rufus Glassco*

22. Prisoners . . . . . . . . . . . . . . . . . . . . . . . . . . . . . . . . . . 181
    *Simon Faulkner*

23. Veterans . . . . . . . . . . . . . . . . . . . . . . . . . . . . . . . . . . 188
    *Terrie King and Kevin Callo*

24. Survivors of Natural Disasters . . . . . . . . . . . . . . . . . . . 199
    *Judy Guthrie and Michelle Taylor*

25. Aboriginal or First Nations Groups . . . . . . . . . . . . . . . . 213
    *Simon Faulkner*

26. Wellness and Personal Growth. . . . . . . . . . . . . . . . . . . 222
    *Christine Stevens*

27. Corporate Groups. . . . . . . . . . . . . . . . . . . . . . . . . . . . 232
    *John Hagedorn*

    *Evaluation Measures. . . . . . . . . . . . . . . . . . . . . . . . . . . 247*

    *Appendix 1: Post Session Questionnaire: Participants . . . . . . 248*

    *Appendix 2: Post Session Questionnaire: Managers. . . . . . . . 250*

    *Appendix 3: Feedback from Third Parties (Teachers, Clinicians,
    Parents, etc.) . . . . . . . . . . . . . . . . . . . . . . . . . . . . . . . . 252*

    *Appendix 4: How Are We Doing?. . . . . . . . . . . . . . . . . . . 253*

    *Recommended Reading . . . . . . . . . . . . . . . . . . . . . . . . 254*

# Introduction

Welcome to this compendium for people wishing to utilize the multiple benefits of drumming and the format of the community drum circle in their work supporting specific populations. The concept for this book came from an understanding of the growing potential of this empowering form of collective music-making to support therapeutic and developmental outcomes; and, alongside this, a growing awareness that for people new to this work there were a range of challenges and potential pitfalls that could undermine their best intentions.

Almost all the contributors to this book have been influenced by the pivotal work of Arthur Hull in developing a range of drum circle facilitation techniques, and an overriding philosophy of service to the participants in your drum circle; a focus on empowering them to work and play together and make harmonious, improvised music in a safe and uplifting way. Arthur Hull, through Village Music Circles,[1] Christine Stevens (a contributor to this book) and others offer drum circle facilitation training in countries across the world, from which many hundreds of people are graduating with these new skills each year. Additionally, the use of drumming in therapeutic contexts has gained increasing prominence in the field of music therapy and to a lesser, but still significant, extent in general counselling and education.

A philosophy of 'serving the circle', focusing on the individual and group needs of participants, is the central tenet of transferring this work successfully to support a wide range of different population groups. In addition, facilitating successful therapeutic or wellness programs and those targeting corporate development requires a clear focus on outcomes, unlike many community drum circles which are facilitated with a more generalized intention of inclusion, fun and a positive shared experience. In these more specifically intentional, focused-outcome circles the facilitator

---

1   www.villagemusiccirclesglobal.com.

is often required to support people through an emotional journey that moves them out of their comfort zone and challenges them in order to reveal new perspective, increase and develop skills, and create an awareness of new potential.

Many of the populations encountered in this compendium experience challenges in the way they interact with others and the world in general. Working with such groups means working with the vulnerable of our society, who often harbour sensitivities which are not externally apparent. A careless or insensitive approach can have serious implications that not only threaten the health of the individuals present but also the reputation of this work generally. All of us connected to this field recognize the extraordinary power of the drum circle to heal and support people, and collectively we need to ensure that this is not compromised by people failing their duty of care to those in their circles. We have a responsibility to put the emotional and physical safety of those in our circle as our highest priority.

Evidence-based research (see Figure 1.1) is increasingly reinforcing what our Indigenous ancestors have known for thousands of years – that the drum is a powerful tool for healing and development when used with sensitivity and consideration. Recent studies have showcased significant benefits for people dealing with mental health issues (including anxiety and depression), for young people with social and emotional challenges, for prisoners, for veterans and for those who have experienced trauma (see Figure 1.1). More studies will surely follow. This research has raised the legitimacy of the drum circle as an evidence-based intervention and is underpinning a growing demand for practitioners who can introduce drumming into a wide range of therapeutic and educational environments. It is an exciting time to be a drum circle facilitator!

For all of the different populations covered in the chapters of this book, there are two universal findings that participants experience when playing and creating music in a drum circle. The first is a strong sense of 'inclusion' – a connection to others on a social and emotional level that is missing from many people's lives. And the second is a surge of spirit and joy; an uplift in mood and associated feelings of vitality.

This book is dedicated to all the therapeutic practitioners
and community helpers who gave of themselves to
support those in need during the COVID-19 crisis,
and into the ongoing recovery period.

*'Words can never reach far enough into music to touch her essence.'*

Carolyn Kenny[1]

---

1  Kenny, C. (2006) *Music and Life in the Field of Play: An Anthology.* Dallas, TX: Barcelona Publishers, p.70.

# Contents

1. Introduction .................................... 9
2. Deepening Awareness through Cognitive Reflection ...... 19
3. A Somatic Approach ............................ 21
4. Group Dynamics and Group Skills ................ 23
5. Duty of Care .................................. 26
6. Evaluating Your Programs ...................... 28
7. Pricing Your Work ............................. 30
8. Managing Challenging Behaviours ................ 31
9. Early Childhood ............................... 33
   *Mary Knysh & Lulu Leathley*
10. Youth ........................................ 45
    *Lucas Coffey*
11. Autism ....................................... 59
    *Nellie Hill*
12. Trauma ....................................... 67
    *Simon Faulkner*
13. Mental Health ................................ 78
    *Dr Jane Bentley*
14. Drugs and Alcohol ............................ 86
    *Bek Wermut*
15. Refugees ..................................... 98
    *Christine Stevens*

16. Neurodiverse Communities . . . . . . . . . . . . . . . . . . . . . 109
    *Ray Watters*

17. Working with Physical and Intellectual Disabilities . . . . . . . 122
    *Jorge Ochoa and Jacqui Barrett*

18. Working with Seniors. . . . . . . . . . . . . . . . . . . . . . . . . . 133
    *Lulu Leathley*

19. Working with Dementia and Alzheimer's . . . . . . . . . . . . 145
    *Jana Broder*

20. Grief and Loss . . . . . . . . . . . . . . . . . . . . . . . . . . . . . . 152
    *Carolyn Koebel and Laura Pawuk*

21. Living with Cancer . . . . . . . . . . . . . . . . . . . . . . . . . . . 166
    *Rufus Glassco*

22. Prisoners . . . . . . . . . . . . . . . . . . . . . . . . . . . . . . . . . . 181
    *Simon Faulkner*

23. Veterans . . . . . . . . . . . . . . . . . . . . . . . . . . . . . . . . . . 188
    *Terrie King and Kevin Callo*

24. Survivors of Natural Disasters . . . . . . . . . . . . . . . . . . . 199
    *Judy Guthrie and Michelle Taylor*

25. Aboriginal or First Nations Groups . . . . . . . . . . . . . . . . 213
    *Simon Faulkner*

26. Wellness and Personal Growth. . . . . . . . . . . . . . . . . . . 222
    *Christine Stevens*

27. Corporate Groups. . . . . . . . . . . . . . . . . . . . . . . . . . . . 232
    *John Hagedorn*

    *Evaluation Measures. . . . . . . . . . . . . . . . . . . . . . . . . . 247*

    *Appendix 1: Post Session Questionnaire: Participants . . . . . . 248*

    *Appendix 2: Post Session Questionnaire: Managers. . . . . . . . 250*

    *Appendix 3: Feedback from Third Parties (Teachers, Clinicians, Parents, etc.) . . . . . . . . . . . . . . . . . . . . . . . . . . . . . . . 252*

    *Appendix 4: How Are We Doing? . . . . . . . . . . . . . . . . . . 253*

    *Recommended Reading . . . . . . . . . . . . . . . . . . . . . . . 254*

# Introduction

Welcome to this compendium for people wishing to utilize the multiple benefits of drumming and the format of the community drum circle in their work supporting specific populations. The concept for this book came from an understanding of the growing potential of this empowering form of collective music-making to support therapeutic and developmental outcomes; and, alongside this, a growing awareness that for people new to this work there were a range of challenges and potential pitfalls that could undermine their best intentions.

Almost all the contributors to this book have been influenced by the pivotal work of Arthur Hull in developing a range of drum circle facilitation techniques, and an overriding philosophy of service to the participants in your drum circle; a focus on empowering them to work and play together and make harmonious, improvised music in a safe and uplifting way. Arthur Hull, through Village Music Circles,[1] Christine Stevens (a contributor to this book) and others offer drum circle facilitation training in countries across the world, from which many hundreds of people are graduating with these new skills each year. Additionally, the use of drumming in therapeutic contexts has gained increasing prominence in the field of music therapy and to a lesser, but still significant, extent in general counselling and education.

A philosophy of 'serving the circle', focusing on the individual and group needs of participants, is the central tenet of transferring this work successfully to support a wide range of different population groups. In addition, facilitating successful therapeutic or wellness programs and those targeting corporate development requires a clear focus on outcomes, unlike many community drum circles which are facilitated with a more generalized intention of inclusion, fun and a positive shared experience. In these more specifically intentional, focused-outcome circles the facilitator

---

1    www.villagemusiccirclesglobal.com.

is often required to support people through an emotional journey that moves them out of their comfort zone and challenges them in order to reveal new perspective, increase and develop skills, and create an awareness of new potential.

Many of the populations encountered in this compendium experience challenges in the way they interact with others and the world in general. Working with such groups means working with the vulnerable of our society, who often harbour sensitivities which are not externally apparent. A careless or insensitive approach can have serious implications that not only threaten the health of the individuals present but also the reputation of this work generally. All of us connected to this field recognize the extraordinary power of the drum circle to heal and support people, and collectively we need to ensure that this is not compromised by people failing their duty of care to those in their circles. We have a responsibility to put the emotional and physical safety of those in our circle as our highest priority.

Evidence-based research (see Figure 1.1) is increasingly reinforcing what our Indigenous ancestors have known for thousands of years – that the drum is a powerful tool for healing and development when used with sensitivity and consideration. Recent studies have showcased significant benefits for people dealing with mental health issues (including anxiety and depression), for young people with social and emotional challenges, for prisoners, for veterans and for those who have experienced trauma (see Figure 1.1). More studies will surely follow. This research has raised the legitimacy of the drum circle as an evidence-based intervention and is underpinning a growing demand for practitioners who can introduce drumming into a wide range of therapeutic and educational environments. It is an exciting time to be a drum circle facilitator!

For all of the different populations covered in the chapters of this book, there are two universal findings that participants experience when playing and creating music in a drum circle. The first is a strong sense of 'inclusion' – a connection to others on a social and emotional level that is missing from many people's lives. And the second is a surge of spirit and joy; an uplift in mood and associated feelings of vitality.

## BENEFITS OF DRUMMING

Research outcomes drawn from targeted therapeutic programs incorporating hand-drumming.

### Physical Benefits
- Increased levels of immunity (disease resistance) – 1, 4, 7
- Reduced blood pressure – 17
- Improved cardio-vascular health – 17
- Increased energy levels – 14, 16, 15, 19
- Reduced pain levels, hedonia – 1, 6
- Improved motor coordination & motor planning – 2, 10, 19

### Psychological & Cognitive Benefits
- Reduction in anxiety/stress – 1, 2, 5, 7, 9, 10, 12, 14, 17
- Reduced depressive symptoms – 1, 5, 7, 9, 12
- Increased attention & focus levels – 2, 9, 10, 21
- Improvements in mood – 5, 11, 12, 13, 15, 17, 18, 21
- Reductions in trauma associated symptoms – 3, 6, 9, 13
- Improvements in mental clarity – 1
- Improved levels of emotional regulation, 3, 12, 13, 21
- Increased levels of self-esteem & personal autonomy, – 1, 3, 8, 12, 14, 21

### Social Benefits
- Increased sense of belonging – 1, 3, 11, 14, 15, 16, 21
- Improved social skills – 8, 12, 18, 21
- Healthier Relationships – 1, 12, 18, 21
- Higher levels of school attendance – 8, 21
- Reductions in anti-social behaviour – 8, 9, 13, 21
- Improved peer relationships – 3, 5, 18, 21
- Improved academic performance (reading & language acquisition) – 20
- Increased levels of social resilience – 1, 2, 7

1. Ascenso, S., Perkins, R., Atkins, L., Fancourt, D. & Williamson, A. (2018) 'Promoting well-being through group drumming with mental health service users and their carers.' *International Journal of Qualitative Studies on Health and Well-being*, 13, 1. https://doi.org/10.1080/17482631.2018.1484219
2. Berger, D.S. (2011) 'Pilot study investigating the efficacy of tempo-specific rhythm interventions in music-based treatment addressing hyper-arousal, anxiety, system pacing and redirection from fight or flight Fear behaviours in children with ASD.' *Journal of Biomusical Engineering*, 2. doi:10.4303/jbe/M110902
3. Bensimon, M., Amir, D. & Wolf, Y. (2008) 'Drumming through trauma: Music therapy with post-traumatic soldiers.' *The Arts in Psychotherapy*, 35, 1, 34–48. https://doi.org/10.1016/j.aip.2007.09.002
4. Bittman, B.B., Berk, L.S., Felten, D. L., Westengard, J., Simonton, O. C., Pappas, J. & Ninehouser, M. (2001) 'Composite effects of group drumming music therapy on modulation of neuroendocrine-immune parameters in normal subjects.' *Alternative Therapies in Health and Medicine*, 7, 1, 38–47.
5. Bittman, B., Bruhn, K.T., Stevens, C., Westengard, J. & Umbach, P. O. (2003) 'Recreational music-making: A cost-effective group interdisciplinary strategy for reducing burnout and improving mood states in long-term care workers.' *Advances in Mind-Body Medicine*, 19, 3–4, 4–15.
6. Dunbar, R., Kaskatis, K., MacDonald, I. & Barra, V. (2012) 'Performance of music elevates pain threshold and positive affect: Implications for the Evolutionary Function of Music.' *Evolutionary Psychology: An International Journal of Evolutionary Approaches to Psychology and Behavior*, 10, 4, 688–702. DOI: 10.1177/147470491201000403
7. Fancourt, D., Perkins, R., Ascenso, S., Carvalho, L. A., Steptoe, A. & Williamson, A. (2016) 'Effects of group drumming interventions on anxiety, depression, social resilience and inflammatory immune response among mental health service users.' *PloS one*, 11, 3, e0151136. https://doi.org/10.1371/journal.pone.0151136
8. Faulkner, S., Wood L., Ivery, P. & Donovan, R. (2012) 'It is not just music and rhythm. Evaluation of a drumming-based intervention to improve the social wellbeing of alienated youth.' *Children Australia*, 37, 1, 31–36. doi 10.1017/cha.2012.5
9. Ho, P.L., Tsao, J.C., Bloch, L. & Zeltzer, L.K. (2011) 'The impact of group drumming on social-emotional behavior in low-income children.' *Evidence-based Complementary and Alternative Medicine: eCAM*, 2011.
10. Homayounpour, P., Kakavand, A. & Mohammadi, A. (2016) 'The effects of Drum music training (Rhythm) on perceptual motor skills in children with Developmental Coordination Disorder.' *International Journal of Humanities and Social Sciences*, 1469–1490.
11. Kaplan, C.D. (2000) 'The short-term effects of group hand drumming on mood, group cohesiveness and rhythm perception.' Doctoral Thesis, University of Connecticut. https://opencommons.uconn.edu/dissertations/AAI9949659
12. Martin, K.E, Wood, L.J., Tasker, J.S. & Coletsis, C. (2014) 'The impact of Holyoake's DRUMBEAT Program on Prisoner Wellbeing in Western Australia Prisons, The University of Western Australia, Crawley, Western Australia.'
13. Martin, K.E. & Wood, L.J. (2017) 'Drumming to a new beat: A group therapeutic drumming and talking intervention to improve mental health and behaviour of disadvantaged adolescent boys.' *Children Australia*, 42, 4, 268–276.
14. Maschi, T. & Bradley, C. (2010) 'Recreational drumming: A creative arts intervention strategy for social work teaching and practice.' *Journal of Baccalaureate Social Work*, 15, 1, 53–66.
15. Newman G.F., Maggott C. & Alexander D.G. (2015) 'Group drumming as a burnout prevention initiative among staff members at a child and adolescent mental healthcare facility.' *South African Journal of Psychology*, 45, 4, 439–451.
16. Perkins, R., Ascenso, S., Fancourt, D. & Williams, A. (2016) 'Making music for mental health: How group drumming mediates recovery.' *Psychology of Well-Being*, 6, 11. https://doi.org/10.1186/s13612-016-0048-0
17. Smith, C., Viljoen, J.T. & McGeachie, L. (2014) 'African drumming: A holistic approach to reducing stress and improving health.' *Journal of Cardiovascular Medicine*, 15, 6, 44–446, https://doi.org/10.2459/JCM.0000000000000046
18. Tague D.B. (2012) *The effect of improvisational group drumming versus general music therapy versus activity therapy on mood, session behaviors and transfer behaviors of in-patient psychiatric individuals.* Florida State University, Electronic Thesis, Treatises and Dissertations, Paper 5220.
19. Thaut, M.H. (2005) *Rhythm, Music, and the Brain.* New York: Taylor & Francis.
20. Tauba, G.E. (2015) 'Effects of improvements in interval timing on the mathematics achievement of elementary school students.' *Journal of Research in Childhood Education*, 29, 3, 352–366.21.
21. Wood, L., Ivery, P., Donovan, R. & Lambin, E. (2013) 'To the beat of a different drum: Improving the social and mental wellbeing of at-risk young people through drumming.' *Journal of Public Mental Health* 12, 2, 70–79.

*Figure 1.1: Benefits of drumming*

Sociologists have long categorized societies into cultures of a 'Collectivist' or an 'Individualistic' nature,[2] describing differences in values, goals and an overarching worldview between the priorities of the group or individual. All of us sit somewhere along a spectrum of connection, with both our fellow man and the natural word. However, increasingly, the dominant pressures of society have been moving us towards separation. The individualistic nature of the modern world, which since industrialization has been dominated by the economic imperatives of production and consumerism, has left many people dissatisfied and isolated. The absence of nourishment for our vital emotional needs within these economic systems, for love, intimacy and connection to each other and the natural world, is at the core of many individual maladies, including an epidemic of loneliness,[3] and many would argue that this undermines the ongoing health of our families and communities.

As human and social beings we all share a yearning for connection. Connection brings with it sharing, understanding, nurturing and collaboration – vital elements inherent in the success of our species on an individual, family, community, national and international level. This primal spiritual need is aligned to the best of human nature which is on full display in a drum circle. Our faith in our fellow human beings is constantly being undermined by many of the dominant structures of the modern world, particularly the fear provoked by the stream of negative news that so many are exposed to, and the growing prevalence of 'othering': a tribalism that divides us and leaves us suspicious of each other. The community drum circle is a welcoming place for all humanity that counters this 'othering' with a message of 'belongingness'. As humans we all share existential anxieties, but we have a choice whether to feed these with the fear and anger that leads to isolation or instead follow a path of empathy and solidarity that promotes togetherness.

The drum circle provides a safe platform for that communal connection, where the emotional power of music is harnessed to reduce the fear that other forms of intimacy require, while sacrificing none of its impact. This conduit to increased social bonding, well known to Indigenous societies across the world, has been recently advanced through research in neuroscience with studies confirming music gives rise to increased levels of the neuro-hormone oxytocin[4] which is linked to increases in trust,

---

2   Tönnies, F. (1957) *Community and Association*. New York: Harper Torchbooks.
3   Holt-Lunstad, J. (2017) 'The potential public health relevance of social isolation and loneliness – Prevalance, epidemiology and risk-factors.' *Gerontological 27*, 4, 127–130.
4   Freeman, W.J. III. (2000) 'A Neurobiological Role of Music in Social Bonding.' In N. Wallin, B. Merkur and S. Brown (eds) *The Origins of Music*. Cambridge, MA: MIT Press.

generosity and empathy.[5] This practice also links us to the grounding and healing qualities of nature, as the rhythm of the music courses through our bodies and merges with the vibrations and rhythms of the natural world around us. These connecting rhythms that unite us have a healing potential all of their own.

Sometimes when I take my drums into a mental health unit, prison or youth service, the first thing I notice are the smiles on people's faces. In situations like these, where depression and feelings of hopelessness are often rife, the drums provide an effective way to energize and uplift people that studies show is long lasting.[6] Scientific research and anecdotal feedback have been consistent in showing improvements in mood and affect for people who join together playing drums.[7] There is clear evidence documenting the release of endorphins and other mood-altering chemicals when playing music, but it still astounds me how quickly this shift in outlook and vitality occurs – far more immediate than a course of anti-depressants.

Another key benefit of utilizing rhythmic musical exercises in a therapeutic or developmental context is the stabilizing impact this has on a wide range of both physiological and psychological states whose previous erratic function were causing an individual difficulties. This effect has been termed 'rhythmic centering' or 'rhythmic grounding' (see Figure 1.2) and is closely aligned to the concept of centring used across the martial arts and more recently by sports psychologists to assist with focus and performance.[8] When someone is 'centred' they experience a sense of calm where distractions, such as anxious thoughts, are banished and replaced by a singular focus, and a sense of stability and security.

'Centring' has a strong somatic component, felt physically as a calm confidence and often reinforced through an awareness and control of the breath. Focusing on the rhythm of the drum and aligning this to

---

5   Tarr, B., Launey, J. & Dunbar, R.I.M. (2014) 'Music and social bonding: "Self-other" merging and neurohormonal mechanisms.' *Frontier Psychology.* https://doi.org/10.3389/fpsyg.2014.01096
6   Fancourt, D., Perkins, R., Ascenso, S., Carvalho, L.A., Steptoe, A. & Williamon, A. (2016) 'Effects of group drumming interventions on anxiety, depression, social resilience and inflammatory immune response among mental health service users.' *PloS one 11,* 3, e0151136.
7   Kaplan, C.D. (2000) 'The short-term effects of group hand drumming on mood, group cohesiveness and rhythm perception.' *Doctoral Thesis, University of Connecticut.* https://opencommons.uconn.edu/dissertations/AAI9949659 (accessed 1 August 2020).
    Tague D.B. (2012) 'The effect of improvisational group drumming versus general music therapy versus activity therapy on mood, session behaviors and transfer behaviors of in-patient psychiatric individuals.' Florida State University, Electronic Thesis, Treatises and Dissertations, Paper 5220.
8   Pam, M.S. (2013) 'Centering.' In *PsychologyDictionary.org.* https://psychologydictionary.org/centering (accessed 19 January 2020).

the cycle of inhalation and exhalation creates a confluence of mind and body, strengthened through repetition and accented by the physical act of drumming. 'Centring' provides a pathway to self-regulation by bringing the mind to a quiet place in which attention is directed away from the overwhelming nature of mental worries and information, on to the body and the composed and unagitated flow of one's breath. Once attention is placed on the body and other distractions are minimized, an individual, whether athlete, client or community member, is better placed to focus on, and address, the challenges ahead of them.

'Rhythmic centring' also takes places on a communal level between people playing music together and connecting through a shared beat and tempo. Playing drumming rhythms together can give rise to the phenomenon of 'entrainment'. Entrainment is seen in a wide range of natural systems and will act on any two or more vibrating bodies as long as they have similar rhythmic cycles. This key outcome distinguishes musical activities from most other forms of social behaviour, with the shared rhythm allowing a synchronization and connection to occur on a biological level.

Drumming together thus connects people at multiple levels, offering the benefits of social communion to many who feel isolated and alone. Performing movements simultaneously with someone else (i.e., synchronizing) is believed to cause a form of integration between self and other, via neural pathways that code for both action and perception.[9] There is evidence showing that synchronization of actions increases people's positive regard for each other.[10] When moving in time with others we experience a co-activation of neural networks with research demonstrating the presence of 'mirror neurons' that are postulated to be central to this process.[11] This social, physical and neural synchronicity has at its core the stable foundation of a grounding pulse, a regular rhythm that brings together otherwise disparate energies.

The process of entrainment can act to align and stabilize both physical and physiological systems. Changes in the human respiratory system, heart-rate and blood pressure have been mediated through exposure to rhythmic auditory stimuli.[12] Physiological states of calm can be induced

---

9   Overy, K. & Molnar-Szakacs, I. (2009) 'Being together in time: Musical experience and the mirror neuron system.' *Music Percept 26*, 489–504.
10  Tarr, B., Launay, J. & Dunbar, R.I. (2014) 'Music and social bonding: "Self-other" merging and neurohormonal mechanisms.' *Frontiers in Psychology 5*, 1096.
11  Acharya, S. & Shukla, S. (2012) 'Mirror neurons: Enigma of the metaphysical modular brain.' *Journal of Natural Science, Biology, and Medicine 3*, 2, 118–124.
12  Chandra, M.L. & Levitin, D.J. (2013) 'The neurochemistry of music.' *Trends in Cognitive Sciences 17*, 4, 179–193.

by slow, steady tempos while energy levels can be raised with faster rhythms. Improvements in vocal dexterity, reading fluency[13] and fine and gross motor movement have also been showcased through exposure to rhythmic input.[14] Entrainment underlies the connection between auditory and motor systems creating a coupled oscillatory system where the firing rates of auditory neurons can entrain the firing rates of motor neurons.[15] This has led to a range of clinical techniques that utilize music to support fluidity of motion in people living with reduced or deteriorating physical movement.[16]

For many people living with psychological challenges there are associated physical issues to deal with and vice versa. For example, an increasing body of evidence demonstrates how a higher allostatic load associated with post-traumatic stress disorder (PTSD) is associated with a significant body of physical ill health in the form of chronic musculoskeletal pain, hypertension, hyperlipidaemia, obesity and cardiovascular disease.[17] Equally, for people dealing with physical challenges the psychological issues are never far away; in particular these individuals are often isolated and this lack of social inclusion negatively impacts their mental health. Rhythm-based therapies have the ability to positively address both these physiological and psychological realms through the grounding and centring element that is core to this practice, restoring equilibrium and homeostasis and providing a unique avenue to positive social connection and better health.

---

13  Bhide, A., Power, A. & Goswami, U. (2013) 'A rhythmic musical intervention with poor readers: A comparison of efficacy with a letter-based intervention.' *Mind, Brain Education 7*, 2, 113–123.
14  Toyka, K.V. & Freund, H-J. (2006) 'Music, motor control and the brain.' *Brain 129*, 10, 2794–2798.
15  Rossignol, S. & Jones, G.M. (1976) 'Audio-spinal influence in man studied by the H-reflex and its possible role on rhythmic movements synchronized to sound.' *Electroencephalography and Clinical Neurophysiology 41*, 1, 83–92.
16  Moumdjian, L., Buhmann, J., Willems, I. & Leman, M. (2018) 'Entrainment and synchronization to auditory stimuli during walking in healthy and neurological populations: A methodological systematic review.' *Frontiers in Human Neuroscience 12*, 263.
17  McFarlane, A.C. (2010) 'The long-term costs of traumatic stress: Intertwined physical and psychological consequences.' *World Psychiatry 9*, 1.

## RHYTHMIC CENTRING

Aligning, stabilizing and strengthening physiological and psychological states through rhythmic exercise.

**PRESENTING SYMPTOMS**

| Dyspraxia<br>Physical instability<br>Co-ordination impairment<br>Motor skill difficulties | ADHD<br>Inability to focus<br>Memory loss<br>Insomnia<br>Organizational and planning difficulties | Emotional dysregulation,<br>Anxiety, fear<br>Reactive, impulsive<br>Obsessive and compulsive behaviours | Post-traumatic stress disorder<br>Mood swings<br>Disorientation<br>Confusion<br>Anger |

Rhythm-based activities: Repetitive musical exercises – clapping, drumming etc., improve co-ordination and motor skills as well as focus and concentration. Movement exercises aligned to rhythm and the breath aid physical stability.

Drumming at specific tempos mediates primal brain function, improving emotional regulation. Drumming focuses attention on the present reducing hyper-vigilance, inducing calm and meditative mind-states, and stabilizing and improving mood.

**OUTCOMES**

| Improved physical attributes – balance and coordination | Improved focus and concentration<br>Improved academic performance | Improved emotional control<br>Reductions in stress and anxiety levels | Increased endorphin levels – improved affect<br>Healthy release of negative feelings |

*Figure 1.2: Rhythmic centring*

Much of the power of music to transform lives lies outside our current scientific understanding, and we do a disservice to its potential when we limit our acceptance to what we can prove with scientific facts. But it is clear that scientific research is slowly revealing some of the mechanisms that have been observed by practitioners using music for developmental purposes for many thousands of years. It is also worth noting that scientific research generally operates on the premise of the objective observation of calculable and measurable effects in a worldview based on an understanding that all actions happen for a purpose. Increasingly however new science (e.g., quantum physics, non-linear dynamics) is showcasing the shortcomings of this underlying philosophy which discredits anything unexplainable within these parameters. Rather than breaking things down into isolated parts impacting each other, the outcomes of rhythmic music circles may be better understood from a science of universal inter-connectivity.

The limitations of judging the benefits of an intervention or method of therapy such as drumming or other expressive therapies is evident in many fields where new understandings are unfolding well ahead of the investment in research. Insistence that treatments be 'evidence-based' can also wrongly imply a superiority which new research insights are calling into question. For example, cognitive behavioural therapies (CBT) are widely endorsed as an 'evidence-based' approach, yet it is well known that these therapies have limited application with many individuals, where expressive therapies succeed.[18] The dominance of CBT is in part because it is one of the most well-funded therapies and favoured by many academic institutions. Large amounts of money are required to engage in the research and testing of treatments according to formal 'scientific' protocols. Many other legitimate approaches are less accessible to 'measurement', and many existing treatments will not be the subject of formal research, not only because of funding constraints, but because the majority of practitioners do not engage in research in any case.[19]

One of the authors in this book, Jana Broder, has a company called Drum Magic. And 'Magic' is perhaps a suitable term for the unexplainable curative impact people give testimony to after drumming with others. The limitations of the medical model in accepting only what can be observed and recorded as statistical data ignores much of the true essence of music and its healing properties – the magic. We can describe the uplift in mood, the release of neurotransmitters in the brain, the change in immune system function, but we can never fully explain in words the magical and spiritual dimensions of music. And to do so would alienate us from many in the health professions and leave our work even more exposed to the sceptics. We spend a lot of time as professionals justifying our work through the standards of scientific rigour but risk losing the essential power of music because its major workings lie beyond description.

Although the main focus of this manual is on working with sub-groups of the general community, it is important to remind ourselves of the bigger picture and the positive role rhythm-based music circles can play on a broader community level, and indeed on a national and international level. It is particularly relevant when we recognize that many of our pathologies are emerging from the dismantling of community life. In the past, drum circles have often been used in ceremonies that bind different tribes and today they can be found in peace-building initiatives in Kosovo, Palestine, Greece, Northern Ireland, Germany, Rwanda, Uganda, El Salvador, and many more. The growth of open and accessible community drum circles offers our broader communities at large the same positive and

---

18  Wylie, M.S. (2010) 'The limits of talk.' (Feature article on the approach of van der Kolk) *Psychotherapy Networker*, 19 October. www.psychotherapynetworker.org/magazine/article/818/the-limits-of-talk (accessed 21 August 2020).
19  Kezelman, C.A. & Stavropoulos, P.A. (2012) *Practice Guidelines for Treatment of Complex Trauma and Trauma Informed Care and Service Delivery*. Adults surviving child abuse. Sydney, Australia.

unifying potential as we offer individuals or organizations when we work on a smaller scale.

There are many experienced practitioners working in these fields and I would encourage anyone who draws inspiration from this introductory book to look further, reach out to others and develop a professional network of fellow practitioners from whom to gain support and encouragement. There is also a growing range of literature from which to learn. Each of the contributors to this manual has significant experience in working with the population group/s of their focus, and all have generously donated their expertise to this project in order to assist those new to this work. Each author welcomes contact and further questioning, and many offer more intensive training. The use of the exercises they have contributed to this book comes with an understanding of the acknowledgement due to each when utilizing their material.

I and all the authors of this book hope, through this compendium, we can make some small contribution to your success in this field.

Simon Faulkner
Rhythm2Recovery

'One day, well into the future, Music will at last become the Great Therapy. And the drums of this present age will then be acknowledged as the first instruments that helped Music to ultimately fulfill Its long-anticipated promise.'

John Diamond, MD[20]

All pages marked with ★ can be photocopied and downloaded at www.jkp.com/catalogue/book/9781787755246

---

20 Diamond, J. (1999) *The Way of the Pulse – Drumming with Spirit*. Vienna: Enhancement Books.

# Deepening Awareness through Cognitive Reflection

*'The parallel between life and music goes perhaps deeper and further than one is able to grasp.'*

Gustav Mahler[1]

Although significant benefits are accrued from the simple act of playing drums and percussion with others, these can often be deepened and extended through the use of metaphors and analogies that link a drum circle activity to a social or emotional learning theme and relevant discussion. Most practitioners, working with participants who have the language skills and developmental capacity (an understanding of theory of mind,[2] i.e., that other people's thoughts and feelings influence their behaviour) to examine ideas, thoughts and feelings, will add this element in varying degrees to their practice. Metaphors and analogies can help simplify complex concepts and reduce some of the inflexibility of literal language.

An integrated approach that combines the multiple benefits of music with the well-established benefits of cognitive behavioural therapy (CBT) creates a powerful combination that marries ancient healing traditions to the latest scientific research. In its elementary form CBT is based on the concept that dysfunctional thinking negatively influences mood and behaviour, and that people can learn to analyse their thinking and broaden their perspective to improve these elements and others in their lives.[3] In order to make long-term change, therapists help people to move away

---

1 Mahler, A.M. (ed.) (1924) *Gustav Mahler Briefe (1879–1911)*. Vienna: Paul Zsolnay Verlag (letter 180).
2 Doherty, M.J. (2008) *Theory of Mind. International Texts in Developmental Psychology*. London: Routledge.
3 Beck, J.S. (2011) *Cognitive Behaviour Therapy: Basics and Beyond (2nd Ed.)*. New York: The Guildford Press.

from the faulty reasoning and false beliefs they hold about themselves, systems, and relationships, and replace or modify these with more positive and realistic alternatives.

Many of the expressive therapies, including art, play and music, increasingly utilize this combination to connect the learning from an activity to a direct personal experience or issue that is limiting the growth of the individual. In corporate, team and organizational contexts the same process is used to assist groups in challenging beliefs and systems that impede growth or creativity. In particular, the drum circle is a wonderful vehicle for examining social interaction, collaboration, cooperation and communication. Dysfunction in any of these areas is often immediately apparent when people are placed together in a drum circle, and a skilled facilitator can help the group recognize and unpack the elements that are undermining these processes and practise new skills and strategies that might help to mend them.

# 3

# A Somatic Approach

There is today an increasing acceptance of the role that our bodies play in managing our feelings. While the cognitive therapies have dominated modern psychotherapy since the advent of Freud, the role of the body has been receiving a growing level of recognition, and many practitioners now specialize in this field. Advances in neuroscience have identified the interconnection between mind and body in relation to the way we process our responses to traumatic events and the role of the vagus nerve as a moderator in this 'mind–gut' axis.[1] Another clear indicator of this link is the high percentage of people living with stress and anxiety who have co-occurring digestive complaints.[2]

Our bodies hold on to past traumas which are reflected in our body language, posture and expressions. We brace for threat, constricting our bodies and sending signals to the brain that the threat persists. These uncomfortable, visceral feelings are relayed back to the brain via the vagus nerve and are party to a chain of reaction that leads both regions to become over-reactive to each other and in a state of constant arousal. In order to cope, many people shut down those areas of the brain that transmit these bodily feelings, repressing them and consequently ensuring that they remain trapped within, long past their use-by date.[3] This form of denial prevents us from healing.

Somatic therapy involves assisting people in managing their bodily responses to emotional distress by helping them become more aware of, and more comfortable with, these often difficult sensations and then learning techniques for releasing the pent-up emotion stored within.

---

1 Breit, S., Kupferberg, A., Rogler, G., & Hasler, G. (2018) 'Vagus nerve as modulator of the brain–gut axis in psychiatric and inflammatory disorders.' *Frontiers in Psychiatry*, 9, 44. https://doi.org/10.3389/fpsyt.2018.00044
2 Hislop, I.G. (1971) 'Psychological significance of the irritable colon syndrome.' *Gut*, 12, 452–457.
3 Van der Kolk, B. (2015) The Body Keeps the Score: Brain, Mind & Body in the Healing of Trauma. London: Penguin.

The use of the drum can serve the practitioner in multiple ways in working through these elements with the client. Specifically, the drum provides a vehicle for the release of trapped feelings. Where a cognitive therapist may ask 'How did that feel?' and potentially elicit no response or one that is open to interpretation. An experiential practitioner can use the drum – 'Would you like to play how that felt?' The drum provides a far greater freedom, and a much safer alternative to the narrow range we have for describing these complex sensations through language.

Somatic therapies and drumming sit side by side as evidence-based approaches to supporting people through the release of trauma held in the body. And in particular, offer an alternative medium to some of the more hazardous treatment regimes. Drumming serves as a natural tool for releasing suppressed emotion, and it is very common to see people in community drum circles with tears streaming down their cheeks. The vibration of the drum permeates the body and acts to loosen the tension of un-discharged stress. Many cultures have traditions of chanting and drumming that simultaneously resonate through the body and restore equilibrium.[4] These practices are generally focused on replicating lower frequencies that reverberate through the lower stomach area and diaphragm. When we drum, we activate the whole body with the sound, as its waves of energy, circulate through, and rejuvenate us.

---

4   Sundar, S. & Parmar, P. (2018) 'Music Therapy Clinical Practice and Research Initiatives in India: Bridge between the Experiences of Traditional Music Healing Practices and its Scientific Validations.' *International Journal of Ayurveda and Pharma Research* 6, 2, 1–7.

# Group Dynamics and Group Skills

This book is not designed to teach you the basics of drum circle facilitation. For that, we would recommend texts by Arthur Hull and others in the Recommended Reading section at the end of this book. It is presumed that most people will have undertaken an accredited training program in drum circle facilitation, music therapy or a related discipline prior to enacting the exercises contained in this book. This is particularly important with groups of people needing your full focus, as confidence in the basics of drum circle facilitation techniques, attained through an accredited training program, will allow more of your focus and attention to go towards observing and meeting the needs of your participants. The need to be attentive to the needs of your group members is another reason why co-facilitation is generally recommended.

However, as most of the work detailed in this book relates to group work, an understanding of group dynamics and therapeutic group facilitation skills will be useful. Much of the work detailed in this book is based on regular sessions where group members gather together over a period of time – this consistency is generally more beneficial than one-off interventions and requires a very different set of skills as the trust that develops in the group enables a much deeper level of introspection and learning. All the positive benefits from the research detailed in this book refer to interventions of an ongoing nature, usually delivered weekly or bi-weekly over eight to 12 sessions.

Most people recognize the work of Bruce Tuckman (1965) who developed a model of group development that proceeded through specific stages, which he named 'forming, storming, norming and performing' (see Figure 4.1).[1] These stages can often be found in targeted developmental

---

1  Tuckman, B.W. (1965) 'Developmental sequence in small groups.' *Psychological Bulletin* 63, 6, 384–399.

drum circles where group members and group dynamics change in relation to how long the group continues to meet. Facilitators align their program content and their facilitation style in accordance to these stages, focusing on activities that are appropriate to the level of trust in the circle and the ability of the group to work together and support each other. See John Hagedorn's chapter 'Corporate Groups' (Chapter 27) for more information.

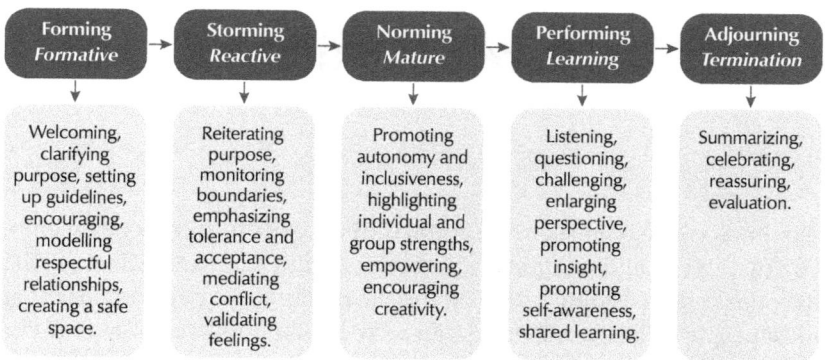

*Figure 4.1: Stages of group development and therapeutic group work skills*

The specific group-work skills of a therapeutic facilitator are those that support the group in moving through the different stages of their time together, while helping them get the most benefit from their experience – paralleling the role of the drum circle facilitation process. An important first step is being clear about the purpose of the group and the outcomes you are searching for. Involving participants and other interested parties (families, care-givers, clinicians, managers) in this task is vital. Monitoring progress towards these objectives, across your time together, allows you to adapt your work to better meet these ends and in doing so offer more meaningful support for your group members. Other important facilitator tasks in the early stages of the therapeutic drum circle include putting people at ease by creating a safe space for all, and modelling respectful, welcoming and inclusive inter-personal skills.

As the group develops it is common to go through turbulence; stages where inter-personal relationships can become tense and individual members may become disaffected. The behavioural management recommendations in Chapter 8 of this book can be useful here; however the main work of the facilitator is to help the group through these challenges in a respectful way – modelling effective problem-solving skills. Reaffirming the group's purpose and reinforcing ground rules and behavioural expectations are also important in keeping the group on track and avoiding a significant deterioration in member relationships.

When sensitively led through this period of discord, a group and its participants will often become more closely bonded, with deeper levels of trust ensuing and greater cohesion and openness appearing. This allows the facilitator to move the group towards deeper learning that often stems from visiting more sensitive and personal subject matter. Extending perspective through open-ended questioning, promoting insight and increasing self-awareness are often roles taken on by the facilitator at this point, as the group extends its autonomy and becomes almost self-managing.

As the group reaches its end, there is a need to acknowledge the journey they have been on together and the learning and changes they have made. It is a time to recognize both individual and group achievement and also to lend a sympathetic ear to feelings that may arise from its conclusion.

# 5

# Duty of Care

As we have noted, working with the drum circle to support specific population groups often means that you will be working with society's most vulnerable, sensitive and marginalized individuals. Each of us has an overriding responsibility when working with these people to prioritize their emotional and physical safety. To be negligent in this area risks not only the wellbeing of the participants, but also the reputation of the drum circle as a positive therapeutic approach, and your own personal reputation and livelihood as a facilitator.

A duty of care is a legal and ethical requirement to act with reasonable care and skill to protect and promote the wellbeing of those in your care or for whom you have responsibility. Reasonable care is the standard of care and skill that an ordinary, sensible person, in your profession or occupation, is expected to take in the same circumstances. In situations where you are contracted by an organization, school or community group, they as your employer have ultimate responsibility. But given that you will generally be directing the structure of the session, it will predominantly be your actions that directly influence people's safety and sense of wellbeing. The concept of providing safety can be seen as a disempowering notion which places people in a passive role at the mercy of others; sometimes it can be better to use the word protection – protect yourself and those around you.

It is important to realize that not all music is beneficial. For certain people, some of whom will be present in the specific populations covered by this book, fast and loud drumming can be particularly unsettling and give rise to anxiety, and may, for some vulnerable people, lead to psychotic episodes or disassociation. Studies of people working with anxious children have shown that loud, fast tempo drumming increased their levels of anxiety.[1] Autistic children and people in mental health settings with

---

1   Flores, K. (2011) 'African drumming as a medium to promote emotional and social wellbeing of children in residential care.' Unpublished DMus thesis, University of Pretoria, Pretoria.

cognitive confusion are also particularly vulnerable to over stimulation. Similarly, rapid rhythms played on the high notes of the drum (Tones or Slaps) can trigger traumatic reactions in some ex-military personnel and refugees from war zones due to the similarity of the sound to gunfire. Many elderly people also find loud drumming discomforting. These are just a few of examples of the issues that can arise when someone is facilitating without awareness. Drumming in a group also has the potential to escalate into volume levels that can damage hearing.

In any situation where you are working with a vulnerable population group it is necessary to seek prior information from the host on the types of issues your participants are dealing with and any specific sensitivity they may have, particularly in relation to sound levels and topics of discussion that could be potentially distressing or re-traumatizing. A preliminary meeting with your employer, or contractor; specifically someone from the service who has a psychological background, will help you avoid 'no-go' areas and provide you with a better understanding of how to structure your session effectively, in the best interests of those present.

Co-facilitation is also highly recommended when working with vulnerable populations, and many organizations will provide staff support to help you manage any incidents that might arise. In these situations, it is highly preferable to meet with your co-facilitators prior to beginning the session to align your goals and delineate areas of responsibility. Co-facilitation can become a nightmare when people are at cross purposes, and particularly when the co-facilitator is not motivated to be there and does not value the exercise. Ensure that you have motivated enthusiastic people supporting you, and where possible someone who has an existing and positive relationship with the group members.

Finally, in your pre-session meetings with your contractor, discuss group make-up and venue considerations – both of which can make or break a successful session. In groups where behaviour can be challenging it is important to think about the combination of personalities and avoid putting too many people together whose challenging behaviours will only reinforce each other. Some people have personality disorders that make them unsuitable for group work and will only destroy the experience for others – this issue needs to be addressed before you start your program. A suitable venue is also critical as poor acoustics, too many distractions, and a lack of privacy can each undermine your work. These responsibilities and tips can often sound onerous, but really they are simply elements of a professional approach and should quickly become part of your standard procedure. Use them to avoid making common errors and have a successful event.

# 6

# Evaluating Your Programs

Obtaining and evaluating feedback about our work is one area that many people in the drum circle facilitation business have not given great priority to. Yet there are many reasons why this should be standard practice. As an ethical consideration, there is an obligation on all of us to understand the impact our work has on others, either in a positive or negative way. Feedback provides us with the information we need to improve our skills and adapt our work to improve its outcomes. Asking participants for feedback also reinforces the empowerment message of the drum circle, where we acknowledge the importance of each individual's input into the success of the session.

In applying the benefits of the drum circle to the support of individuals facing specific social, physiological or psychological issues, evaluation becomes even more critical. Often there are limited financial resources for supporting these populations and being able to demonstrate the worth of a particular activity becomes critical. Although doing formal research can be quite onerous in terms of organizational requirements, less formal evaluation can often be implemented very easily by simply handing out questionnaires at the end of a session or by comparing people's experiences prior to and following an intervention, using the same questions. Obtaining feedback in this way can be critical in helping an employer justify your services for future contracts.

There is a wide range of philosophies, methods, therapies and, frankly, vested interests that all compete with, and sometimes actively undermine, each other for space across the personal and corporate development field. In many quarters the drum circle is not recognized as a modality for behaviour change or personal growth, but seen instead as a fun recreational tool. Evaluation is a key strategy in changing these misconceptions – the greater the body of evidence showing its impact, the harder it will be for people to dismiss this work as complementary rather than what we all know its potential to be – transformative. We all have a part to play in this mission.

At the end of this book there are some simple evaluation measures you are welcome to use or adapt. Additionally, I would recommend talking with any prospective contractor prior to starting your sessions about their ability to assist you in evaluating your work. Managers of services working with specific populations will often have access to validated measures that are better tailored to the populations they support and can evaluate their needs more effectively than would be the case using the generic questionnaires provided here.

# Pricing Your Work

Many people, when they first begin as drum circle facilitators, have doubts about knowing how to suitably charge for this work. And the truth is there is no one answer, as every situation is different and needs to be approached as such. One of the keys to pricing your service is to understand the scope of the contract – Is it a one-off event for 50 people or a weekly event over six months for 20? Does it require serious travel time or is it close to home? Will you have to employ a co-facilitator or hire additional drums, etc.? Your time at an hourly rate is probably the first place to start in beginning to formulate a quote, and the scale of the event should also have some weight. Another factor may be how many sessions you may do on the same day – schools and other services can often contract you to work with several different groups scheduled across a day, and I will always reduce my fee for consecutive programs like this as the travel is lessened.

Unlike corporate organizations, many social service organizations have very limited budgets and are wary of spending on an unknown product. It can be beneficial to offer free introductory sessions to help people judge the value of your work to their organization or the clients they support. There may be value in bartering with services which have low budgets, offering a cheaper rate in return for their support in evaluating your work, and thus providing you with an independent evaluation report that can serve as a useful marketing tool for future contracts. I have always had a policy of never doing a free session twice for the same organization – if they appreciate its worth then they can find the money to pay you adequately the next time.

When people ask you 'What does it cost?' remember to find out first what their intention is and then develop your quote around meeting their needs. It may well be that you can offer them a range of options with differing price tags that they can pick from. Never rush into providing a figure without the full facts behind you.

# 8

# Managing Challenging Behaviours

Many of the contributors to this compendium have experienced the difficulties of managing the challenging behaviours of certain population groups. 'At-risk' youth, people with behavioural and personality disorders, seniors with Alzheimer's or dementia, and those with cognitive impairment are among the most likely to test your ability to stay calm and maintain a positive attitude. It is important to understand that these behaviours are rarely caused by your actions but are generally the result of a myriad of complex factors.

Probably the primary cause of behavioural issues in these groups is an individual's sense of insecurity. Your response, however, may have a significant impact on whether that problematic behaviour is maintained, escalates or subsides. So, it is important not to take these things too personally and to learn how to stop them from escalating.

Key recommendations in behaviour management in drum circle situations include:

- Asking the contractor to supply an experienced co-facilitator to take responsibility for and manage group behaviour if this is a known issue. Sometimes people will need to be escorted from the room.

- Having some input into group make-up where there are known behavioural issues – talk to the organizer and let them know that the group process can be undermined if too many people with defiant behaviours are placed together.

- Where necessary, start your sessions by establishing group rules that address personal safety, both physical and emotional, and asking people to articulate how they can support and respect each other in the circle.

- Always keep your responses to challenging behaviour calm and validate people's feelings.
- Keep the momentum of your sessions going. Keep the group actively involved in the musical activities and try to avoid 'down time' where people become restless and have time to provoke trouble.
- Build on success – ensure that group members achieve quick success by starting with fun games and simple rhythm play. Many people entering a drum circle are nervous and harbour doubts about their musical ability that can lead to resistance and anti-social behaviour.
- Be careful about challenging people with exercises or rhythms that are overly complex – people's frustrations in these scenarios are often revealed as aggression.
- Be realistic about your expectations and do not overreact to small misdemeanors.
- Offer leadership opportunities or other forms of recognition to those participants whose challenging behaviours represent a need for greater attention.
- Never shame an individual in front of the rest of the group or give them an ultimatum that backs them into a corner – offer choices and a way of saving face.
- Focus on the fun.

# Early Childhood

## MARY KNYSH & LULU LEATHLEY

**OVERVIEW**
Children love to make music and the drum circle is an excellent means to that end. Drum circles are very popular in schools, community centres, after-school programs and summer camps. When you bring drums, percussion toys, Boomwhackers™ and found sounds into a group of children from three to eight years old, you will have instant participation… then your facilitating skills go to work! Keeping the children's attention can be a challenge and having a lot of activities in your back pocket to bring out at a moment's notice will help keep them with you. Chaos can erupt in a second so having some signals and boundaries (such as using a Samba whistle for attention or hands up to speak) established at the very beginning helps.

One fun thing about working with young people is that you can be one yourself. If you're real with children and get right where they are, then they will respond. If you find your sense of fun and joy, they will join you. If you look them right in the eye (where culturally appropriate) and get down to their level, they will join you. Mary Poppins had it right – she spoke honestly to the Banks children and her inner child shone though, drawing the children to her.

## POSITIVE OUTCOMES

Music education can help teachers and parents discover a child's potential. The positive effects of music-making are numerous. Speech development and listening skills are enhanced through music.[1] Muscle development and motor coordination are strengthened when playing instruments and dancing. Hand/eye coordination and left/right brain activation are developed as well.[2] Being part of a happy learning environment allows the children to express themselves, build their self-esteem and increase their concentration skills as they are at ease and enjoying themselves. Additionally, music making is beneficial to the parent/child relationship as well as the child's peers, siblings and community.[3]

In her pivotal book, *The Power of Music*, Professor Susan Hallam writes:

> The research shows there is compelling evidence for the benefits of music education on wide range of skills including: listening skills which support the development of language skills, awareness of phonics and enhanced literacy; spatial reasoning which supports the development of some mathematical skills; and where musical activities involve working in groups a wide range of personal and social skills which also serve to enhance overall academic attainment even when measures of intelligence are taken into account.[4]

Rhythmic music is probably the most accessible form of music for younger children and for teachers who may have limited musical backgrounds.

---

1   Hyde, K., Lerch, J., Norton, A., Winner, E. *et al.* (2009) 'Musical training shapes structural brain development.' *Journal of Neuroscience 29*, 10, 3019–3025.
2   Norton, A., Winner, E., Cronin, K., Lee, D. & Schlaug, G. (2005) 'Are there pre-existing neural, cognitive, or motor markers for musical ability?' *Brain and Cognition 59*, 2, 124–134.
    Orsmond, G. & Miller, L. (1999) 'Cognitive, musical and environmental correlates of early music instruction.' *Psychology of Music 27*, 1, 18–37.
3   Myers, R. (2019) 'Music is an important ingredient for child development and parent–child relationships.' Child Development Institute. https://childdevelopmentinfo.com/development/music-is-an-important-ingredient-for-child-development-and-parent-child-relationships/#gs.d7976f (accessed 21 August 2020).
4   Hallam, S. (2015) *The Power of Music: A Research Synthesis of the Impact of Actively Making Music on the Intellectual, Social and Personal Development of Children and Young People*. Great Britain: Music Education Council, p.103.

## SETTING UP FOR SUCCESS

Before starting, I send a contract to the contact person or teacher with definite stipulations such as easy access to the room if possible, help with unloading and loading, and a general lesson plan. I explain that the lesson may not always be as planned and that I will remain flexible to the needs of the children. I also sensitively state that it is preferable if the teacher doesn't admonish anyone for misbehaving as I can usually work something out with the child to change their behaviour and maintain their engagement. It is a good idea to also find out beforehand if the teacher has any children with additional needs who might require some extra help.

Ask as many questions as possible. Find out what the expectations of the teachers or parents are, which room you are going to be using, whether or not the event will be near other classrooms that you may be disturbing with the music-making, and the number of children in the group. I have arrived at a school and found out that we were to be placed in a large gym, which isn't ideal. If this happens, I will go to one corner of the room so the sound can bounce off the two walls instead of the middle of the large room where the sound will travel outwards and resonate uncomfortably. A visit to the school beforehand to lockdown all your requirements and meet the staff is always valuable.

## COMMON CHALLENGES AND HOW TO MINIMIZE THEM

I like to have the room set up well before I start with a group but it rarely happens due to time constraints and room access. Often, I have my instruments outside a classroom door waiting to get into the space before my event. When this happens, I ask the children to help move the instruments into the room, placing the drums in one corner of the room, bells in another, wood instruments in another and shakers in another. I then have them come into the middle of the room in a circle, do an ice-breaker activity such as 'Stomping in the mud' (see below) and then invite one child to find a drum, the next in the circle to find a bell, the next a wood instrument, and the next a shaker, then a drum again and so on. There is a little chaos but when they return to their chairs they are in a drum, bell, wood, shaker circle which makes for a nice balance of sounds.

Many children will complain that they don't want a certain instrument so I tell them right away that they will all get a chance to play every type that we have. Every third or fourth activity I will stop everyone and say 'Life is change! Please pass your instrument to the person on your right.' Don't forget to do these changes, as even small children will remember if you say something and fail to deliver on it – it might be a good idea to ask one of the complainers or a fellow teacher to keep track and let you know when it's time to change. Some activities will work and some won't, so it's important to have a lot up your sleeve to pull out when you need it. I often end with a quieter exercise such as a 'sound-scape' (a sound collage that mimics a real or imagined environment) or a guided visualization (a guided journey of the imagination, employing all the senses) so as not to pass overly excited children back to the teacher.

## PRACTICAL APPLICATIONS OF THE DRUM CIRCLE
### Creating a brain-based activity sequence for young children

When designing a session for young children it is very important to consider the sequence of activities, the flow from one activity to another and the opening and closing rituals. The brain seeks familiarity to enter safely into an activity; therefore providing young learners with predictable, accessible and fun opening activities will ensure that the group is engaged from the very beginning of your session. It is most beneficial to share opening activities that eventually can be led by the children themselves, providing them with leadership experiences during each session.

Once the session begins in this predictable manner, then the brain seeks novelty or new experiences and ideas to keep the level of engagement high. It is beneficial to have open-ended activities where children's creative ideas, movements and rhythms can continually fuel fresh new variations of familiar songs, games and movement sequences. This balance between the familiar and the novel is essential in shaping a best practice activity sequence for young children.

### Breath to boom

- Place hands out in front of you on the floor and invite students to join you as you say the word '*PREPARE*'.
- Bring hands all the way up in the air in front of the body, give a good stretch and wiggle fingers up in the air.
- At the top of the voice (the highest pitch) make a sound and siren down as your hands fall to the floor, saying '*BOOM*' loudly when you reach the floor.

- Second time, invite students to look around the room and see if they can reach the ground and say '*BOOM*' at exactly the same time.
- Third time, do the same thing. It is usually the third time around that the group is able to land on the floor simultaneously.

## Heartbeat

- Begin by asking students to put both hands on their chest and to listen to and feel the drum that lives inside their bodies. By asking students this question, you are empowering them to discover for themselves that the heart is like a drum beating inside the body.
- Tap hands over heart at a steady pulse saying the word:
  - '*HEART-BEAT HEART-BEAT*' – one hand after the other.
  - This will lead into walking hands drumming when they begin to play on the drums.
- Move the body percussion rhythm to the legs and use *both* hands on the legs, saying:
  - Say '*LEGS, LEGS, LEGS, LEGS*' – one tap for each word.
  - Then freeze the group and explore a new idea, sequence or rhythm.
- Leader taps each leg (R hand on R leg and at the same time L hand on L leg) and then crosses hands and taps the opposite legs (R hand on L leg and L hand on R leg) and asks the students 'What letter does this looks like when my hands are playing the opposite legs?' (A great curriculum connector.)
  - Students say this looks like the letter '*X*' and now the pattern is spoken as:

    | Legs    X         Legs      X        |
    | legs    opposite legs   legs   opposite legs |

  - This is a simple cross the mid-line activity but can reveal much about the cognitive development of students. It can serve as an excellent developmental indicator for teachers as they observe their students doing this activity.

### Extension
Developing a solid sense of steady beat is a fundamental skill that will support children in all areas of learning, including their ability to track words across a page.

- You can build upon this simple activity by inviting children to create many body drumming variations such as:
  - LEGS, LEGS, HEAD, HEAD
  - or:
  - FEET, FEET, LEGS, LEGS.
- The more time children spend experiencing steady beat patterning, the better prepared their brains will be for learning.

## Hello Song
I wrote this song many years ago while working in many inner-city early childhood centres. It is great for children to hear such a variety of ways that people around the world greet one another. This song has now become one of my opening rituals and is always a favourite for both the students and myself!

- Students echo each phrase of the song. I like to vary the way that I sing each greeting so that children can explore a wide range of vocal possibilities.
- Try singing high, low, in a funny voice, opera voice, whisper, or any idea that you or they may dream up!

### Lyrics

*'Hello, hello, Buenos dias, Bonjour, Guten tag.*
*Hello, hello, Konichiwa, Selema page, Ciao ciao*

*Around the world each and every day*
*we greet each other, smile and say...'*

(chant the following)

*'Hello hello...that is English*
*Bonjour...that is French*
*Hello Hello...that is English*
*Selama pagee...that is Indonesian*

*Buenos dias...that is Spanish*
*Guten tag...that is German*
*Konichiwa...that's Japanese*
*Ciao ciao...that's Italian.'*

## Body percussion

- Begin this song by sitting 'crisscross applesauce' on the floor and playing legs with both hands. I usually say the leg pattern. *Cross* = hands crossed over one another and play opposite leg (an excellent 'cross the mid-line' activity).
- Children enjoy offering their own ideas for varying these body percussion patterns and have come up with some wonderful ideas of their own over the years.
- Invite children to come up with ideas and patterns of their own! The body makes a most delightful drum. Always 'say what you play'. This is not only a powerful rhythmic tool but also a great way for young children to discover new places to drum on their bodies.
- While students are tracking this simple body percussion pattern, the leader sings the Hello Song and students echo each phrase in the song.
- In the middle of the song, the leader invites students to explore other places on their body that can be played like a drum (head, shoulders, belly, heart, legs, floor, shoes, etc.).

When the song is sung the second time, the body percussion pattern changes to:

| 'Legs | X | Clap it | Up' |
|---|---|---|---|
| (Hand taps legs) | (Hands cross and tap opposite legs) | (Clap 2 times moving up) | (Clap high!) |

- Invite students to add to this pattern: 'What shall we add?' 'Head?' 'How many times?'
    - It is a good idea to suggest four times or less, as any more than that and the patterns gets pretty complex.
    - It is also always fun to see how fast students can say and play the patterns, and how slowly they can say and play them as well.

## Extension

If you have students from other cultures in your group, add their greetings to this song. The song can become a reflection of your classroom community.

### Bend your elbows
This activity is especially fun with Preschoolers, Nursery and up to Grade Three (7 years and younger). Ask the children to 'Do as I do…'

- Bend your elbows, shoot them straight
- Bend your elbows, shoot them straight
- Bend your elbows, shoot them straight
- These are my elbows and aren't they great!
- Bend your knees and shoot them straight
- Bend your fingers, toes, wrists, ankles, waist…

An extension to this could be to ask the children to give you other bending parts of the body or bending ideas and link them all together in one long movement/chant.

### Stomping in the mud
This activity is great with children from five years old to age eight…and beyond. A circle formation is best with everyone standing.

- Invite the group to step from one foot to the other.
- Repeat after me: 'Stomp, stomp, stomp, stomping in the mud.' Ask the group to say it over and over.
- Sculpt (divide into groups) one-third of the students. Stop them on a '4, 3, 2, 1 Stop'. Ask that group to repeat after you: 'Hey, you… get out of that mud!' Keep on saying it over and over until you tell them to stop.
- The next third of the group can repeat 'Sliding through the mud'. Ask them all to say their words a little louder, with attitude and some type of movement then move around the room.
- The children can pick other themes such as snow, swimming, skiing, movies, food, etc.

### Expressive rhythm stories
Expressive rhythm stories are a fantastic way to engage children and adults in rhythm making. Using stories as the basis for the session engages the group in a process, a journey, which in itself contains elements of rhythm

and song…somehow because the focus is not entirely music based, the music part becomes just that…a part. That part then becomes an expression of language within a story rather than a piece of music in itself and so the engagement with young children is higher than it would be for a solely rhythm-based activity.

Using both verbal and non-verbal forms of communication, the facilitator engages the group and encourages them to become expressive. Stories give us the freedom to become characters and to explore our creativity openly and in a fun way.[5]

### The mouse house
In my story telling, I use a large 'Gathering Drum' and ask the children to gather around and listen to the story:

> Once upon a time there was a little mouse. This mouse didn't have a house! He longed to have a house so decided to go into the forest and see if he could find a house. He walked and walked all over the forest (I play a steady walking beat on the drum) and lo and behold he came upon a big house in the middle of a clearing in the forest! He knocked at the door (knocking on the drum) and slowly stepped in. He called out to see if anyone was at home but nobody answered so he ran up the stairs and all over to check out the house (quick beats on the drum).
>
> The mouse thought this house was a perfect place to have a party. He needed some friends for this party so he went in search for his friend, another mouse. They both ran all over the house (running beats on the drum). The second mouse said they needed some more friends for the party so she went off to find her friend the rabbit.
>
> The rabbit hopped all over the house (hopping beats) and thought it perfect but wanted to ask her friend the horse who clip-clopped over (1, 2, 3 repeating beats on the drum). The horse asked his friend the snake who slithered around (fingernails on the head of the drum) and agreed that they should definitely have a party in this house. The snake asked her friend the elephant to join in.
>
> When the elephant came up the stairs of the house he was very, very noisy (loud bass notes on the drum). He knocked at the door and went in to see the snake (finger nails on the drum), the horse (1, 2, 3 beats), the rabbit (hopping beats) all ready to party but when the elephant (loud bass notes) saw the mice he jumped up, ran all around the house and out the door in a big hurry! Elephants are afraid of mice!

---

5   For more information on expressive rhythm stories visit www.rhythmbridge.com.

I then ask the children which animal they would like to be...the mouse, rabbit, horse, snake or elephant. We go over the sounds of each animal and then they go to their drum if they have one or play on the 'Gathering Drum' if there aren't too many people, or play on a table or the floor. We all tell the story together and play.

## Dance conducting

- *Leader introduces conductor role*: Leader models the conductor role to the group by standing in the middle of the circle and designating which part of their body will conduct which group of instruments. For example:
    - DRUMS follow the movement of the FEET
    - WOODS follow movement of the HEAD
    - SHAKERS follow movement of the HANDS
    - BELLS and METALS follow movement of the HIPS.

- *Leader models a variety of conducting possibilities*: Leader models possibilities for movement from very small tip-toe (very quiet drum sound) to a very exaggerated JUMP (a vibrant, loud sound on the drum that matches the movement of the foot EXACTLY). The circle participants play their instrument when they see their designated body part move.

- *Students become the conductors*: Once the group understands the game, the leader turns over the conductor's role to a student. Student conductor leads the orchestra by moving his or her body in and around the centre of the circle as the orchestra carefully tracks each movement of their designated body part in sound.

- *Student conductor chooses new conductor*: When the student conductor's composition comes to a close, the students choose the next conductor for the game.

## CLOSING THE SESSION
### Goodbye Song
I always end my sessions singing to the tune of Woody Guthrie's 'So Long' song.[6]

I go around and look every child in the eye and shake their hand singing:

> 'So long, it's been great to drum with you
> So long, it's been great to sing with you
> So long, it's been great making music with you
> Keep singing and playing along.'

## ADDITIONAL ADVICE
If you are hired to do a group of classes or have an entire school contract over a period of a week or more, you could ask the children to invite their parents to a 'Family Jam' if the teachers are willing. Invite the children to bring an instrument that they have made out of something in their home or environment for their parents to play. You could have some of the children facilitate the entire group, which would build huge self-esteem! If that isn't possible you can still ask some of the children to facilitate in the class that you're doing. Often the shy reticent children will step up and do a little volume up and down and feel very special.

## AUTHOR BIOGRAPHIES
### Lulu Leathley, BA
Lulu is an author, speaker and founder of LuluJam, based in Vancouver Canada. With over 35 years' experience. Lulu has designed music programs and drum circle events for diverse populations from children and cancer patients to college students and seniors. She is the co-author of the recent book, *1, 2 Let's All Play* with Mary Knysh.

With a BA from the University of Victoria, she also holds post-graduate diplomas, certificates and advanced training with Village Music Circles, Rhythm2Recovery and Health Rhythms. Her unique approach, which draws upon her background in Orff and Montessori, helps people make music for health, wellness and therapeutic benefits.

Email: lulu@lulujam.com
www.lulujam.com

---

[6] See www.youtube.com/watch?v=zqiblXFlZuk.

## Mary Knysh

Mary is the founder of Rhythmic Connections, an innovative company advancing education, health, and creative development through drum circles and music improvisation. Mary is a cutting-edge workshop facilitator, with a speciality in education, trainer and consultant who uses music as a means for personal and organizational transformation through creativity, leadership and non-verbal communications.

She is a professional musician, recording artist and international author. An international teacher/trainer with the Music for People organization, Mary is also an Orff Schulwerk clinician and teaching artist for the Pennsylvania Council of the Arts, Young Audiences of NJ, and New York BOCES. She is endorsed by Remo Inc and Rhythm Band Instruments. Mary travels throughout the United States, Europe and Asia offering conference presentations, clinics, teacher-trainings, performances and workshops.

Email: maryknysh@gmail.com
www.rhythmicconnections.com

## RECOMMENDED READING

Cass-Beggs, B. (1980) *Your Baby Needs Music*. New York: St Martins.
Jensen, E. (2005) *Teaching with the Brain in Mind*. Alexandria, VA: ASCD Publications.
Knysh, M. & Leathley, L. (2017) *1, 2, Let's All Play: Music Activities for Pre-School and Primary Grades*. Vancouver, BC: LuluJam Publishing.
Willis, J. (2020) *Research Based Strategies to Ignite Student Learning – Insights from Neuroscience and the Classroom*. Alexandria, VA: ASCD Publications.

# Youth

## LUCAS COFFEY

**OVERVIEW**

There is a diversity of opportunities for running drum circles with youth – everything from birthday party celebrations to multi-week/year school residencies. To make this section clear I will focus predominantly on schools with students aged five to fifteen, where most of this work is being done. Given that schools cater to large numbers of students, they are commonly identified as one of the best places to provide mental health support.[1] From school to school there can be large differences in the availability of resources and exposure to the arts. One school may have a general music teacher, a choir and a band with all the necessary equipment; another school may have none of those things. Being flexible, understanding and having a good grasp of the individual needs of each school can help navigate this diversity.

Many schools find the engaging, hands-on, and metaphor-rich nature

---

[1] Connecting Social and Emotional Learning with Mental Health (2008) Prepared for the National Center for Mental Health Promotion and Youth Violence Prevention by the Collaborative for Academic, Social, and Emotional Learning at the University of Illinois at Chicago. https://files.eric.ed.gov/fulltext/ED505361.pdf (accessed 21 August 2020).

of drum circles to be an excellent addition to community celebrations, diversity, and anti-bullying and mental health events. As well, longer-term artist-in-residence roles can be a great way to enrich subjects like history, social studies, health and music. Most youth immediately respond to the hands-on nature of the rhythm circle, and the majority will find a place suitable for them given the time and space to do so. Having large numbers of students of different ages and abilities engaged and participating in a meaningful activity is always a winning combination for school administrators.

## POSITIVE OUTCOMES

Group drumming programs for school-aged children like 'Beat the Odds©' or the 'DRUMBEAT©' program reveal that group drumming, integrated with activities from group counselling and psycho-education, can improve a wide range of social and emotional markers.[2] These and similar programs can also reduce depression and anxiety and improve social resilience.[3] The physical activity of hand drumming and its social nature are also positive features that resonate with the needs of schools, allowing for a safe outlet for the exuberant energies of children, especially testosterone-driven boys, and for the development of important social skills and a sense of community.[4]

Drumming and other musical programs can also have a significant impact on a young person's academic performance. Neurologists have been studying the link between interval timing, working memory and mathematics through Interactive Metronome (IM) training. Participants who received the IM training showed statistically significantly higher scores on the multivariate maths post-test (controlling for the maths pre-tests) compared to the control group participants.[5] This link between

---

[2] Ho, P., Tsao, J.C.I. & Zeltzer, L.K. (2011) 'The impact of group drumming on the social-emotional behavior of low-income children.' *Journal of Evidence-Based Complementary & Alternative Medicine.* https://doi.org/10.1093/ecam/neq072
Wood, L., Ivery, P., Donovan, R. & Lambin, E. (2013) 'To the beat of a different drum–improving the social and mental wellbeing of at-risk youth with drumming.' *Journal of Public Mental Health* 12, 2, 70–79.

[3] Fancourt, D., Perkins, R., Ascenso, S., Carvalho, L.A., Steptoe, A. & Williamson, A. (2016) 'Effects of group drumming interventions on anxiety, depression, social resilience and inflammatory immune response among mental health service users.' *PloS one* 11, 3, e0151136.

[4] Wood, L., Ivery, P., Donovan, R. & Lambin, E. (2013) 'To the beat of a different drum–improving the social and mental wellbeing of at-risk youth with drumming.' *Journal of Public Mental Health* 12, 2, 70–79.

[5] Tauba, G.E. (2015) 'Effects of improvements in interval timing on the mathematics achievement of elementary school students.' *Journal of Research in Childhood Education* 29, 3, 352–366.

rhythm and memory should not be surprising given much of our earliest learning has been done with the assistance of rhythmic cues, e.g., rhymes for remembering our maths tables. Other research has shown rhythm activities, such as drumming, can assist with language acquisition and improve reading.[6]

As the studies on the neurological and physiological benefits of group drumming grow, so does our understanding that social emotional learning (SEL) plays a critical role in improving children's academic performance and life-long learning.[7] Drumming is a shared creative experience that can facilitate insight and empathy, which enables changing perceptions of self and others, social connection, and individual and collective empowerment.[8] In addition to students feeling better about themselves, and feeling more open,[9] drumming workshops markedly improved participants' affective states and enhanced their capacity for personal agency, mastery and self-expression, as well as improving levels of social interaction and social regulation.[10]

Other key outcomes that come from drumming programs include:

- *Learn while having FUN!* Physical and mental play-based activity is essential for overall healthy child development, with drumming contributing to cardiovascular health and improvements in motor-coordination.[11]

- *Motivating students through creative music-making*: When people reach their own insights and conclusions, solve their own problems, or come up with their own ideas, the reward centres of the brain get a rush of the pleasure chemical dopamine, which helps facilitate action.[12] This biological reward, added to the social benefits of group membership and the personal incentives of freedom of expression

---

6   Anvari, S.H., Trainor, L.J., Woodside, J. & Levy, B.A. (2002) 'Relations among musical skills, phonological processing, and early reading ability in preschool children.' *Journal of Experimental Child Psychology 83*, 2, 111–130.
7   Zins, J.E. (2004) 'Building Academic Success on Social and Emotional Learning: What Does the Research Say?' Teachers College, Columbia University.
8   Ho, P. (2015) *Out of the Box: Positive Development and Social Change through the Arts.* Berkman Center Research Publication.
9   Snow, S. & D'Amico, M. (2010) 'The drum circle project: A qualitative study with at-risk youth in a school setting.' *Canadian Journal of Music Therapy 16*, 1, 12–39.
10  Flores, K., van Niekerk, C. & le Roux, L. (2015) 'Drumming as a medium to promote emotional and social functioning of children in middle childhood in residential care.' *Music Education Research 18*, 3, 254–268.
11  Stegelin, D.A. (2005) 'Making the case for play policy: Research-based reasons to support play-based environments.' *Journal of Young Children 60*, 2, 76–85.
12  Radecki, D. (2018) 'Psychological safety: Managing the hidden drivers of individual behavior and team success.' The Academy of Brain-based Leadership. https://academy-bbl.com

and recognition, combine to make drumming programs particularly engaging for young people that are often hard to reach.

- *Developing communication skills*: Group drumming develops relationship skills, providing children with the tools they need to establish and maintain healthy and rewarding relationships. Competence in this domain involves communicating clearly, listening actively and cooperating.[13] Drumming has traditionally been a communication medium and involves utilizing and developing a wide range of communication skills.

- *Building resilience through teamwork challenges*: There is a growing interest in teaching 'grit' or 'growth mindset' within schools. This reflects an increasing awareness that richer, deeper learning can flow from having students struggle with a challenging task and persist until completion.[14] Working together in the drum circle to learn rhythms, play games and develop performance pieces requires this form of commitment and persistence.

## SETTING UP FOR SUCCESS

Schools tend to be large and sometimes insular institutions, and this can make it difficult to market your service through common channels like social media, email, phone, and written letters. As an alternative, I would recommend giving a free demonstration to the school or youth organization as means of generating interest, building personal relationships, getting helpful feedback, spreading word-of-mouth marketing and finding clients who are a genuine fit.

### Tips

- Set up free demonstrations with clear boundaries on the size, length and who should be in attendance (I suggest 20–30 students, an administrator/decision-maker, and a guest from the parent community).

---

13 Durlack, J.A. (2015) *Handbook of Social and Emotional Learning Research and Practice.* New York: Guilford Press.
14 Ermeling, B., Hiebert, J. & Gallimore, R. (2015) 'Beyond growth mindset: Creating classroom opportunities for meaningful struggle.' *Education Week Teacher.* www.edweek.org/tm/articles/2015/12/07/beyond-growth-mindset-creating-classroom-opportunities-for.html (accessed 3 August 2020).

- Give demonstrations in the year preceding the potential residency or well in advance of an event.
- Set a time after the demonstration to describe the value of your work, the booking process, and any potential grants or assistance that might be available to the school or organization.
- Ensure that there are at least two people from the hosting organization involved in all communications.

Also, always ensure that you are using equipment that is suited for a younger demographic and is well protected. Often you will have students helping you load your equipment. Drums that have legs, stands, or holes in the bottom for maximum sound without tilting are preferable. Be careful with sharp sounding bells, blocks and sticks when playing with youth under nine or other special populations. Sticks can become weapons and can also be used to damage hand-drums.

## COMMON CHALLENGES AND HOW TO MINIMIZE THEM

Larger youth organizations and schools do not necessarily have effective internal communication. I have arrived at events where teachers were not informed I was coming, had never been sent a schedule, or had a field trip the same day. I suggest asking the coordinator to send a note (that you craft) to all the staff giving an outline of expectations, including organizational needs and the benefits of your program. Ensure that you have two staff copied in in case one of the staff becomes unavailable. Make sure to recognize their busy schedules and offer an invitation for them to join the event. The more informed and invested the staff are, the more likely you will have a successful event. Many worthy music programs have been undone by being undervalued and sometimes deliberately undermined by other staff.

Some of your first gigs with youth may include drop-in centres. There are two different styles of circles you may encounter here, a set program where youth must attend, or an optional transient circle where youth may come and go as they please. The transient circles can be a difficult place to build relationships and momentum. When I am faced with this challenge, I will first ask the centre organizers if I can spend some time hanging out with the youth – playing sports and games at the centre, or having some snacks so I can get to know them. Then I will work on creating an environment where I can get as many young people as possible to participate for a short window (5–10 mins) of fun rhythm games. I will then give the option to stay after to play and learn more. If you say 10 minutes, make sure it is 10 minutes; this is a crucial time to build trust. Have a strong 10 minutes of fun and when the time is up, celebrate and thank them. Build on these small successes until they are ready for a bigger commitment.

When it comes to managing behaviour in youth groups, a number of different strategies can help. The first is to make the whole experience safe and fun in the first place – many difficult behaviours stem from feelings of insecurity. It also pays to talk to the organizers to ensure that they will provide someone who can manage any seriously disruptive behaviour – preferably someone who has a good and respectful relationship with the young people present. Remember, if you are an outside contractor, it is not your job to manage this aspect of the work. If you are working with 'high-risk' youth across a longer time period it can also be beneficial to agree on some boundaries (involving the whole group in this process) that will allow the group to run well.

The opening of the circle is a crucial time to establish boundaries, assess potential behaviour issues and build rapport. Rushing your opening due to classes being late, announcements, or pressure from teachers can seriously impact your circle. Here are a few things you can do to ensure a successful opening.

## Set the circle with care

Circular seating arrangements can help instil a sense of belonging within classroom communities with overall positive effects on learning, emotions and wellbeing.[15]

Setting up the circle:

- Have everyone in the room before entering the circle.
- Set the chairs for the exact number of participants.
- Have everyone in the circle (no spectators).
- Have drums in the middle of the circle and out of reach.

## Create a ritual for your opening

Rituals reduce young people's uncertainty and anxiety about an intervention due to their consistency. They provide a clear path for action and reduce

---

[15] Falout, J. (2014) 'Circular seating arrangements: Approaching the social crux in language classrooms.' *Studies in Second Language Learning and Teaching* 4, 2, 275–300.

an individual's personal response to failure.[16] Using and maintaining an opening ritual to create a predictable and safe environment will help set the stage for creative risk-taking.

Types of opening rituals

- check-ins
- welcoming and closing songs
- body percussion warm-ups
- entering and exiting the circle in a specific way
- a set opening rhythm.

Working with an exceptionally large age range can be difficult as effective classroom management for a five-year-old is different to that for a 13-year-old. Do some research and/or find a mentor to get some insight on best practices with an age group and then do multiple circles with that group. This will allow you to see behaviour patterns as they emerge and enable you to refine and employ a set of management techniques appropriate for that age. As you explore different ages you can then build management strategies that are effective and tailored to each circle. Better management skills will allow you to focus on the drum circle work and maximize its benefits.

## Tips for each age group

### 5–8 years
Have a good mix of movement activities, vocal activities, and drumming activities. Depending on time of day or mood of the group the balance of that combination may change.

### 9–12 years
Create as many opportunities as possible for them to have input into the games, activities and rhythms you will do. A lot of students in this age group are beginning to claim their independence and need to be empowered by being offered choices and leadership roles.

---

16  Hobson, N.M., Bonk, D. & Inzlicht, M. (2017) 'Rituals decrease the neural response to performance failure.' *PeerJ* 5, e3363.

**12-15 years**
Begin with teaching a rhythm and rhythm games. Introducing group improvisation to this age range too fast without building trust and confidence can leave them in 'student crisis' mode. Once confidence is lost in this age group, it is hard to get back.

## PRACTICAL APPLICATIONS OF THE DRUM CIRCLE
### Activity: Poison rhythm group mastery (communication, resilience, fun)

Musical objectives
Detect and echo specific rhythm patterns, learn a commonly used West African 'break', teach volume dynamics, and use mnemonics as a tool to learn patterns (see Table 10.1).

Social objectives
Use positive body language to communicate with peers, learn to maintain a positive mindset through failure and set-backs, develop ways to build the confidence of your teammates.

Group objectives
Move through the different levels to achieve your black belt (see Table 10.2).

Rules

- There is no talking, only communicating non-verbally.
- Students cannot play the specified poison rhythm.
- The poison rhythm: all six notes must be played in the correct order. (If there is a bass note in the rhythm, the teacher must include that note.)
- If anyone 'Blames, shames, or calls names', the teacher takes points away.

Procedures

- Play poison pattern with mnemonics (words attached to the rhythm).
- Have the students repeat the pattern while saying the words until they get it.

- Play the poison pattern until they do not play it back (silence).
- Use 'Call and response' and play several different patterns, eventually playing the 'Poison rhythm'.
- Introduce the warning signal (One index finger pointed high in the air).
- Once participants understand the game, they receive their white belt.

**Table 10.1: Rhythm phrases for 'Poison Rhythm' exercise**

| Timing | 1 + 2 + 3 + 4 + | 1 + 2 + 3 + 4 + |
|---|---|---|
| Poison rhythm (Facilitator) | T t T t T  B | |
| Students answer | Silence | |
| Universal break (Facilitator) | T t T  t  T | t  T t T |
| Students answer | B | |
| Dynamic contrast (Facilitator) | T t     T t T | (play loud) |
| Students answer | T t     T t T | (Play soft) |

T – Tone note – dominant hand
t – Tone note – non-dominant hand
B – Bass note – dominant hand

**Table 10.2: Colour belt table**

| Level | Musical criteria | Social goals | Teacher's notes |
|---|---|---|---|
| White | Do your best not to play the poison rhythm. | Fun | Demonstrate rhythm with mnemonics: 'This one is the poison', then demonstrate without. |
| Yellow | If less than three play the poison you get a point. If you get three points (in-a-row) you get your yellow. | Work as a team by using the 'warning signal'. The warning signal is putting your index finger high in the air. The clearer your body language the more likely you will have team success. | Note the importance of not only listening to the rhythm but watching and listening to your peers for support. |

| Level | Musical criteria | Social goals | Teacher's notes |
|---|---|---|---|
| Orange | If no one plays the poison you get a point. If you get three points (in-a-row) you get your orange. Teachers can take points away if there is blame, shame or calling names. | Blame, shame and calling names: everyone makes mistakes. When we shame or blame someone for making a mistake the team will likely make more. | Watch for behaviour change. Encourage students that stop themselves from blaming others by giving an extra point. |
| Green | To get a point, no one can play the poison; with teacher distractions. | Building up your team: Instead of blaming or getting angry at your team, find a way to build their confidence; fist bumps, pats on the back, smiles, words of encouragement. | Types of distractions:<br>• play with one hand<br>• volume dynamics<br>• play it on your neighbour's drums<br>• use your voice<br>• look them right in the eyes<br>• tempo |
| Blue | To get a point, no one can play the poison; with teacher distractions. Also, if one person does not play a rhythm they are supposed to, you lose all your points. | Resilience: the capacity to recover quickly from difficulties. After we have 'failed' 20 times, how do we keep going? | Play variations of the rhythms that are slightly different, so students really must know the poison. Watch for anyone not playing the rhythm they are supposed to. |
| Brown | All previous rules apply plus students must play 'the note' after the break. | Success is something that happened because of your hard work and effort. | Increase or decrease the tempo based on the level of your group. |
| Black | All previous rules apply, and students must play a dynamic contrast rhythm. | Mastery: ask the masters, they know learning never ends. | If a group is struggling, take some time to practise the rhythms, or not! |

## Notes about 'special needs' populations
### For students 4–6 years old and with developmental delays

- Begin without instruments and by just having them show the warning signal when you say the mnemonics: 'this one is the poison'.

- Once they have that, do a simple call and echo (with just the voice) and after a few measures say the poison rhythm again.

- Add instrument; still using voice while you play.
- Take away mnemonics.
- Play strictly as a listening game (show warning signal if you hear the poison rhythm).

For students with physical disabilities have them choose a warning signal that is comfortable for them or have them vocalize the warning signal.

**For students with behavioural challenges**
For this group, the blaming and shaming can be very intense and the emotional resilience for failure can be really low.

- Start by talking about negative impact of blame, shame and calling names.
- Begin with exercises that guarantee success (icebreaker games).
- Make the first challenges, individual challenges.

Ways to help if they are struggling:

- Set a time limit.
- Take a mental refocusing break.
- Take a minute to practise with them.

## Activity: Change the note (communication, creativity, fun)
**Musical goals**
Improvise different note selection over a pattern that has been taught, explore different textures, movements, and sounds.

**Social goals**
Listen to and clearly articulate the rhythms of another classmate.

This activity bridges the gap between 'teaching a rhythm' and having students improvise on their own while keeping a common group rhythm for support. For this activity to be the most effective follow the steps below. 'Creating a rock-solid rhythm' at the beginning of the procedure is essential until the group can play on their own without speeding up.

**Procedure**

- Teach an easy pattern.

- Have students demonstrate that rhythm.
- Have students explore all the different sounds and movements they can think of with their instrument.
- Have them demonstrate.
- Show how those ideas can replace the low and high notes of the original rhythm.
- Have them replace the new ideas over top of the initial rhythm.
- Have the class play their rhythms together.
- Have students observe and copy one of their classmate's rhythms as precisely as possible.

## Activity: Rumble race car (communication, creativity, fun)
**Musical goals**
Develop sensitivity to subtle movements and dynamic changes; explore volume dynamics through body language.

**Social goals**
Follow non-verbal instructions, deliver clear and controlled non-verbal signals; explore the motions/emotions of different types of drivers; create your own way to drive.

**Procedure**

- Model the movements of driving a fast-moving car.
- Have all participants mirror your movements as if they are the passengers in your car.
- Driving straight: use a gentle two finger rumble on the front of the drum.
- Turning right: move your body to the right and hands into a full rumble on the right edge of the drum.
- Turning left: move your body to the left and hands into a full rumble on the left edge of the drum.
- Going through a dark tunnel: move your body down as close to the drum as possible while rumbling on the bass note.

- Honk the horn: play the bass note twice while saying 'beep, beep'. Have the group respond with a 'beep, beep' of their own.
- Speed up: have both hands rumbling on the front of the drum. As the drum gets louder, move your body and head back until you are looking at the roof.
- Going over bumps: play a sharp note as you bounce your but off the seat.
- Crashing the car or being pulled over by the police happens when the teacher/facilitator begins a loud rumble or makes a siren sound.
- Donuts: move your hand and body around in a circle.
- Gravel road: knuckles on the drum while you bump up and down on your seat.
- Radio: have them crank an imaginary knob and start singing a tune you have been playing in class.

*Note*: When you are demonstrating the movements, do them slowly, with controlled body language. (If the 'passengers' can't keep up with the 'driver's' movements that's a good sign the driver is out of control!) Model quality participation rather than chaos.

## ADDITIONAL ADVICE

Take your set-backs with a giant smile! Working with young people can at times be challenging but don't take it personally. Drum circles can be a phenomenal way to connect and uplift youth. Every school (and class), however, has different dynamics, special populations and a wide range of ages and needs. One circle may leave you and the participants feeling on top of the world; the very next class, using the same program, can leave you feeling exhausted and perplexed. The toughest circles are the ones with the most to learn from, try to take as much as you can from them. They will begin to show you the subtle needs of each group, and the ability to facilitate success in the toughest groups.

## AUTHOR'S BIOGRAPHY
### Lucas Coffey

Lucas is the founder and lead facilitator of 'Rhythm Rhythm Rhythm', an artist-in-residence program that has shared rhythms and improvised music with over 100,000 students in Alberta and throughout North America. He is the co-founder of Rhythm for Youth, a training program designed to assist youth educators in launching or enhancing their own rhythm programs. He has apprenticed for several years with renowned facilitator and djembe instructor Cameron Tummel and is a certified global trainer with Village Music Circles.

    Email: rhythmalberta@gmail.com
    www.rhythmrhythmrhythm.com
    www.rhythmforyouth.com

## RECOMMENDED READING

Knysh, M. (2017) *Innovative Drum Circles: Beyond Beat into Harmony*. Millville, PA: Rhythmic Connections Publications.

Siegal, D.J. (2014) *Brainstorm – The Power and Purpose of the Teenage Brain*. London: Scribe Publishing.

Smyth, P. (2017) *Working with High-Risk Youth: A Relationship-Based Practice Framework*. London: Routledge.

# Autism

## NELLIE HILL

**OVERVIEW**

Autism Spectrum Disorder (ASD) is a life-long developmental disorder that affects the way an individual relates to their environment, and generally includes difficulties with social skills, written and verbal communication, and repetitive behaviours. The Center for Disease Control estimates the one in every 54 children in the USA is autistic, and similar figures are found in many other western countries.[1] As the child develops, managing ASD so that they can function often requires a range of interventions such as intensive social skills training, physical and occupational therapy, speech and language support and sometimes medications to ease their anxiety and improve attention issues. The chances of encountering someone with ASD in a drum circle are high, and musical interventions like drum circles are increasingly being used as a tool to work with people on the spectrum.

There are many studies showing that both children and adults with ASD respond well to music. Research has found that music as an intervention used with children and teens with ASD can improve social

---

1   Center for Disease Control (2016) Data and Statistics on Autism Spectrum Disorder. https://www.cdc.gov/ncbddd/autism/data.html (accessed 21 August 2020).

behaviours, increase focus and attention, increase communication attempts (vocalizations, verbalizations, gestures and vocabulary), reduce anxiety, and improve body awareness and coordination.[2] It may take a while for these individuals to adjust to this new experience – a new environment, new instruments, new sounds, etc. – but most will. The wonderful thing about drumming is that, when given the correct materials and environment, ASD is an ability and not a disability.

It is very helpful to know the different characteristics of ASD. Not every person with ASD manifests all behaviours and in many cases ASD is not the only issue to be considered.[3]

- *Restricted behaviour and play.* This includes repetitive body movements, obsessive attachment to an unusual object, a strong need for sameness, order and routine, odd movements, a fascination with things that move and hyper or hypo reactions to sensory input.

- *Social behaviour and social understanding.* This could be unusual or inappropriate body language, gestures or facial expressions, a lack of interest in sharing, a lack of empathy, and/or resistance to being touched.

- *Speech and language.* This would include speaking with an atypical tone or rhythm, using repetitive words or phrases, having difficulty in starting a conversation, taking statements very literally and not understanding simple questions or statements.

## POSITIVE OUTCOMES

One of the key focus areas for people supporting those with autism is helping them improve their ability to develop social relationships, interact at a functional level socially in order to negotiate the world around them and develop nurturing friendships. Research has shown that regular drumming sessions with a therapy focus can lead to neurobiological change that increases functional brain connectivity and improves social communication and connection.[4] Group drumming activities are social in

---

2   Sharda, M., Tuerk, C., Chowdhury, R., Jamey, K. *et al.* (2018) 'Music improves social communication and auditory–motor connectivity in children with autism.' *Translational Psychiatry 8*, 231.
3   Smith, M., Segal, J. & Hutman, T. (2019) 'Help guide: Autism Spectrum Disorders.' www.helpguide.org/articles/autism-learning-disabilities/autism-spectrum-disorders.htm (accessed 3 August 2020).
4   Sharda, M., Tuerk, C., Chowdhury, R., Jamey, K. *et al.* (2018) 'Music improves social communication and auditory–motor connectivity in children with autism.' *Translational Psychiatry 8*, 231.

nature but without the stress factor of language. Inclusion in a drum circle helps reinforce social cues and skills as people interact through a focus on music and learn to play in harmony together. The skill set needed to work as part of a musical team replicates many of those necessary to negotiate inter-personal social interaction generally.[5]

The drum also offers a highly useful medium for practising emotional communication, developing emotional awareness and improving emotional regulation.[6] Research has shown that that highly structured rhythmic interventions at a slow tempo can improve levels of systemic pacing, motor planning, visual contact, attention, and general functional adaptation while reducing levels of anxiety and repetitive behaviours.[7] Note the key recommendation of slower tempo rhythms that are known to be calming – higher frequency tempos can cause irritation and anxiety.

Growing evidence indicates that neurological dysfunction may be associated with abnormal movements seen in individuals with autism. Recent research points towards rhythmic therapies being useful in addressing motor coordination, motor planning, and functional motor skill development.[8] Musical rhythmic stimulation activates motor areas of the brain including the pre-motor cortex, supplementary motor areas, pre-supplementary motor area, and the lateral cerebellum. This can lead to improved synchronization and fluidity of movement when linked to an external rhythmic cue for people with this neurological disability.[9]

Other benefits I have seen through my work in this area include:

- a sense of accomplishment that participants receive when they create their own sound and music and there are no mistakes

---

5   Yoo, G.E. & Kim, S.J. (2018) 'Dyadic drum playing and social skills: Implications for rhythm-mediated intervention for children with autism spectrum disorder.' *Journal of Music Therapy 55*, 3, 340–375.
6   Srinivasan, S.M. & Bhat, A.N. (2013) 'A review of "music and movement" therapies for children with autism: Embodied interventions for multisystem development.' *Frontiers in Integrative Neuroscience 7*, 22.
    Sharda, M., Tuerk, C., Chowdhury, R., Jamey, K. et al. (2018) 'Music improves social communication and auditory–motor connectivity in children with autism.' *Translational Psychiatry 8*, 231.
7   Berger, D.S. (2011) 'Pilot study investigating the efficacy of tempo-specific rhythm interventions in music-based treatment addressing hyper-arousal, anxiety, system pacing and redirection from fight or flight fear behaviours in children with ASD.' *Journal of Biomusical Engineering, 2*, 2, 1–15.
8   Hardy, M.W. & Lagasse, A.B. (2013) 'Rhythm, movement, and autism: Using rhythmic rehabilitation research as a model for autism.' *Frontiers in Integrative Neuroscience 7*, 19.
9   Thaut, M.H., Kenyon, G.P., Schauer, M.L. & McIntosh, G.C. (1999) 'The connection between rhythmicity and brain function.' *IEEE Engineering in Medicine and Biology Magazine: The Quarterly Magazine of the Engineering in Medicine & Biology Society 18*, 2, 101–108.

- a high degree of comfort and ease with these types of instruments and sounds
- an increased level of grounding through connection to the pulse that helps control the need for repetitive body movement
- improvements in cognitive function.

## SETTING UP FOR SUCCESS

In a community drum circle I am always prepared with some earplugs. I am pretty careful about sound levels in all my circles but this is particularly crucial when working with community groups that include ASD participants. When I notice someone covering their ears, I have earplugs (or sometimes headphones) available for them in order to reduce their sensory pain. I also always have in my kit, mallets with padding on the handles for participants with texture or grip issues. It is useful to provide a range of different instruments, of different sizes and textures, to help people with ASD find the right sensory feedback. And if they come with a helper, it is easier for them to help find just the right feeling and sound for those in their care. My kit has many different types of shakers, and wooden instruments that are not shrill, and bells that can be shaken, rather than hit.

When setting out your instruments you need to know the ages that will be participating. Are your instruments safe to be put in the mouth? Is there a potential choking hazard? (Test: if it can go through a toilet paper tube it is a choking hazard!) Can you sanitize them? Make sure anything you use can be cleaned both before and after your circle. It is not unusual for hands to be put in the mouth and then on the instruments. Wiping them thoroughly with sanitizing wipes every time is a good habit to have.

Before working with children or adults with ASD, seek out information on the individuals you will be serving as every individual is different and it can be helpful to know each person's idiosyncrasies. Ask those in charge what markers (body language) you should know or be alert for. If there are signs that are commonly used for stop, listen, watch – learn them. Be aware of the dangers of over stimulation and try and create an environment in your area that reduces unnecessary distractions. Sometimes over-enthusiasm needs to be moderated. (Solo rumble drumming is not unusual but can be disruptive if not moderated!) A bass frame drum is calming and helps keep the group grounded and together. Be as predictable as possible – same starting and finishing times, same introductory and closing exercises. And give your instructions as clearly and concretely as you can. Keep it simple!

## COMMON CHALLENGES AND HOW TO MINIMIZE THEM

The biggest challenge I have found when working with people with ASD is knowing how to use what they give you. Understand that eye contact is difficult but that smiles are not. Know that repetitive movement and sound is good in a drum circle. Do not think that all loud sounds are banned; they just can't be constant. When the group knows they are coming they can be a joy. Telegraphing what you are going to do is extremely important. Know that the variety of your kit is your saving grace. If you can, turn instrument selection into a musical game. You will find that as the drum circle progresses, the abilities of the group will greatly improve. The more you connect through rhythm the more they will be connected.

As a drum circle facilitator it is important to recognize an individual's hypo or hyper reactions to sensory input; this means being alert to high levels of sensitivity to sound, touch, textures, etc. Get to know your group members' needs in this area and find ways of helping them feel comfortable. Repetitive body movements (known as stimming), such as flapping, rocking or just constantly moving, are also common in the circle and may be distracting and sometimes anxiety provoking – it is important to find ways to stay calm. The more you can feel comfortable with simply experiencing whatever the group members bring to the music-making, the more relaxed and creative you will be as a facilitator.

In working with this population, I have found two important elements are 'telegraphing' and variety. Telegraphing is making your movements large and obvious, thus signalling your intention prior to any action. This helps to reduce any surprise and the anxiety that may be aroused. Selecting groups of players with different sound types (wood, metal, shakers, drums) is a great way to help them focus and also gives them a break from playing all the time. Keep your interventions and explanations short. Be clear in your directions – tell what will happen, show what will happen, and then do it. Do it more than once. Reinforce the strong bass beat frequently to keep the group grounded.

This is not a group that you would generally pass out parts! 'Call and response' can be very successful. It also gives breathing room in the circle. Your highest success will come from letting each person find their music and be the music. Soloing can be very successful and you can use it to turn an impulsive movement into a positive experience. Constant variety is a wonderful characteristic that in a drum circle allows for lots of great sounds and movement.

I have also found that with younger age groups, there will be some who will, at times, need to move away from the circle. I always have a spot for these individuals to step away. I make sure this spot has sensory items. When they hear something that draws them back, they return. Always ensure that you have someone with them to support what they need at that moment.

## PRACTICAL APPLICATIONS OF THE DRUM CIRCLE

One of the things I do to open the circle is play a steady beat on a low drum and ask everyone to join in. I then ask everyone to add to my beat. This is where I can evaluate where the participants are developmentally, i.e., their tolerance for sound, eye contact, willingness to be active in the group and other variables. I will usually follow this with a 'call and response' activity. (I play a simple pattern and the group echoes!) I start with really simple calls using not only my drum but adding some vocal silliness, body percussion, etc. This leads to letting individuals do the 'call' and the group responding. The wonderful part of this action is that it activates both social and emotional interaction between the group participants. It also readily involves the non-verbal drummers.

Taking this activity one step further I extend the 'call and response' beyond just instruments to the voice and the body. Silliness and joy arise spontaneously when you use body percussion and movement that everyone has to copy. Again, guidelines about appropriate behaviours may be necessary.

Practising getting steadily softer or louder is a simple way of helping these children with emotional control. As individuals or as a group, we can learn to lower our volume gradually and then increase again with greater and greater control.

Another intervention that is very rewarding and reinforces social skills and emotional awareness is the use of dialogue games where people have to have a conversation on their drum with another person in the circle. In these exercises they practise making eye contact, turn-taking, and responding at a similar level (attuning volume and feeling) to that of their partner. And guessing games where one individual can play a feeling on their drum and the rest of the group have to guess what they were playing can assist with emotional awareness.

Drumming exercises that utilize two hands and involve crossing the mid-line (body centre-line) can be very useful in overcoming the developmental delay caused by avoiding this technique. Implementing exercises where you reach over with one hand, across your own body, and play a beat on your neighbour's drum, swapping sides each time are one fun way of doing this. If you bring the circle in tight there are many different rhythms that can be played together while crossing the mid-line, and at the same time, building bilateral integration skills. *Note*: I will only use this intervention when I know the participants well. Otherwise you can wind up in crisis mode due to sensory issues around touch, inappropriate touching and other person boundary dilemmas.

I often ask people to play their feelings on the drum and we may try to name these. A fun game that addresses emotional awareness is 'Freeze' – in this game one person chooses a feeling. Everyone plays along until the facilitator calls down to STOP. When the music stops everyone has to 'Freeze' with the emotion on their face – the person with the best expression gets to choose the next feeling and so the game repeats.

Other fun instruments I have in my kit are a 'pentatonic' set of Boomwhackers – coloured plastic tubes of different length arranged tonally, because when you play these anything goes (no notes clash) and they are very accessible. They can be played immediately and in many different ways, which bolsters confidence and allows for varying degrees of sensory stimulation, e.g., playing on the body can be useful for somatic awareness. They are colourful and you can give people different parts based on their colour (tone) and arrange these in multiple fun ways.

## ADDITIONAL ADVICE

Music extends the possibilities for communication and reduces the boundaries associated with language. This can be particularly important for those with ASD who are non-verbal or borderline verbal. Music can be used as a representation of some aspect of a person's experience. It allows them to paint a picture of an experience, a feeling or a journey. The drum circle provides an opportunity to converse without words. It allows for personal expression without words getting in the way. Always be alert and respond to any sounds or signs that the participants offer during these activities as they can be the beginnings of new pathways to connection.

Either in a community circle or as a specialist group, working with people with autism is never something to fear. When the music of the circle brings them into community, wonders happen. Appreciate what wonderful things they bring to your drum circle and what their smiles and body language tell you of the joy that your circle has inspired in them.

## AUTHOR'S BIOGRAPHY
### Nellie Hill, MA (Music Education)

Nellie is an accredited drum circle facilitator and operates as 'Playful Spirit Adventures'. She is the co-author of the *Drum Circle Facilitator's Handbook*, along with Arthur Hull. She is a retired music teacher and has facilitated many populations from preschool to special needs, and the elderly. She is a long-time board member of the Drum Circle Facilitator's Guild – the professional organization dedicated to supporting DCFs. Nellie, with her partner, also has first-hand experience of raising an autistic child, something that, though at times is demanding, gives her great pleasure.

Email: playfulspirit@mac.com
www.playfulspiritadventures.com

## RECOMMENDED READING

Autism Spectrum Disorders, A Parent's Guide to Symptoms and Diagnosis of the Autism Spectrum Disorder. www.helpguide.org.

Berger, D.S. (2017) *Kids, Music 'N' Autism, Bringing Out the Music in Your Child.* London: Jessica Kingsley Publishers.

# Trauma

## SIMON FAULKNER

**OVERVIEW**

Our understanding of the way trauma impacts people's health and behaviour has increased significantly in recent years, primarily due to an improved understanding of the way the human brain reacts to stress. Neurological research has revealed the way people who have had experiences of violence, abuse, neglect, or extreme fear, helplessness or horror, maintain vulnerabilities linked to these experiences well into the future. In mental health settings, drug and alcohol rehabilitation, prisons, behavioural centres and other environments where facilitators may be working, the likelihood that certain individuals within your groups have histories of trauma is high.

The use of expressive therapies, including drumming, in trauma recovery is increasingly valued by therapists as neuroscientific research reveals the limitations of talk-based approaches and the central role of the body and bodily feelings.[1] Effective therapies then should include elements of sensorimotor processing (physical and sensory responses,

---

1   Ogden, P., Minton, K. & Pain, C. (2006) *Trauma and the Body: A Sensorimotor Approach to Psychotherapy.* New York: Norton.

sensations and movement). The drum circle also provides a highly accessible pathway to cementing the critical phase of safety and stabilization that is recognized as the essential first stage of any trauma-informed practice.[2] One of the key research outcomes from drumming therapies is the importance of slower tempos in creating this safe space.[3] Tempos that replicate the mother's heartbeat at rest (60–80bpm) are thought to sub-consciously recreate the safe associations of the womb, and may assist with re-stabilizing primal brain structures dysregulated through exposure to trauma.[4]

This focus on safety and stabilization, so critical for working with this demographic, requires a facilitation approach focused on empathy and understanding, which aims to assist in helping stabilize those emotions that interfere with daily functioning. Creating a safe, respectful and predictable environment is central to this outcome. Unfortunately, people who have experienced trauma and may be suffering from post-traumatic stress disorder (PTSD) can have unpredictable sensitivities, or triggers, that can lead to a recurrence of the initial trauma-evoking experience and the behavioural characteristics that people use to combat them, sometimes categorized as fight, flight or freeze. This means that working with this group requires sensitivity and flexibility, as well as ensuring that access to additional therapeutic support is available if needed.

## POSITIVE OUTCOMES

Because of the complexity and different manifestations of trauma, it can be highly challenging to measure specific change, and where research is forthcoming it often focuses on only one area of adversity.

Many of the positive benefits identified by practitioners stem from the work of trauma theorists like Bessel van der Kolk and Pat Ogden who advocate the benefits of introducing somatic, experiential processes to complement traditional cognitive therapeutic approaches. McFerrin and her colleagues have suggested that the beneficial outcomes of rhythmic

---

[2] Kezelman, C.A. & Stravropoulos, P.A. (2012) *Practice Guidelines for treatment of complex trauma and trauma informed care & service delivery*. Adults surviving child abuse. Sydney, Australia.

[3] Berger, D.S. (2011) 'Pilot study investigating the efficacy of tempo-specific rhythm interventions in music-based treatment addressing hyper-arousal, anxiety, system pacing and redirection from fight or flight fear behaviours in children with ASD.' *Journal of Biomusical Engineering 2*, 2, 1–15.

[4] MacKinnon, L. (2012) 'Neurosequential model of therapeutics: Interview with Bruce Perry.' *The Australian & New Zealand Journal of Family Therapy 33*, 3 210–218. http://childtrauma.org/cta-library/interventions (accessed 3 August 2020).

music, specific to the drum circle, for those managing the impacts of trauma, may be divided into four areas:[5]

- *Stabilizing* – the playing of predictable and stable patterns can potentially help stabilize and calm an over-sensitive central nervous system.[6]
- *Entrainment* – providing both a physiological and inter-personal synchronization that bypasses trauma-impacted cognitive processes and delivers a safe avenue for connection.[7]
- *Expressive* – the opportunity to express and explore feelings through the medium of music, including a focus on regulation;[8] this outcome is often extended through the addition of reflective discussions.
- *Performative* – the use of performance to reconstruct identity and improve self-construct.[9]

Two important studies by Bensimon[10] and his colleagues in Israel, and Martin and Wood[11] in Australia have found reductions in PTSD symptoms with very different population groups (soldiers and high-risk youth). In both of these studies, psychological distress and levels of aggression diminished, while feelings of belonging and social acceptance increased. Additionally, the use of drumming as a focus for mindfulness has significant applications within trauma treatment, in reducing avoidance and disassociation, and is supported by an increasing body of evidence.[12]

Other benefits noted through my own personal observation and feedback from clients that is supported by drum-related research with other population groups include:

---

5   McFerran, K.S., Lai, H., Chang, W.H., Acquaro, D., Chin, T.C., Stokes, H. & Crooke, A. (2020) 'Music, rhythm and trauma: A critical interpretive synthesis of research literature.' *Frontiers in Psychology 11*, 324.
6   Porges S. (2011) *The Polyvagal Theory*. New York: W.W. Norton & Co.
7   Ogden, P., Minton, K. & Pain, C. (2006) *Trauma and the Body: A Sensorimotor Approach to Psychotherapy*. New York: Norton.
8   Van der Kolk, B., McFarlane, A. & Weisaeth, W. (2007) *Traumatic Stress: The Effects of Overwhelming Experience on Mind, Body and Society*. New York: Guilford Press.
9   Butler, J. (2010) 'Performative agency.' *The Journal of Cultural Economics 3*, 2, 147–161.
10  Bensimon, M., Amir, D. & Wolf, Y. (2008) 'Drumming through trauma: Music therapy with post-traumatic soldiers.' *The Arts in Psychotherapy 35*, 1, 34–48.
11  Martin, K.E. & Wood, L.J. (2017) 'Drumming to a new beat: A group therapeutic drumming and talking intervention designed to improve mental health and behaviour of disadvantaged adolescent boys.' *Children Australia 42*, 268–276.
12  Thompson, R.W. Arnkoff, D.B. & Glass, C.R. (2011) 'Conceptualizing mindfulness and acceptance as components of psychological resistance to trauma.' *Trauma, Violence & Abuse 12*, 4, 220–235.

- improved sleeping patterns
- a reduction in hyper-vigilant thoughts
- reductions in stress and anxiety
- improvements in emotional regulation
- improvements in psychological wellbeing, including mood and affect
- instillation of hope.

Because isolation is such a common issue for people dealing with trauma, the ability of drumming groups to provide support and reconnection for members is particularly important for recovery.

## SETTING UP FOR SUCCESS

When I am invited by a service organization or school to run a drum circle and the nature of the enquiry relates to supporting people with social and emotional needs, I will seek information from the organizer about the participants and their presenting needs. 'Are you aware of any of the participants experiencing significant trauma?' And if so 'Are you aware of any specific triggers that I might need to avoid?' In certain contexts, it is a given that a high number of people will have PTSD – veterans groups, or domestic violence survivor groups for instance. Knowing in advance of potential triggers can help you avoid re-traumatizing susceptible individuals.

Often trauma groups are set up to help people share experiences, reduce isolation and validate feelings. Drum circles can work with each of these aims. Setting up clear boundaries at the beginning of the circle and setting a tone of acceptance, respect and tolerance for all will help create a sense of safety for participants. Ensuring that people who are experiencing or have recent histories of psychosis or high-level paranoia, or who are over-stimulated by groups, or who are particularly sensitive to sound are not forced to attend is also important – pre-group assessments by organizers can assist with identifying these individuals.

## COMMON CHALLENGES AND HOW TO MINIMIZE THEM

Avoiding re-traumatizing group members: this is probably our chief responsibility when we work with this population group. The last thing we want to do is further damage. Luckily for us as drum circle facilitators most of the danger that leads to re-traumatization stems from people revisiting their experiences verbally with a group leader. In the drum circle re-traumatization can occur if people feel overwhelmed by the level of sound, or the complexity and speed of the rhythm – soft, slow, simple rhythms are always preferable, with a strong grounding pulse.

Managing challenging behaviours and distress is an important skill when working in this field; many people, young and old, who have experienced trauma present with difficult behaviours, often driven subconsciously, that stem from the way they react to stress. They maybe hypersensitive to feelings of threat, socially anxious and avoidant, or have low levels of impulse control. Again, ensuring physical and emotional safety becomes critical. Other issues that relate to safety include a focus on predictability and generally trying to avoid too many new things. Avoid reacting to disruptive behaviours unless they impact emotional or physical safety – a degree of tolerance and patience is critical as rhythmic alignment may take time and trauma can also impact motor coordination and timing. If people do react to the drumming and become overwhelmed, it is vital that the organization provides trained therapists to be on hand and to support them away from the circle.

One of the common ways that trauma manifests itself is through disassociation, where an individual mentally separates themselves from the reality of a situation to avoid the emotional pain and distress it evokes. Drumming as an activity is useful for many people with dissociative tendencies because it helps people maintain a focused awareness in the present moment, as they play, connect and learn together. However, there is always the potential for experiences to become overwhelming and some people may move into a state of disassociation as a means of psychological defence. In these situations, it is helpful to bring people back to the current reality by using calming strategies – helping them focus on their breath, ground their feet, and relax any tension in the body.

Working with people who have experienced horrible ordeals can put facilitators at risk of 'vicarious trauma' – identifying with what your group members have been through and suffering similar consequences. Signs of this occurring are when you find yourself struggling with sleep, feeling guilty or shamed, indulging in rescue fantasies or just becoming overly sensitive to others' experiences. Empathy is a fundamental quality for this form of work, but if you have your own trauma history it can also lead to revisiting your own experiences. Ensure that you are emotionally stable before accepting this work.

## PRACTICAL APPLICATIONS OF THE DRUM CIRCLE

Most of the work a drum circle facilitator will do in supporting people with trauma symptoms comes under the mantle of 'early stage interventions' where the focus is predominantly on 'safety and stabilization'.[13] The 'processing' and 'integration' stages of recovery should not be initiated until this 'stabilization' phase is secured, particularly the ability of the client to regulate their emotions.

### Mindfulness exercise

*Note*: Mindfulness needs to become a regular practice in order to be effective. Many facilitators make this a regular part of their sessions.

One of the most useful exercises I utilize in my work with people recovering from trauma is to bring the music of the circle down to a single pulse and then go into a mindfulness routine. Mindfulness practice has been shown to help people dealing with trauma relax and find a measure of acceptance towards the traumatic memories that continue to impact them, reducing hyper-vigilance and stress, as well as supporting reductions in disassociation.[14] To the beat of a slow bass pulse (facilitator plays around 60–80 bpm) I ask people to first stop drumming but to tap the slow pulse on their leg and relax into their chair, lower their gaze or lightly shut their eyes and focus first on the sound of the pulse and then move that focus to their breath and deepen and slow the breath. A short script that looks at acceptance – making room for the trauma without being beholden to it can be useful.

#### Acceptance

Use a simple and very soft bass pulse (60–80 bpm) for this awareness exercise. Give instructions in a mellow, clear voice, speaking slowly in time to the rhythm. Remember, the script below is just a guide – make it your own.

- Relax your body.

- Adjust your body until you feel comfortable and relaxed. You may wish to close your eyes or focus your gaze on one spot. Focus on

---

13 Kezelman, C.A. & Stravropoulos, P.A. (2012) *Practice Guidelines for Treatment of Complex Trauma and Trauma Informed Care and Service Delivery*. Adults surviving child abuse. Sydney, Australia.

14 Kimbrough, E., Magyari, T., Langenberg, P., Chesney, M. & Berman, B. (2010) 'Mindfulness intervention for child abuse survivors.' *Journal of Clinical Psychology 66*, 17–33.
Follette, V.M., Palm, K.M. & Hall, M.L.R. (2004) 'Acceptance, Mindfulness, and Trauma.' In S.C. Hayes, V.M. Follette & M.M. Linehan (eds) *Mindfulness and Acceptance: Expanding the Cognitive-Behavioral Tradition*. New York: Guilford Press.

and relax any tension in your neck, shoulders, chest, arms, hands, back, hips, thighs, lower legs, and feet.

- Slow your breathing – focus on your breath, aligning it to the pulse, becoming still.
- Now move your focus to the sound of the bass note.
- Then slowly transfer your focus back to your body and those parts where you may be feeling sensations – observe any bodily feelings, tingling, warmth, etc., with curiosity and interest, like an explorer or birdwatcher. Focus closely on these sensations in all their different states, letting any other thoughts that come to mind pass gently by.
- Breathe gently, slowly and in time with the pulse.
- As you breathe and focus on these feelings, try to make some space for them, allowing them just to be there – breathe in and around them. Maintain your focus on these feelings but see them from a detached perspective, where you control the view.
- Breathe gently and slowly, and in time with your breath make individual statements of acceptance of your feelings and sensations – these are normal.
- Now move your thoughts to the idea of acceptance, allowing a warmth to settle over these feelings. A warmth of understanding, even to those feelings of angst, pain or distress – breathe.
- Picture yourself now, free from the dominance of these feelings and instead more accepting and appreciative of them – their right to exist and be a part of you without overshadowing or dominating you.
- Breathe gently, slowly.
- Slowly move your focus back to the bass note.
- Hold your focus on the bass note as it slowly fades away.

If possible, sit in silence for 40–60 seconds, or if doing this as part of the rhythmic wave exercise below, you may prefer to rebuild the rhythm you were playing in the beginning.

Discuss the challenges and benefits of acceptance.

## Grounding exercise

Grounding techniques are important skills for people working with traumatized individuals and can help defuse an escalating situation and calm an anxious client. Grounding strategies share the same therapy focus as mindfulness – helping a person stay connected to the present, so as to minimize the distress caused by difficult memories and emotions.

### Body – pulse – grounding

Have each person accent the bass pulse on their drum at a tempo of 60–80bpm.

- Become aware of your breath and align it to the pulse – breathing slowly, deeply, relaxed and regularly. Take your time to align the rhythm of your breath. If you lose your focus that is perfectly OK – you are alert to that and can find your way back.

- Now joining on the bass, see if you can bring in your other hand. Make sure the bass pulse stays slow and steady. (Facilitator demonstrates double hand bass pulse first, then playing between the pulse on the tone – maintaining the bass pulse at the same tempo while adding a simple fill, e.g., B O O O repeat.)

*Note*: this section is unnecessary if using frame drums.

- Feel the pulse move through the body like a warm vibration. Take your time moving both hands to the grounding pulse.

- Now see what other parts of the body we can connect to the rhythm, starting with our feet, legs and thighs – tapping, stepping, moving in sync to the beat. Take your time and keep your breath steady, go at your own speed.

*Note*: if using frame drums you may decide to walk to the rhythm at this point.

- Now move up through the body – moving the torso; swaying, or rocking to the pulse.

- Now relax the shoulders and let them join in and then extend this to your neck and head as your whole body synchronizes to the mother pulse – one rhythm linking you, unifying, grounding, stabilizing, loosening, accepting.

- Fade slowly away and allow a moment's stillness.

*Note*: you can add voice (chants) as well if people are comfortable.

## Emotional regulation exercise

More than any other factor, being able to manage the emotional roller coaster of traumatic memories is the first critical step in recovery. Being able to self-monitor, intercept and then manage one's emotions is central to an enduring sense of safety. Assisting people to maintain their emotional states within a 'window of tolerance'; avoiding the extremes of hyper- and hypo-arousal is a key objective within trauma support programs.[15]

### The rhythmic wave

An exercise I find useful for working with clients, in both group and one-to-one situations, is to alternate volume and tempo from high and fast to slow and soft and have the client/s practise this several times over the course of a session. The loud, high tempo playing represents the heightening of emotional arousal and is connected by analogy to a loss of control, and the transition to slow soft playing, (usually a single bass pulse of 60–80 bpm) a taking back of that control. Additional calming strategies can be applied at the calm end of the cycle including instructions to lengthen the breath and relax the shoulders. Client consent and close monitoring of the reaction of each individual to the loud and fast drumming is critical in exercising this technique as some people may find it anxiety inducing, but generally it is a comfortable way to practice moving between the extremes to a position of control. After practice on the drum, this routine can be extended to the body, and I have had many clients utilize this calming technique in times of stress.

Remember to always finish your sessions in a soft and tranquil way.

## Strength-based/resilience exercise

Working from a strength-based approach and recognizing the resilience in the individual provides a foundation for future growth. Recognize that many of the negative symptoms and behaviours that a client engages in are actually adaptive responses rather than problems. A common outcome of trauma is a feeling of powerlessness – focusing on an individual's strengths helps them to re-establish the sense of autonomy and control required to move forward with their lives.

### Bounce back

Pre-discussion: It would be fair to say, that across our lives there will be many events that 'knock us down' and set our lives back – all of us have

---

15  Van der Kolk, B.A. (2014) *The Body Keeps the Score: Brain, Mind, and Body in the Healing of Trauma.* New York: Viking.

experienced these at different times and often we feel as though there is no return. But think about a time where you have been knocked back and found a way to get back on your feet – what are some of things that have helped you?

In this exercise we are going to hear one rhythm that knocks you down (a crisis) and have a period of recovery (8 counts) that allows us to get back on our feet (resilience). As you slump low think about the types of things that 'get you down' and as you rise up out of your chair think about what helps you 'bounce back'.

We start with a simple, steady rhythm, representing life going on as normal and then the facilitator plays a loud sharp rumble representing a crisis (12 quick Tones followed by a sharp Flam (a sharp accent note played with two hands)). When you hear that you have to stop playing and slump in your chairs as low as possible (representing being knocked back). After a reasonable pause the facilitator counts out 1, 2, 3, 4, 5, 6, 7, 8 aloud as you slowly regain your strength and sit upright – by the number eight you should be standing. Then we all hit the bass notes three times (representing 'back on track') and then resume our seat and re-enter the foundation rhythm.

The facilitator demonstrates the process and leads the first crisis call before giving others an opportunity. The exercise finishes with everyone yelling out as they hit the three basses 'back on track!'

## ADDITIONAL ADVICE

When working in this sphere a lot of positives can come from the activity of improvised music-making, particularly when we can connect that activity to overcoming some of the social challenges people are facing due to their trauma, and to helping reconnect to others in a safe way.

The drum is also a wonderful tool to help people share and release feelings without the judgement and misinterpretation that often accompanies the verbal expression of feelings. Instead of asking, 'How did that feel?' we can instead ask, 'Would you like to play how that felt?' It is not necessary for people to articulate their feelings or experiences; instead the drum becomes a safe alternative form for this cathartic expression. Always work from an empowering and strengths-based approach and ensure that you work with co-facilitators or other supportive personnel who have experience managing these types of groups.

## AUTHOR'S BIOGRAPHY
### Simon Faulkner BSocSc (Psychology & Addiction) MCouns.

Simon is the director of the therapeutic service, Rhythm2Recovery, and has worked extensively with people who are living with the repercussions of trauma, in child protection services, refugee trauma services, prisons, and drug and alcohol rehabilitation services. Simon trains professionals internationally in a model of therapy based on his book *Rhythm to Recovery*, which combines rhythmic music with cognitive reflection.

   Email: simon@rhythm2recovery.com
   www.rhythm2recovery.com
   Facebook: www.facebook.com/rhythm2recovery

## RECOMMENDED READING

Ogden, P., Minton, K., & Pain, C. (2006) *Trauma and the Body: A Sensorimotor Approach.* New York: Norton.

Van der Kolk, B.A. (2014) *The Body Keeps the Score: Brain, Mind, and Body in the Healing of Trauma.* New York: Viking.

# Mental Health

## DR JANE BENTLEY

**OVERVIEW**

Because of the social, cooperative, connecting nature of group drumming, it lends itself especially well to mental health settings, and can be a fertile ground for engaging social and communicative development, as well as being an activity that has a high level of intrinsic motivation and reward. Broadly, work takes place in either community or hospital settings. In the community, settings include mental health support groups – geographical, gender or issue-based; carers groups; recovery groups; and day hospital; outpatient clinics; and community mental health centres.

In hospital, there are usually several different types of ward:

- Acute – short-term stays in times of crisis, with high patient turnover

- Intensive Psychiatric Care Unit – longer-term, for people experiencing more severe symptoms

- Rehabilitation/recovery – longer-term: geared towards rebuilding life skills

- Forensic – secure care for people whose mental health has brought them into contact with criminal justice settings, or puts them at risk of offending. A significant proportion of this population have a learning disability
- Older adult – also brings the physical challenges of ageing. Wards can be separated into functional/organic wards (equivalent to an acute setting), and dementia-specific wards
- Child and adolescent (CAMHS) – care for young people.

Often the Occupational Therapy Department will be your point of contact.

Presenting needs can include: low confidence; low motivation; difficulty in concentration/task persistence; hyperactivity and challenges with self-management; noise sensitivity; difficulties with social/group interaction; social anxiety. Further needs include: recognition as an individual; genuine praise where it's due; a chance to shine; a chance to hide; structure and safe boundaries; authenticity of relationship; humour; appropriate challenge; opportunities to connect; and freedom to withdraw.

## POSITIVE OUTCOMES

Researchers are showing increasing interest in this area, with several large, well-organized studies showcasing the potential of this type of intervention in mental health recovery. Drumming has been identified by participants as energizing and liberating; as a form of non-verbal communication; as a catalyst for belonging, acceptance and positive relationships; increasing self-efficacy and agency, confidence in the learning process, focus and flow; creating positive self-identity, and physical wellbeing.[1]

Using psychological testing, Dr Daisy Fancourt and her research colleagues at University College London have shown that regular drumming interventions can increase wellbeing and social resilience and reduce depression and anxiety over a 10-week period.[2] In the same experiment, accompanying biomarker research identified a shift from a pro-inflammatory

---

1 Perkins, R., Ascenso, S., Atkins, L., Fancourt, D. & Williamon, A. (2016) 'Making music for mental health: How group drumming mediates recovery.' *Psychology of Well-Being* 6, 1, 11. Ascenso, S., Perkins, R., Atkins, L., Fancourt, D. & Williamon, A. (2018) 'Promoting well-being through group drumming with mental health service users and their carers.' *International Journal of Qualitative Studies on Health and Well-Being* 13, 1.

2 Fancourt, D., Perkins, R., Ascenso, S., Carvalho, L.A., Steptoe, A. & Williamon, A. (2016) 'Effects of group drumming interventions on anxiety, depression, social resilience and inflammatory immune response among mental health service users.' *PLoS ONE* 11, 3.

to an anti-inflammatory immune profile, which has broader implications for long-term health outcomes.[3]

Very little explicit research is available on the contraindications of drumming – mental health is a sensitive area and there is potential for drumming to escalate mental health challenges – particularly with people experiencing schizophrenia or psychosis. Each person is completely individual in this regard, however, and so negative outcomes should be approached rapidly and responsibly, but on a case-by-case basis with trained professionals.

## SETTING UP FOR SUCCESS

Small groups work well – between seven and 20 people. Sometimes just being in the room is a big deal: don't pressure people to participate, as long as they are not disrupting the group. Be flexible with time – 20 good minutes are better than an hour of half-hearted participation. Manage the instruments and help people to avoid injury by teaching good technique, and the ability to start, stop and modulate volume right from the start. Take extra care with bell sounds and instruments with sticks until you know your group.

If there are opportunities to succeed at something early on, however simple it may be, it builds a foundation for taking the next step. Help the group recognize their successes. If just a couple of staff or group members have had a positive experience, they will tell others about it, and will often be a lot more successful in convincing people to join! Be prepared to be vulnerable – it's so much more empowering than appearing to be a 'perfect' facilitator. Shift between playing together as a group and exercises that offer space for more individual turn-taking and attention, then back again. If you can, build in a social element, e.g., a refreshment break – often the act of playing music can help to reduce social inhibitions and enable people to feel more confident during non-drumming time.

## COMMON CHALLENGES AND HOW TO MINIMIZE THEM

These tend to fall at either end of the energy spectrum – either apathy and lack of confidence, or over-confidence and continual interruption. For ebullient members of the group, self-management exercises such as copying someone else, raising and lowering volume together, and turn-

---

[3] Fancourt, D., Perkins, R., Ascenso, S., Atkins, L., Kilfeather, S., Carvalho, L., Steptoe, A. & Williamon, A. (2016) 'Group drumming modulates cytokine response in mental health services users: A preliminary study.' *Psychotherapy and Psychosomatics 85*, 1, 53–55.

taking become important. Try and avoid energetic extremes – have a way down off the 'high' and be aware of how excited or stimulated people are getting; be able to return in a connected way to a gentler pace if necessary.

For people who are self-conscious, have a 'get-out' of turn-taking games, etc., that allows less participation or exposure, but maintains just a little challenge, so that it's not really a get-out entirely. For example, in the pass the beat game (below), someone could simply choose the next person to take a turn, rather than play their drum and point. Or play just one sound on their drum, rather than try a rhythm.

There can often be an incredible diversity of competence in a group – you might have someone who struggles to coordinate their two hands sitting next to someone who's highly musical and rhythmical. For this reason, improvisation can be useful, allowing people to play at their own level. It is important to have ways to include a whole spectrum of ability. If you're demonstrating or teaching rhythms, always start simply and have one up your sleeve that's super-accessible and close to the pulse.

## PRACTICAL APPLICATIONS OF THE DRUM CIRCLE
### A typical session protocol
#### Set up – before the workshop

Take a look at the space – try and enable participants to sit in a circle. This allows people to see and hear each other clearly. It enables turn-taking exercises, and for participants to act as role models for each other. As a facilitator it allows you to make eye contact with everyone in the circle and to be a part of the group, rather than in a conspicuously hierarchical physical position.

Some participants can also find that sitting in a circle feels exposing. I remember one of my first workshops in a prison, where the men absolutely did not want to be seen or be visible to each other, as they had the perception of the potential for humiliation or conflict. After some negotiation, we eventually ran the first few sessions in 'lecture' mode, with the 'teacher' in front of a line of all the men. Once trust had been built within the group, it was then possible to progress to a semicircle, and eventually a circle.

#### For new participants

Drumming can seem intimidating, and there is often a fear of getting it 'wrong' in front of people. If someone is new, it's always worth going over the basics, and making it explicit that this is a beginner-friendly activity. More experienced members can be invited to help with this introduction, and explain and introduce the drum, etc. A standard introduction might be:

- *Welcome.*

- *How to hold the drum* (allowing for repositioning and use of stands if necessary).

- *Hand position for playing drums* – using a flat hand – and BOUNCE!! (Think of the drum as a trampoline to be bounced on, rather than a nail to be hammered.) Creating two sounds using the middle and edge of the drum.

- *Practise a 'rumble' (drum roll) together* – including starting and stopping on cue.

- *Practise taking the volume up and down together* (a great lesson in self-management, and a hugely helpful skill to master for the remainder of the session!).

- *Explaining the pulse* – that we all have it, where we would naturally tap our feet or fingers.

- *Explaining how to find your way back into the beat if you get lost* – stop, listen for the pulse, match it, and come back in).

- *Introductory jam* – all try the pulse together to begin with, then encourage people to explore and change what they are doing, but stay connected. Encourage people to copy each other if that helps! For two to five minutes, everyone plays, *supported* by the facilitator on the bass drum, who alternates between simple pulse playing (support and consolidation), and small solos (adding moments of interest and excitement). Mostly the facilitator's role here is to offer predictability and stability to let people find their confidence in playing along.

## Protocol for ongoing groups

- Open with a *supported* (but not overtly facilitated) *drumming groove*, allowing people to 'land' in the session, but not to have to think too much yet. Keep it light on instructions.

- *Relational games/exercises* that engage:
  - attention
  - listening
  - awareness of others
  - self-management in a group
  - building group connection.

- *Facilitated drumming* – another groove, perhaps inspired by some of the work just done; perhaps a little more overt facilitation, or not! Read the group energy – what does the group need at this time?
- *Musical development games/exercises* – these can work on concepts such as:
  - pulse
  - dialogue
  - space
  - time signatures
  - rhythm creation
  - roles of instruments
  - playing one thing while someone else is playing another.
- *Ongoing work* – this might be learning a song or a rhythm piece, or devising your own! In a weekly group it doesn't all have to happen at once. Build confidence a little at a time.
- *Closing achievement*, which could involve:
  - playing what you've just learned
  - having a brief, joyful jam
  - singing a favourite song
  - one big bang/drum roll
  - a quiet, mindful moment
  - passing the talking drumstick and sharing a sentence about what you learned/how you feel this week.

## Other exercises
### Call and response
This is an ideal exercise to follow an opening introduction, for beginners and seasoned participants alike. The facilitator plays a four-beat phrase, which the group plays straight back; then the facilitator offers another, and so on. In this setting it's helpful to start with a very simple four beats and then to gradually increase the complexity of the patterns. It's helpful to let the group know that it's not a test – there's no penalty for not getting it, we're all probably likely to fall off the rhythm at one stage. The point of the exercise is to experience trying different (unfamiliar) patterns out with the hands, which can act as starting points for drumming together and creating one's own rhythms later on. As a facilitator, try and resist the temptation to throw down your most complex moves; keep pace with

the group and take it to a point where it's just slightly more challenging, and then revert back to secure, simpler patterns. The aim is to build confidence rather than technical proficiency at this stage.

Variations include (from simple to more challenging):

- I play, you play (no timing at all, just fundamental turn-taking)
- I play for 4, you play for 4 (not necessarily copying, just starting and stopping in time)
- I play, you copy (with permission not to get it exactly right)
- I play, you play a response (musically relevant to the previous phrase, in time)
- Pass the leader (going around the circle, each participant gets to play a simple phrase which the others copy – this can be taken right back to a simple hit or rumble on the drum, without any particular rhythm)
- Pass the leader – each willing person gets to lead the group four times, before passing on the leadership.

**Bop around**
Everyone gets to play one sound on their drum, in turn, round the circle. Try it both ways around the circle, listening to the different sound made by each drum. In the next round, each member of the group gets to control which direction the sound goes either by eye contact, body language, or using names – it's easiest to work with this by just keeping it going side to side for a few rounds; then finally opening it up so that people can send it across the circle to someone else.

VARIATIONS
Try this with:

- a rumble
- a simple rhythm that gets copied each time
- a round, where everyone plays their own rhythm phrase before passing it on
- a round, where each person gets to 'solo' before passing it on.

ADVANCED VARIATIONS

Devise and practise a sonic signal that indicates which way the sound goes, or if you're 'bouncing' the sound back to the person who sent it to you. This takes significant concentration, so it's helpful to be very consistent about the meaning of each signal, or try practising just one, before introducing another.

## ADDITIONAL ADVICE

Try and avoid the stereotypical 'get your emotions out on the drums' activities unless you're a trained therapist and know how to pick up or de-escalate what could be released. Trust that the act of coming together to drum in a group is therapeutic enough, and that people are able to name their emotional release for themselves, without being led into it. A more responsible journey to make with a group is to work on exercises that gently turn attention away from a preoccupation with our own selves, sounds and performance, into listening, accepting, responding and relating to the sounds of others, and to the group as a whole. Rebuilding and reconnecting self and community is powerful medicine.

## AUTHOR'S BIOGRAPHY

**Dr Jane Bentley BA (Community Arts) PhD (Musical Interaction)**

In 2007 Jane founded the award-winning drumming group 'The Buddy Beat' for mental health and social inclusion, which continues to this day. She trains musicians, music therapists, and medical staff worldwide, and is a consultant and speaker on the subject of drum circle facilitation and the potential of music-making for social development.

>   Email: art.beat@me.com
>   www.artbeatmusic.org
>   Facebook/YouTube: Renfrewshire's The Buddy Beat

## RECOMMENDED READING

Procter, N., Hamer, H.P., McGarry, D., Wilson, R.L. & Froggatt, T. (2013) *Mental Health: A Person-Centered Approach*. Cambridge: Cambridge University Press.

Sacks, O. (1985) *The Man Who Mistook His Wife for a Hat*. London: Macmillan Publishers.

# Drugs and Alcohol

BEK WERMUT

## OVERVIEW

Drum circle work with people managing alcohol and other drug issues (AOD) can take place in a variety of settings. Some examples include short-stay inpatient withdrawal units (one to two weeks), longer-term inpatient rehabilitation programs ranging from a few weeks to a number of months, and ongoing community and family support programs.

There are many variables to consider when designing a drumming program for AOD populations. Depending on the type of setting, the duration of the treatment, the focus of the contracting service, and other life-factors, different approaches will be required. Considerations include whether participation is compulsory or voluntary, whether participation takes place as a single session intervention (such as in short hospital stays for withdrawal management) or over a number of sessions, and whether the participants of the program are a transient (open) or resident (closed) group. Personal factors such as comorbidity with mental illness and/or trauma as well as possible withdrawal symptoms and medication side effects are other important considerations. After initial stages of treatment, which are focused on detox and withdrawal, the general focus of therapy shifts to relapse prevention and social and family integration.

AOD clients can often feel isolated, disempowered, stigmatized and lack self-esteem, so creating a safe, supportive and inclusive environment, fostering positive connections within the group and creating a culture of empowerment are paramount to ensuring positive engagement and access to the benefits drumming can provide.

## POSITIVE OUTCOMES

On a social level, it is well documented that drug and alcohol addiction often contributes to relationship breakdown, a reduced sense of belonging, social isolation and a reduced ability to develop healthy relationships and social networks.[1] Group drumming and rhythm-based activity have been reported to increase social connection, sense of belonging, social skill development such as teamwork, cooperation and collaboration, and reduce social isolation.[2] Low self-worth is another common issue for people suffering with drug and alcohol addictions, and group drumming has been shown to increase participant self-esteem.[3]

Many people with substance use disorders use drugs or alcohol as a way to minimize or avoid intense negative emotions as well as to regulate these feelings. Drumming provides a safe and healthy outlet for people with AOD issues to explore, express and release emotions, as well as to aid in emotional regulation, resulting in a reduced need to rely on drugs or alcohol to manage these. Other emotionally-based positive outcomes of drumming and rhythm-based activity with AOD populations include

---

1   Faulkner, S.C. (2018) 'Therapeutic applications for integrating rhythm and reflection in support of people with co-occurring drug and alcohol, and mental health issues.' *Dual Diagnosis Open Access 3*, 5.
2   Winkelman, M. (2003) 'Complementary therapy for addiction: Drumming out drugs.' *American Journal of Public Health 93*, 4, 647–651.
    Wood, L., Ivery, P., Donovan, R. & Lambin, E. (2013) 'To the beat of a different drum: Improving the social and mental wellbeing of at-risk young people through drumming.' *Journal of Public Mental Health 12*, 70–79.
    Fancourt, D., Perkins, R., Ascenso, S., Carvalho, L.A., Steptoe, A. & Williamon, A. (2016) 'Effects of group drumming interventions on anxiety, depression, social resilience and inflammatory immune response among mental health service users.' *PloS ONE 11*, 3, e0151136.
3   Benisimon, M., Amir, D. & Wolf, Y. (2008) 'Drumming through trauma: Music therapy with post-traumatic soldiers.' *The Arts in Psychotherapy 35*, 34–48.
    Martin, K.E., Wood, L.J., Tasker, J.S. & Coletsis, C. (2014) The impact of Holyoake's DRUMBEAT program on prisoner wellbeing in Western Australian prisons.' The University of Western Australia, Crawley, Western Australia.
    Maschi, T. & Bradley, C. (2010) 'Recreational drumming: A creative arts intervention strategy for social work teaching and practice.' *Journal of Baccalaureate Social Work 15*, 5–66.

stress and anxiety reduction,[4] relaxation, and mood enhancement,[5] all of which are associated with treatment success and relapse prevention.

## ADDITIONAL THERAPEUTIC OBJECTIVES

In addition to the outcomes of rhythm-based work with AOD populations listed above, it is important that practitioners are aware of the types of behaviours and concepts that existing AOD treatment and relapse prevention approaches commonly focus on, and work to integrate musical interventions with these existing treatment approaches.[6]

Finken (2010) states that some of the skills that are required in order to prevent relapse include skills in stress management, communication, emotional expression, self-belief, developing a positive attitude, commitment to change, building healthy relationships and support systems and developing and adhering to self-care regimes. Gallagher and Steele (2002) add to this list objectives such as education around healthy drug-free living, values clarification, leadership, self-esteem building, relaxation and coping skill development and state that treatment approaches for AOD patients should address physical, social, emotional, mental, spiritual and family aspects of life if recovery is to be sustained.[7]

Specific therapeutic models can provide facilitators with a structure that integrates rhythm-based activity with education and skill development around behaviours and concepts that are central to recovery, relapse prevention and social and family integration. Some examples of how rhythm-based activities can be tied to relevant life themes through analogy as well as how client reflection and discussion around these themes can be infused into rhythmic activities are detailed in the section below entitled 'Practical applications of the drum circle'.

---

4   Ascenso, S., Perkins, R., Atkins, L., Fancourt, D. & Williamon, A. (2018) 'Promoting well-being through group drumming with mental health service users and their carers.' *International Journal of Qualitative Studies on Health and Well-Being 13*, 1. https://doi.org/10.1080/17482631.2018.1484219

5   Kaplan, C.D. (2000) 'The short-term effects of group hand drumming on mood, group cohesiveness and rhythm perception.' Doctoral Thesis, University of Connecticut. https://opencommons.uconn.edu/dissertations/AAI9949659 (accessed August 3 2020).
    Baker, F., Gleadhill, L. & Dingle, G. (2007) 'Music therapy and emotional exploration: Exposing substance abuse clients to the experiences of non-drug-induced emotions.' *The Arts in Psychotherapy 34*, 4, 21–330.

6   Finken, T. (2010) 'Music Therapy with Chemically Dependent Clients: A Relapse Prevention Model.' In D. Aldridge & J. Fachner (eds) *Music Therapy and Addictions*. London: Jessica Kingsley Publishers.

7   Gallagher, L.M. & Steele, A.L. (2002) 'Music therapy with offenders in a substance abuse/mental illness treatment program.' *Music Therapy Perspectives 20*, 2, 117–122.

## SETTING UP FOR SUCCESS
Apart from the program facilitation itself, there are a number of factors that contribute to the success of an intervention. These include:

- *Organizational support* – Having staff members within the organization who are supportive of the program, understand the program objectives and display a positive attitude towards the program has a huge impact on its success. This can influence the clients' attitude towards the program and their level of engagement. Ideally a staff member should be present in sessions to provide any support that may be required as well as assisting with participant attendance prior to session commencement where appropriate.

- *Space requirements* – The session room should be acoustically sound (i.e., not too much echo), free from distractions, and not be situated somewhere where the noise of the drumming may disturb others. Comfortable upright chairs without arms should be provided for each participant.

- *Safety* – Facilitators should be made aware of any clients who pose a potential threat to their safety (e.g., those, with a history of aggression) and a safety plan may need to be put in place. In hospital settings in particular, sanitizing instruments after each session is recommended to minimize the risk of spreading infectious disease.

## COMMON CHALLENGES AND HOW TO MINIMIZE THEM
### Anxiety
Initial feelings of anxiety are very common, as participants often don't know what to expect, fearing they may 'fail', be pushed out of their comfort zone, put on the spot or criticized. A verbal introduction that communicates the values of expression, creativity, connection, inclusiveness and diversity, rather than focusing on right or wrong, challenging people or forcing participation, as well as maintaining a warm and friendly demeanour, can help to reduce anxiety from the outset. Starting with simple rumbling activities can release tension and create an atmosphere of fun, light-heartedness and connection.

### Resistance/Disengagement
In addition to the points above addressing anxiety-related resistance, respecting people's choice not to participate while still including them in the group and gently encouraging participation often leads to increased

participation and reduced resistance. Giving all participants the option to 'pass' on any turn-taking activities also reduces resistance by empowering them to make their own decisions around their level of participation. Keeping sessions fun, light-hearted and maintaining a warm and friendly demeanour will also help to reduce resistance and positively engage participants. The use of a variety of drums and other percussion instruments as well as incorporating a varied range of activities into each session is another strategy that can help to maintain engagement for the duration of a session.

Resistance and disengagement are common where attendance is compulsory and music or drumming are not of particular interest to the client. Tying in relevant life themes with the drumming activities through analogy can be a useful strategy to engage those clients as they begin to perceive the sessions as being relevant to their lives rather than being about drumming per se.

### Disruptive behaviour
While there are many strategies that can be adopted to minimize disruptive behaviour, ensuring sessions are fun and engaging, allowing individuals to express themselves and celebrating their unique contributions can often be enough to initiate cooperative behaviour.

### Overstimulation/Triggering
For some people with a history of trauma or psychosis, high-energy drumming may be overstimulating or triggering. Minimizing high-intensity drumming and emphasizing low-volume, slow-tempo drumming can help to reduce the risk of overstimulating or triggering clients.

### Lack of confidence
Using encouragement, creating successes, highlighting strengths, encouraging expression, creativity and leadership, and empowering participants to find their own rhythms, not only builds confidence and self-esteem but also helps to create a culture of encouragement, cooperation and camaraderie within the group. This in turn contributes to increased confidence and self-esteem.

### Cognitive impairment
Clients may present with some level of cognitive impairment as a result of extended substance use or medication side effects. Focusing on

improvisation rather than set rhythms can ensure successful engagement for all, regardless of differing levels of functioning.

## PRACTICAL APPLICATIONS OF THE DRUM CIRCLE
### Rumble de-stress
In the early stages of a session or program, activities that are fun, easy and guarantee success build a sense of safety, trust, confidence and positive engagement, and reduce anxiety and resistance. Rumble-based activities are ideal introductory activities as rumbles are associated with anxiety reduction, tension release and instilling a sense of safety – one cannot fail at a rumble.

This activity combines a simple introduction to the basic strikes of the drum (in order to build confidence and comfort with the instrument) with rumbles. After demonstrating a bass and tone strike, instruct the group to repeatedly play each strike with alternating hands, starting slowly in conjunction with a common pulse and gradually getting faster. As the tempo increases and moves towards a rumble, instruct participants to use the rumble to release any stress or tension. This is a simple way to change a simple drum lesson into a fun, mood-enhancing, and de-stressing activity.

### Pass the beat
This is another activity that works well as a session or program opener due to the fact that, similarly to the 'Rumble de-stress' exercise above, it is fun, musically easy (participants are only required to play a single beat of the drum) and guarantees success, thus minimizing anxiety around failure and increasing participation and positive engagement.

Participants are instructed to play one beat on their drum and gesture that they are passing the beat to another person in the group by directing their hand towards that person after playing the beat, while making eye contact with that person. The person who receives the beat then does the same thing, playing one beat and directing it towards another person in the circle. This continues, with one beat getting passed from person to person randomly around or across the circle.

This activity requires participants to be aware of, pay attention to and connect with the other participants. So not only does it act to bring the participants together in a positive and fun way, instilling a sense of connection, but it also exercises social skills relating to communication, eye contact (where culturally appropriate) and social awareness.

Once people are feeling more comfortable within the group and more confident playing the drum (say in subsequent sessions), the activity can be extended to include more complex rhythms than just a single beat. Each person can make up any short rhythm when it's their turn to play, passing the rhythm to someone else, who then adapts it or makes up their own short rhythm before passing it on, and so on. Encouraging creative self-expression in this way empowers participants as it celebrates each person's unique voice, highlighting their value and worth in the group. The creative process is also a critical one in therapy as we seek to assist people to change problematic behaviours.

## Call and response with emotional check-in

'Call and response' is another great confidence-building, introductory activity. After an initial facilitator demonstration, I offer participants the opportunity to play a 'call' and have the group 'respond' (with the option to 'pass'). This contributes to a sense of empowerment and self-esteem, as well as providing leadership opportunities; elements which have been identified as goals of therapy in AOD treatment.[8] In order to communicate the values of creativity, expression and no right or wrong, encourage participants to focus on making the 'calls' creative and expressive rather than about timing. And make it clear that the responses are open to creative interpretation rather than needing to reflect the call exactly, removing any pressure to 'get it right' and therefore reducing any anxiety people may have around failure.

With emotional identification and expression being other well-documented therapeutic objectives in AOD treatment[9] a useful extension to this involves having the 'call' reflect participants' emotional states coming into the session. This acts as an emotional check-in, giving participants the opportunity to identify and creatively express their feelings through the drum in the form of simple 'call', and have their feelings validated through the group's 'response', which echoes their call. Expressing feelings through the drum helps to release these in a safe and healthy way, and provides an alternative option to using words, which many people struggle to articulate and feel unsafe expressing.

---

8   Gallagher, L.M. & Steele, A.L. (2002) 'Music therapy with offenders in a substance abuse/mental illness treatment program.' *Music Therapy Perspectives* 20, 2, 117–122.
9   Baker, F., Gleadhill, L. & Dingle, G. (2007) 'Music therapy and emotional exploration: Exposing substance abuse clients to the experiences of non-drug-induced emotions.' *The Arts in Psychotherapy* 34, 4, 321–330.
    Faulkner, S.C. (2018) 'Therapeutic applications for integrating rhythm and reflection in support of people with co-occurring drug and alcohol, and mental health issues.' *Dual Diagnosis Open Access* 3, 2, 4.

## Conflicting rhythms

In this activity, half the group are playing a simple 3/4 time rhythm while the other half are simultaneously playing a simple 4/4 time rhythm. The simplest rhythms to use for this activity involve playing a constant pulse, accenting the first beat of each bar with a bass tone while all other beats are played with Tones. For the 3/4 group the rhythm would be a repeated pattern of 'Bass Tone Tone' and for the 4/4 group the rhythm would be a repeated pattern of 'Bass Tone Tone Tone'. For an extra level of challenge, participants might like to yell 'hey' every 12 beats, when the bass notes of the two rhythms align.

Participants must stay focused in order to hold onto their rhythm without getting pulled into the opposing rhythm, and work together with those playing the same rhythm in order to stay on together and in time. The variation, where participants recognize their unified bass note with the word 'hey' on every 12 beats, acts to further unify participants, fostering connection, camaraderie, collaboration, belonging and a sense of collective achievement.

An analogy can be added to this which connects the idea of holding onto one's rhythm with peer pressure. This can then lead to discussions around various aspects of peer pressure and clients can draw from their experience of participating in the activity to discuss real-life examples of how others may try to draw them into opposing 'rhythms' (i.e., values, behaviours, etc.) and explore strategies they may use to resist this pull.

It is important to note that this activity requires a reasonable level of cognitive functioning, both in playing the set rhythms and in the level of focus required to hold onto one rhythm while an opposing rhythm is being played simultaneously. Even for cognitively able people, holding onto your rhythm under pressure from others to change is challenging, hence if people lose their way it is important that the facilitator acknowledge the difficulty of this activity – both in the game and in real life. This activity would not be recommended for clients whose cognitive function is significantly impaired.

## Relaxation jam

It is well-documented that stress is a strong contributing factor to drug and alcohol use as well as relapse, so stress management and relaxation are a common focus of many AOD treatment approaches. Low-volume, slow-tempo rhythmic music is known to have a calming and relaxing effect.[10]

---

10 Berger, D.S. (2011) 'Pilot study investigating the efficacy of tempo-specific rhythm interventions in music-based treatment addressing hyper-arousal, anxiety, system pacing and redirection from fight or flight fear behaviours in children with ASD.' *Journal of Biomusical Engineering 2*, 2, 1–15.

This activity involves setting up a rhythmic music improvisation where a slow tempo and low volume are maintained for the duration of the jam. Often peoples' natural inclination is to gradually speed up and get louder, so by making it clear that the intention is to resist this inclination and maintain a low volume and slow tempo, participants are required to practice regulatory constraint, thus building regulation skills. This activity can be done with hand drums and un-tuned hand-held percussion instruments, or if available, instruments such as chimes, singing bowls, xylophones and more resonant drums such as buffalo or bass drums can be added.

To enhance mindfulness and relaxation, participants are instructed to remain aware of what is happening in the present moment, paying attention to the sounds, vibrations and sensations in each moment. Giving the option to stop playing at any time throughout the relaxation jam and purely receive the music as a mindful listening activity can add to the relaxation experience. Some participants may continue to play throughout the jam, others may go in and out of playing, and some may choose to simply listen. Instructing people to observe the changes in the music as people enter and exit the improvisation is another option for mindful practice. Given that there may be a lot of change in the music as people enter and exit the music and explore different sounds, it may be useful for the facilitator to hold a steady bass pulse in order to give the music stability.

**Reflection jam**

This exercise combines percussion improvisation with verbal reflection on a wide range of themes that are relevant to AOD clients and their families. It can be used with groups at any stage of recovery, from short- and long-term treatment and relapse prevention programs to social and family integration programs, due to the wide scope and flexibility around the themes that can be explored.

The activity is based on an exercise called 'The speakers chair' from the Rhythm2Recovery model. A question that relates to a relevant life theme or therapeutic objective is posed to the group, and each individual is asked to reflect on that question and come up with an answer that relates to them, in only a few words. This method encourages clients to take an active role in therapy, drawing on their own insights and solutions, which has been shown to lead to more successful client outcomes than practitioner reflection alone.[11] To start, the group enters into a rhythmic improvisation on mixed drums and hand-held percussion instruments. The group is instructed to stop the music at regular intervals, and each time the music stops, another participant answers the question (going around the circle). One round of the activity is complete when everyone has answered the question that has been posed to the group (i.e., there is only one question posed to the group each time the activity is conducted).

As the music is improvised and there is no right or wrong, this activity is accessible to anyone, regardless of musical expertise and level of cognitive functioning. As clients need to work together to co-create the improvised rhythmic music, building skills in cooperation and collaboration and fostering a sense of connection and belonging are intrinsically built into the activity. The sharing of insights also builds trust, group cohesion and contributes to learning.

A few examples of questions that could be used for this activity, which relate to AOD treatment objectives include:

- If you have relapsed in the past, what is one pattern of thoughts, feelings or behaviour that led to relapse?
- What is one thing that causes you stress and one healthy activity that helps you to relax?
- What is one healthy activity you can integrate into your life on a regular basis?
- What are three things you most value in life right now? (E.g., health, family, freedom, etc.)
- What are three values you would like to bring into your relationships? (E.g., honesty, open communication, integrity etc.)
- What is one strength you possess?
- What are three things you are grateful for?

---

11   Duncan, B.L. & Miller, S.D. (2004) *The Heroic Client: Principles of Client Directed, Outcome-Informed Therapy (revised edition)*. San Francisco, CA: Jossey-Bass.

- What are three self-care strategies you would like to adopt on a regular basis?

There are many questions that could be added to this list. The key is they must relate to treatment goals and be designed to give short answers, so that clients feel comfortable enough to contribute verbally, and musical play can be quickly resumed (for the sake of maintaining momentum and client engagement).

Variety maintains interest and engagement and this is one activity that can be repeated over a number of sessions in a multitude of ways, not just by asking a different question each time the activity is conducted, but also by varying the instrumentation, the nature of the improvisation and the overall set-up of the activity. For example, when working on themes around relaxation, mindfulness or stress management, the musical interludes could be set up to be low in volume, slow in tempo and include instruments that are more conducive to relaxation such as chimes and other tuned percussion instruments if available, as with the 'Relaxation jam' above.

To explore leadership and empowerment and build self-esteem, participants may initiate the starting and stopping of the music by taking turns to count the group in and out of the music, or lead the music by playing a bass drum on their round, prior to speaking.

Variations in the set-up or structure of the activity could include passing instruments to the next person before recommencing the music, so that every time the music resumes, each participant has a different instrument to play. A varied range of percussion instruments and different types of drums makes for a more interesting experience.

A range of tools and techniques from Arthur Hull's model of community drum circle facilitation[12] may be used within each musical interlude to facilitate variations in the music and showcase different musical elements and players in order to deepen participants' sense of connection, listening, empowerment and fun. Examples of the types of interventions that may be facilitated within these short musical interludes between each participant's verbal sharing include changing volume or tempo, showcasing different instrument types or timbres, showcasing different segments of the circle, or even individual players if they are comfortable.

---

12 Hull, A. (2007) *Drum Circle Facilitation: Building Community through Rhythm.* Santa Cruz, CA: Village Music Circles.

## ADDITIONAL ADVICE

Conducting drum circles with AOD populations is a challenging yet rewarding experience. Drum circles have the potential to give clients, who are often in a state of crisis, the ability to access joy, connection and relief from the stress of their current situation. The keys to successfully working with this population are ensuring a safe environment, building a trusting rapport, being sensitive to each individual's needs and approaching sessions in a fun and light-hearted way. With these things covered, clients can feel safe and comfortable enough to positively engage in rhythmic activities and access a world of benefits.

## AUTHOR'S BIOGRAPHY
### Rebecca Wermut BA (Music & Psychology) Grad Dip MT, RMT

Bek has been working as a registered music therapist in clinical and community mental health care and AOD treatment programs since 2007. She is a teacher trainer of the Rhythm2Recovery model and lectures on therapeutic rhythm facilitation and percussion skills at Western Sydney University for the music therapy program.

Email: bek@rhythmosis.com.au
www.rhythmosis.com.au

## RECOMMENDED READING

Bernstein, G. (2012) *Spirit Junkie: A radical road to self-love & miracles*. New York: Harmony Books.

Faulkner, S.C. (2018) 'Therapeutic applications for integrating rhythm and reflection in support of people with co-occurring drug and alcohol, and mental health issues.' *Dual Diagnosis Open Access*, 3, 2, 1–6.

Hari, J. (2015) *Chasing the Scream: The First and Last Days of the War on Drugs*. New York: Bloomsbury.

# Refugees

## CHRISTINE STEVENS

### OVERVIEW

Because many refugees herald from rhythmic cultures where musical expression, drumming, and dancing are woven into the fabric of life, drum circles are a perfect fit for community building and trauma recovery. With human displacement currently at an all-time high, whether due to climate change, war, trauma or natural disasters, the opportunity to work with refugee populations in drum circles is needed now, more than ever before. The facilitator's role is unique: both as an 'empathic outsider' as well as 'leader', being able to honour the emotionality and sensitivity to trauma, along with the explosive joy and creative freedom that often comes in music-making with world cultures.

Working in partnership with translators, human rights and relief organizations helps provide services that give voice to the inherent musical knowledge of these cultures and at the same time address psychological challenges. In my experience of over two decades working cross-culturally, I have heard from participants how drumming offers hope, a sense of freedom, relationship building, and a relief from the language barriers common to other interventions. In many cases, the rhythms literally take people home.

Together with a team that includes ethnomusicologist Dr Craig Woodson, facilitator Mary Tolena, drummer Kristina Sophia and filmmaker Constantine Alatzas, we have collaborated with a wide range of refugee support services. At one of these sessions, a drum circle training with the Lost Boys Center in Phoenix, Arizona, we were surprised that on the second day of the program, the participants called their relatives and friends during the lunch break. The second half of that day was filled with refugees from Sudan living in Phoenix, drumming up regally in their cultural attire. They brought food and instruments, and we danced, drummed and sang the rest of the day until dinner, which became a pot luck of cultural cuisine. The point is – be prepared for surprises and trust the cultural flow more than your own agenda.

Here are five key reasons why music and drumming are important modalities to support work with refugees and peace-making:

- Music is a language of global diplomacy.
- Being of service shifts us from performers to reformers.
- Music is magnetic and draws people in, removing shame, judgement and resistance.
- Words communicate thoughts; while music communicates energy.
- Being in rhythm together promotes kindness, compassion, and helpfulness.

## POSITIVE OUTCOMES

Unfortunately there is little formal research on drumming outcomes with refugee populations; however, many of the outcomes we have noticed from our own experiences working in this field and from the testimonials and feedback from group members, are supported by formal research with other population groups. These can be grouped into five main areas.

### Relationship building

Community integration occurs as refugees form new relationships. Someone who plays the drum connects to someone who sings, and they form a bond. During a break time, you notice the music continue between them and jamming occurs. Several significant studies have noted the positive connections that are made through drumming programs and the sense of community they inspire.¹

## Stress reduction

Drumming offers health benefits in terms of moving through the negative energy associated with trauma, pain, loss and grief. Surprisingly, breathing is one of the most important things refugees have reported on after drumming programs. Participants would often comment that they didn't realize how much they were holding their breath until we used the drumbeat to support deep relaxed breathing for about three minutes while stretching. The cathartic process of releasing feelings through the drum and the in-the-moment experience of drumming reduces the hyper-vigilance and tension that many refugees from war-torn countries carry with them. Several studies have shown the calming potential of drumming with anxious client groups. The use of different forms of mindful, meditation practice aligned to a slow drum pulse is an age-old remedy for stress and common across a diverse range of cultures.²

## Conflict resolution and peace-making

Drumming makes space for cross-cultural bonding. This can even include enemy groups, as was the case in our three-year project in northern Iraq. Music can break down barriers where words fail. Drumming engages people in a common activity that requires collaboration and cooperation, offers insight into the way differences can be resolved and re-emphasizes our common humanity. Former South African president and champion of social equality and nonviolence, Nelson Mandela attests, 'Artists reach areas far beyond the reach of politicians. Art, especially entertainment and

---

1   Ascenso, S., Perkins, R., Atkins, L., Fancourt, D. & Williamon, A. (2018) 'Promoting well-being through group drumming with mental health service users and their carers.' *International Journal of Qualitative Studies on Health and Well-Being 13*, 1. https://doi.org/10.1080/17482631.2018.1484219
    Perkins, R., Ascenso, S., Fancourt, D. & Williams, A. (2016) 'Making music for mental health: How group drumming mediates recovery.' *Psychology of Well-Being 6*. https://psywb.springeropen.com/articles/10.1186/s13612-016-0048-0 (accessed 4 August 2020).
    Wood, L., Ivery, P., Donovan, R. & Lambin, E. (2013) 'To the beat of a different drum – improving the social and mental wellbeing of at-risk youth with drumming.' *Journal of Public Mental Health 12*, 2, 70–79.
2   Kane, L. (2017) 'Drumming for mindfulness and healing: A simple way to calm the mind, remove stress and heal.' *Buddha Weekly*. https://buddhaweekly.com/drumming-for-mindfulness-drumming-for-healing-mind-and-body-a-simple-way-to-calm-the-monkey-mind-remove-stress-and-heal-how-science-and-different-buddhist-traditions-use-the-drum-for-everything-fr (accessed 4 August 2020).

music, is understood by everybody, and it lifts the spirits and the morale of those who hear it.'[3]

## Empowerment and self-expression

Drumming honours the beauty of musical traditions, the richness of cultures, and renews power by giving disempowered people a voice. Several studies have emphasized the way that group drumming gives people a sense of autonomy.[4] For refugees, who find themselves in a strange place, far from home, and often at the mercy of local authorities and complex bureaucratic constraints, this is a rare feeling, but one that offers hope for the future, and reinforces a sense of identity.

## Trauma recovery

Drumming creates a sense of nurture and support in a music-circle, allowing deep pain or grief, to be released. Many refugees have experienced shocking violence and other deprivations, which continue to haunt them and leave them emotionally vulnerable. The drum circle, particularly when led by someone with a therapeutic understanding, can provide people with a safe place to reconnect to others and release feelings. There is often a significant disconnect between western and other traditional approaches to treating mental health and music can help bridge that gap. After the genocide in Rwanda, western agencies were criticized by locals when they flew in western-based counsellors – 'What we wanted said one, was drumming – something to get our blood flowing again, something that brought people together again.'[5]

Less researched, though obvious through our work, is the power of music and rhythm to literally 'take people home' – that longing pain for those cultural memories, a feeling of a dance or the sound of a certain song.

---

3   Mandela, N. quoted by Heckman, D. (2006) 'Hitting replay on Mandela's life, times.' *LA Times*, 30 July. http://articles.latimes.com/2006/jul/30/entertainment/ca-worldspotlight30 (accessed 4 August 2020).
4   Martin, K.E., Wood, L.J., Tasker, J.S. & Coletsis, C. (2014) 'The Impact of Holyoake's DRUMBEAT Program on Prisoner Wellbeing in Western Australian Prisons.' The University of Western Australia, Crawley, Western Australia.
    Ascenso, S., Perkins, R., Atkins, L., Fancourt, D. & Williamon, A. (2018) 'Promoting well-being through group drumming with mental health service users and their carers.' *International Journal of Qualitative Studies on Health and Well-Being 13*, 1.
5   Leach, A. (2015) 'Working in development. Exporting Trauma: Can the talking cure do more harm than good?' *The Guardian*, 05 February. www.theguardian.com/global-development-professionals-network/2015/feb/05/mental-health-aid-western-talking-cure-harm-good-humanitarian-anthropologist (accessed 4 August 2020).

Music evokes memories and emotions and participants may weep or cry. This is known as 'reunion grief', happy tears which are bitter-sweet. In its capacity to connect people across the barriers of language, place and culture, or to inspire social consciousness and change, or in its ability to heal the scars and injustices of conflict, music is a powerful force.

## SETTING UP FOR SUCCESS

Make sure you research how to dress appropriately prior to your program. Learn to say key words and phrases in the language of those you are with, such as hello, goodbye or see you again, good job, thank you, and *yes*! Be aware of cultural drum patterns and attune your ears to the musical lineage of the cultural group, through research online. By collaborating with organizations and building relationships with experts and counsellors you will be better prepared for what to expect. I like to ask questions like: 'Any tips on working with the group?' 'What is one mistake I can avoid?' 'Anything else I should be aware of?' 'Are there any musicians in the group?'

When I was setting up for an event at 'Hands of Peace', working with Palestinian and Israeli youth in a California location, I simply brought a Middle Eastern doumbek drum over to the circle and started to play. Immediately the group pointed at a young man who came over and played along with a second drum I left waiting. Soon, a cultural dance and song emerged with Palestinians jumping into the groove. I had formed my pit-band, found my ringer, and before the group even started, I was given an important insight into the culture.

In this work I do not start with a traditional 'Drum Call'[6] unless it is a recreational event. On the following page is the protocol I generally follow (see Figure 15.1), beginning with a 'welcome experience' and concluding with a 'closing' routine – often, there is a cultural goodbye song, if not, it's important to do a closing sequence, e.g. drum roll – rumble, or ask each participant to share in one word (in their language) the learning or feeling that they are taking with them from our time together.

---

6 Hull, A. (2007) *Drum Circle Facilitation: Building Community through Rhythm.* Santa Cruz, CA: Village Music Circles, p.68.

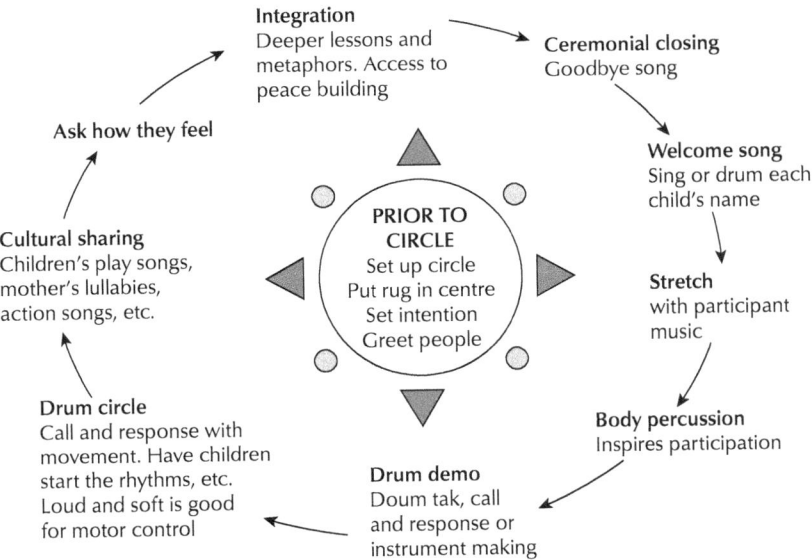

*Figure 15.1: Peace protocol diagram*
Based on 8 shields model.
Jon Young *et al.* www.8shields.org
Christine Stevens, Mark Montygierd

## COMMON CHALLENGES AND HOW TO MINIMIZE THEM
There will be challenges, which help you grow.

### Language barriers
Learn some simple phrases – 'start' and 'stop', and 'let's go!'. These will be important cues for your drum program. Find a translator, and as much as possible use music to communicate. I often find words limiting in these settings and the music often becomes a much more immediate and reliable tool for communication.

### Trauma
Because the sound of drumming can revive memories of gunfire and trigger traumatic memories, you must be alert to group members who may find loud, fast drumming distressing. At the beginning ask the group to play slowly and softly and manage the volume. At the same time, cultures I've worked with have a style that can become wild and exuberant; this is

a good thing! Don't block that joy. Read the group and manage the tempo and volume accordingly. Also, where possible, ensure that there are trained professionals alongside you who can manage people's distress if required.

## Grief

Music is a form of emotion and drumming, particularly when it invokes cultural traditions lost to conflict and displacement, can give rise to grief and overwhelming feelings of loss. It's a bitter-sweet experience when refugees sing, drum and dance the music from their homeland. I remember a woman drumming, and at the same time sobbing and wailing with grief, until all the women gathered around her for support. I didn't need to do anything, it resolved itself after 15 minutes with the women offering her tea and snacks. Again, the group will often help you through this process but it can pay to have professional support alongside you.

## Cultural sensitivity

In some cultures, women do not drum. There are also specific drums that are only used for spiritual ceremonies. It's important to educate yourself in cultural practices with respect to drumming, music and social norms. Sometimes it may be better to utilize non-traditional drums, particularly when working with mixed cultures, as the wrong use of a traditional instrument can be a significant breach of etiquette and lead to a breakdown in trust. Additionally, the concept of cultural appropriation is a sensitive issue. Always consult with the organizer and a cultural elder when planning your session.

## Compassion fatigue

The roots of compassion fatigue come from an awareness of the depth of need in the group you are working with. Be gentle with yourself and honour the results. Know that your work is helpful and it is enough. In working with refugees, I've experienced gratitude for the simple things in my western life: freedom, female empowerment, my vehicle and my home. Keep a journal and find ways to express your emotions so that you can stay clear and present to be of service to the group.

Remember too that your own issues can be triggered from working with people whose grief and loss are close to the surface. If you are vulnerable to your own emotions this work can trigger thoughts and feelings that are otherwise manageable. A duty of care is required whereby you recognize your own fragilities and avoid situations where they can impact the work you do in supporting others.

A useful debriefing tool I've used comes from The Phoenix Rising Yoga Therapy Institute. It includes three questions and a fourth question I added.

- What happened?
- What did I learn?
- How do I apply this to my life?
- What magic moment stands out for you?

## PRACTICAL APPLICATIONS OF THE DRUM CIRCLE

We often start with a 'pit band' playing a cultural beat to welcome participants for relationship building, trust and safety. I recruit participants to join me by simply starting a beat and leaving a few drums and empty chairs next to me. With an obvious hand gesture invitation, I await the right people to step up and play for the group.

While the beat plays, we do basic stretching without any words, for stress reduction, leading by example, and accompanied by slow and steady breathing. This is good for the fine motor skills of hand drumming and the breathing exercise has benefits for any individuals experiencing stress or anxiety. This exercise will then often flow into a body-percussion routine; many cultures have their own special body-percussion sounds and techniques; from the flamenco hand clapping of Spain to the snapping fingers of the Arab world.

Before handing out drums, I sometimes use shakers and do a follow the leader ice-breaker game for stress reduction, trust and relationship building. The benefit of this is the feeling that we all have the same instrument, the shaker. There is no one best drummer at this point, and this equality helps build community.

Once drums are handed out, the basic sounds on the drum are reviewed, such as 'bass and tone'/'doum and tak'. It's a good idea to review the basic sounds on the drum, no matter how advanced people may be, as it gives everyone a starting position and spills into group entrainment as people start to play the different sounds on their drums together.

Next, I use 'call and response' as a powerful way to emulate conversation beyond language barriers. I play a short phrase and cue the group to copy me on the beat. Repeat four times and then cue a new leader to play their beat and the group responds. This passing of leadership roles is a key element of empowering the group, and avoiding the problematic power dynamic of leader/follower. 'Call and response' routines flow easily into creating a rhythm with a leader from the group starting a beat. Once you get the rhythm entrained, try and maintain the rhythm for at least four minutes. Some facilitation is helpful, and most cultures understand the basic body language of loud and soft; up and down; and start and stop.[7] By this point, as the group has come together, I will often then introduce cultural sharing as an important tool for hope and empowerment, asking if anyone is happy to showcase a rhythm, dance, or song from their culture. Again, this empowers someone else as a leader. A woman once brought a rhythm from Baghdad called 'Choni' which is played at weddings and celebrations. The whole room erupted in a circle-dance, arms linked, with shrill cheers as I sat in the centre, playing the beat. This went on for a long time, as different women took a turn dancing solo in the centre of the circle, something that is common to their culture.

I would recommend taking a short break if you have a few hours or a day-long session with a group. These breaks often open up new opportunities for social connection between people that may have been initiated through the safe platform of the drum circle. Food breaks are also important opportunities for cultural sharing for conflict resolution. Often during this free time, you will see refugees connect with the music; a drummer, singer and dancer might suddenly jam together. Allowing this spontaneous magic to occur may be the most important aspect of your program.

For trauma recovery, I ask a question and invite participants to answer on their drum. Known as 'inspirational beats' in the HealthRHYTHMS® program, this can be applied with questions like, 'What do you miss most about your homeland?' 'What has been the biggest challenge coming to this country?' 'What has been the biggest gift coming to this country?' 'What does peace sound like; play it on your drum?'

It's important to end programs with a clear closing routine. I invite participants to share one word about what they are taking from the program, in any language. From an Iraqi goodbye song to a Japanese hand clapping pattern, to a Sudanese group dance, world cultures often have a way to end.

I created a video reflecting on my experience working with Iraqi refugee women in a project called 'Shifa', which means healing in both Arabic and Kurdish.[8]

---

[7] Here is a useful YouTube video tutorial on cultural rhythms used in Call and Response: 'Drum circles call and response: Take the rhythm challenge.' https://youtu.be/8AHaDW1AGDY

[8] 'Refugee rhythms of women's empowerment by Christine Stevens.' https://youtu.be/Amm0YPLN36s

It's worth being aware of five additional elements of drum circles with refugee populations.

- *Reconnection* – Refugee experiences often force people to separate from their families, communities and culture. As younger generations become more easily acculturated, it is more challenging to maintain family bonds.
- *Values* – Refugees often enter communities where values may be different – it can be good to emphasize common core values that link the old and the new.
- *Tolerance* – Activities that promote tolerance and respect for people across cultures are important.
- *Trust and hope* – Exercises such as drumming and community meals build trust and look towards a positive future.
- *Catharsis* – Exercises that allow people to express how they feel about their journey, situation, etc. on the drum or in their language. We have had participants write poetry and read it to the group during our drum circles.

## ADDITIONAL ADVICE

Always debrief your programs with someone from the hosting organization who can offer objective feedback, or at the very least be a good listener. Avoid 'compassion fatigue' by maintaining good self-care. Be aware of inner and outer learnings that occur in this work. For me, it's been a road map to unity consciousness – discovering that we really are one, despite language, culture, race and religion. Sometimes gifts are exchanged and I have often brought food to share. It's important to prepare, prepare, prepare. I considered learning a rhythm from Iraq to be as good a language course as any vocabulary I could have mastered.

## AUTHOR'S BIOGRAPHY
### Christine Stevens, MT-BC, MSW

Christine is the author of *Music Medicine*, *The Healing Drum Kit* and *The Art and Heart of Drum Circles*. In 2007, Christine led the first drum circle training in the war zone of Iraq. Her work was featured in NAMM magazine, The Rex Foundation, and the DVD *Discover Your Gift*. She has continued to work with refugees from Sudan, Iraq, Afghanistan, Iran, and Syria. Through her company, UpBeat Drum Circles, she offers training in conflict resolution and peace building through drum circles.

Email: christine@ubdrumcircles.com
www.ubdrumcircles.com
Refugee Drum Circles: https://ubdrumcircles.com/about/peace-building
YouTube: https://www.youtube.com/user/ubdrumcircles

## RECOMMENDED READING

Hesser, B. & Heinemann, H.N. (2015) UN Global Compendium of Music as a Global, (4th Ed.). https://musicasaglobalresource.org/2016magrcomp.pdf (accessed 4 August 2020).

Powers, C. (2006) *Spiritual Traveler: Journeys Beyond Fear*. USA: GL Publishing. www.cameronpowers.com.

Stevens, C. (2009) Keynote Address on Peace Drum Circles at International Sound Healing Conference. www.youtube.com/watch?v=KyOhJREauDw (accessed 4 August 2020).

# Neurodiverse Communities

## RAY WATTERS

**OVERVIEW**

It has proven difficult to find a term that would encompass the area of specialization that I spend most of my time working in, covering the extensive diversity among human brains and minds. Most recently the term 'neurodiversity' is being used to explain this variance in human consciousness that has existed for thousands of years but which we are now becoming increasingly aware of. Different people think differently not just because of differences in culture, social or peer influences or life experience, but because their brains are simply 'wired' to work differently. In the past, particularly within the health services, our focus has been on fixing and curing these differences, but more recently this has begun to change in favour of accommodation, acceptance and being able to adapt to include these variations within our societal structures. As well, we are learning to appreciate many of the positive contributions people who think outside the norm make to our world.

Working with this hugely diverse and engaging population is perhaps one of the most rewarding and, at times, the most challenging environments you can find yourself in. It is important to remember that although we live in a world where labels are allocated to assist with identities, groupings, medication and to inform our generalized understandings of populations, each one of these people is a unique individual with wants, desires and needs and a right to be treated as such. They are human beings, fundamentally no different to us, despite their cognitive and behavioural dissimilarities and how our labels segregate them.

You will find yourself working with this community in a variety of settings, which tend to be grouped into residential/care settings, day/drop-in centres, schools geared towards specific needs, summer camps and evening clubs, usually within specific caring settings or community centres. Within these facilities you may find yourself in the dining area, hall or a classroom or if you are lucky, on a sunny day, outside.

## POSITIVE OUTCOMES

Before delving into the myriad of positive outcomes associated with using drums with these specific participants it is important to look at the foundation upon which these positive outcomes are based. That foundation is accessibility, the ability to access the functionality and benefits of a service. And within the context of the drum circle, it also pertains to the safety and simplicity of these forms of musical interventions that offer a degree of active participation within a social setting that is regularly denied to many people from the neurodiverse world.

This can be explored on a group, personal and facilitator level. In some areas, particularly those inner-city urban areas of social deprivation, it is one of the few occasions that classes, whole year groups, schools or communities come together and play together. And it can also extend to involvement with their parents or siblings as the occasion allows. Evening groups in many support centres often have an ongoing rolling program of separate activities, so, again, a drum circle may provide one of the few occasions where all come together in one creative activity. However, in many cases, the provision of musical activities within today's 'neurodiversity' support curriculum is sparse, bordering on nonexistent, so your work with these groups can sometimes be their first experience of improvised and/or structured music-making.

On a personal level, accessibility to the instrument is vital and the drum is one of the most inclusive and accessible instruments there is. Ensure while working with these participants that the instruments you bring are practical; for example, use adapted mallets (see image on the following page) and drums that are suitable for the clientele that can be placed on their lap or the table of a wheelchair and ensure that the client is supported correctly. There is a lot of especially adapted equipment that can be used with members of this group. Remember, no actual rhythmical ability is necessary in order to be able to join in – this is always emphasized in the sessions that I lead; It is simply impossible to make a mistake. There is no judgement and everyone's contribution is valid and valued.

Most of us have had an experience of the crippling effect of judgement on our performance and feeling of self-worth, and members of the neurodiverse community are particularly sensitive to these issues. It is likely that a number of the group will have challenges with their abilities and have previously encountered negative feedback. For some, this is an ongoing issue that eats away at their self-confidence and sabotages their social comfort. As the facilitator, you must ensure that the session and the work undertaken by the group are delivered at the right developmental level, the right pace and with the right attitude to maximize accessibility, personal confidence and enjoyment; this cannot be over-stated.

In his book, *Rhythm, Music and the Brain*, Thaut (2005) wrote that: 'We know that in all societies throughout human history music has been used to express emotions, ideas and feelings not revealed through ordinary discourse.'[1] This has particular relevance for many of my clients, who struggle with articulating their emotions and also with attuning to the emotions of others.

There is a broad range of research that supports the benefits of drumming and music making with various populations including those on the autistic spectrum.[2] A pilot study coordinated by the University of Chichester using rock drumming sessions once a week over five weeks with autistic children led to a decrease in hyperactivity as well positive changes in social skills, behaviour and self-confidence.[3] It is common in my work to be advised by other staff of the newly displayed focus that attendees

---

1 Thaut, H.M. (2005) *Rhythm, Music and the Brain, Scientific Foundations and Clinical Applications.* London: Routledge, p.113.
2 Litchke, L.G., Dorman, R., Willemin, T.A. & Liu, T. (2019) Mental Health Benefits of a Service-Learning Group Drumming between College Students and Children with Autism Spectrum Disorder. *Journal of Service-Learning in Higher Education* 9. https://journals.sfu.ca/jslhe/index.php/jslhe/article/view/185 (accessed 4 August 2020).
3 Lowry, R.G., Hale, B.J., Draper, S.B. & Smith, M.S. (2018) 'Rock drumming enhances motor-coordination and psycho-social skills of children with emotional and behavioural difficulties.' *International Journal of Developmental Difficulties* 65, 3, 1–10.

show through these sessions even though generally their attention span is minimal and they are usually highly distracted.

A number of parallels can be drawn from the outcomes of various research papers that are applicable to neurodiverse groups, remembering that many of the perceived differences from neurotypical (NT) people are often exaggerated through the labels that are applied to them. An adolescent labelled with profound difficulties is still an adolescent trying to cope with being an adolescent and the pressures and emotions associated with that, as well as a person with their own unique abilities. Common findings of an improved sense of belonging, improved mood, improvements in collaboration and reductions in anxiety are all outcomes that I have seen first-hand and that are regularly quoted as outcomes from research into drum-based therapies.[4]

A lot of the members of these groups are working one to one with support workers and life coaches and these core relationships are vitally important to the quality of their day-to-day living. So, to share positive and fun experiences alongside their carer is hugely beneficial to this bond. Associated with this connectedness and group experience are the positive benefits for their mental health. We are, after all, gregarious people who crave, enjoy and thrive with human contact and it has been proven that bringing people together to make music in a life affirming and supportive environment can have a positive impact on people's mental wellbeing.[5]

Therefore, as a facilitator, the creation and pacing of these sessions and exercises to ensure maximum participation is so vital. One of the organizations that I developed a drumming workshop for shared this feedback on the session they had been also been part of:

> 'For us as staff there were some really magical moments watching some of the young people we support find confidence that they didn't realise they had.'

The client groups that I work with tend to suffer from particularly high levels of stress and anxiety when just interacting with people, the world and completing normal day-to-day tasks that we take for granted. The toll that this takes can be severe to the point where they are unable to function. They can sometimes arrive at my sessions in an agitated state or with already heightened stress levels. For the short time that we are together the drumming is able to lessen these symptoms. A number of these clients,

---

[4] Wood, L., Ivery, P., Donovan, R. & Lambin, E. (2013) 'To the beat of a different drum – improving the social and mental wellbeing of at-risk youth with drumming.' *Journal of Public Mental Health* 12, 2, 70–79.

[5] Fancourt, D., Perkins, R., Ascenso, S., Carvalho, L.A., Steptoe, A. & Williamon, A. (2016) 'Effects of group drumming interventions on anxiety, depression, social resilience and inflammatory immune response among mental health service users.' *PloS one* 11, 3, e0151136.

though I hasten to add not all, do also have a relatively sedentary lifestyle so, not only does the participation in drumming activities significantly decrease stress, but it may also help to increase cardiovascular fitness.[6]

It is therefore clear that a correctly facilitated drum circle with neurodiverse participants can have huge benefits on a personal and relational level. Allowing people to express their emotions, release stress and frustrations, celebrate success, have fun, connect to others, improve their motor coordination and other physiological conditions, and simply benefit from the fun and beauty of recreational music-making. As Seashore wrote in his seminal work on music and psychology, some 60 years ago:[7]

> All our mental life works rhythmically...rhythm gives us a sense of balance the sense of rhythm gives us a feeling of freedom, luxury and expanse... It gives a sense of achievement in moulding [sic] or creating... Rhythm gives us a feeling of power... Rhythm finds resonance in the whole organism...

## SETTING UP FOR SUCCESS

Be aware if you can of the make-up of your particular group and the individual issues and skills that you may be presented with, but do not use that as an excuse to reduce your expectations of an individual, they never fail to surprise. Be aware of processing problems; in short know as much about those in your group as possible. Do proper and thorough research and understand the labels that people use. Research the organization and their facilities if at all possible before attending; arranging a preliminary visit prior to starting can be beneficial. Always arrive early and engage clients and staff as you come across them. An organization's receptionist can be a treasure trove of information.

If possible, make sure that you have a suitable room to work in with easy access and movement for those in electric and manual wheelchairs and suitable seating for those that require it. Most venues that invite you in are well able to cater for this, but be aware if it is a neutral venue. I have a small portable PA speaker and iPod and I usually have suitable rhythmical music playing when people arrive. I prearrange my instruments in an inner circle in the room with a mallet on each drum. It is beneficial to have a bright and welcoming space with the chairs and instruments set up, the music playing and you there to greet everyone with a smile. When the staff arrive, they will

---

6   Smith, C., Vilijoen, J.T. & McGeachie, L. (2014) 'African drumming: A holistic approach to reducing stress and improving health.' *Journal of Cardiovascular Medicine (Hagerstown)* 15, 6, 441–446.
7   Seashore C.E. (1967) *Psychology of Music.* New York: Dover Publications, Inc., p.145.

then instantly know how you would like them arranged around the circle of drums. Invest in your relationship with the care team – support workers and occupational therapists, etc. – who work with your participants. Be aware that they will often be supporting the members of your group so their participation and enthusiasm are essential. Ensure that they understand that they are needed and not at liberty just to walk off and leave you with a group of clients. Be prepared to give drums out and suitable mallets. This can take some time, so encourage people to play along with the music as they settle in.

Be open, available and engaging to all of those in the room; use eye contact and address the person, not the carer or support worker, and learn their names if you are at the location over a number of sessions. Name badges can be useful. Liaise closely with the support workers and personal carers so they understand what their role is and encourage their enthusiastic participation. Help participants select the most suitable instrument, ensuring you empower the client to make the choice.

Be comfortable in the chaos that ensues, sometimes it can be harmonious but often with this kind of group and with diverse abilities there will be mayhem – this is normal. Smile and encourage.

Invest in proper adaptable equipment and drums; some examples are below:

- proper mallets (adjustable grip types and larger handled mallets for people with poor grip, nothing too heavy, be aware of poor muscle tone in some of the client groups)
- frame drums that can be placed on laps or wheelchair tray tables
- table top Cajon drums are excellent for sound variety, easy to play and clients can get lots of different sounds with mallets, hands and fingers
- REMO® paddle drums are excellent for a care worker or family member to use supporting a client
- REMO®, or other make, drum stands (see following page) that lift the drums off the floor to give them more height
- REMO® Large Timbau drums placed in a REMO® basket frame are excellent as they raise the drum quite high off the ground and allow easy access for wheelchair users
- REMO® Djembe's also placed in frames to lift them off the ground and give them stability
- a plentiful supply of cleaning wipes to keep the equipment clean.

## COMMON CHALLENGES AND HOW TO MINIMIZE THEM

Often the facilities you encounter are unsuitable, particularly in the early sessions when the management is unaware of your needs. So make sure proper contact has been made with those responsible and that you have talked through what works best for them and for you – the emphasis is always on what works for them. It can be useful to have a set list of your venue requirements and other necessities, that you can pass onto the organizer as part of your contract, specifying things like size and soundproofing, chair types, etc.

Be equipped for a number of noise-related challenges and have a couple of sets of over-ear defenders (headphones) for participants that are especially sensitive to noise – they are easily available, cheap and cleanable. I always try and ensure that there are instruments available for all, even those that throw things. I have worked with groups who have clients who want to join in, but like to throw things either for attention or frustration. I have a number of shakers that are sown into padded socks that cause no injury should they be thrown.

Be aware of personalities in the group and that you are not responsible for crowd control; melt-downs can and will happen, as will issues between clients. Ensure that staff understand their responsibilities and leave these types of issues for them to deal with. Nine times out of ten the support workers will ask you to keep going, so keep going. Use your experience to determine your response, every situation is different, and sometimes it may be wise to acknowledge if a significant event has happened and check that people are OK.

If people do not want to play that is fine, just place a drum and mallet in close proximity and they will join in when they feel ready. Some people may be unable to drum or hold any instruments at all, so it can be good to include some simple songs or vocal work, the funnier the better, depending on the age of the group.

As mentioned previously, your relationship with the carers and support workers is vitally important. Occasionally you can come up against some resistance; carers who underestimate or negate their client's ability and what their client is capable of, or willing to do. Recently, while working with a group, some of whom had profound difficulties, I had this issue with apathetic carers who didn't believe the person in their care would be able to participate. I did my introduction to everyone in the circle and gave out some shakers and then walked outside the circle to where this young lady (participant) and her reluctant support workers were sitting. I gave the workers a shaker each and left one next to the girl. I fixed my gaze on the workers and said to them 'you shake along and this lovely lady will shake along as well'. And sure enough, she did. Later I moved to include drums and I walked over to the carers and gave a drum to each of them before kneeling down to the same young lady and letting her know that I was just leaving a drum that she could hit whenever she wanted, or not. And you know she played along, she shook her shaker and played her drum – imagine if I had listened to those support workers? How much fun would she have missed? Sometimes it pays to challenge these sorts of defeatist judgements in a subtle way.

Time keeping is always something to bear in mind – be sure to build plenty of time around the session. Life for this group of people is often complex and things rarely go to plan because of their uniqueness. Extra time is always beneficial as common undertakings often require additional time. For some, just getting to the session can be a struggle and coordinating their special needs, arranging the availability of a care/support worker to help them, and many other factors have to combine to get them there. So be aware of this when booking the session, giving yourself additional leeway between any other commitments you have on the day. And be patient when things start late or run over time.

## PRACTICAL APPLICATIONS OF THE DRUM CIRCLE
My sessions tend to be individually planned from start to finish and then I usually throw these plans away as the session develops. I often play rhythmical music with a strong beat (either African or Samba) through a small PA as people arrive and settle in and also when I am setting up the room beforehand. The music travels down the corridor beckoning people to join me.

At the start of the session I engage with each of the clients at the door as the group assembles, giving out different shakers depending on my initial perception of the client's ability. We then carry out a few simple shaker games and rhythmical exercises to build confidence and familiarity, and for me to assess the developmental level of each person and the group as a whole.

At the conclusion of the warm-up I work with the support staff to hand out drums and mallets, ensuring that everyone has a suitable instrument. I will then move through drumming 101 – teaching how the mallet is held and the notes available on the drum. No matter how many times I visit some centres, I always go through this procedure as these beginning routines can be comforting and also in case we are also joined by new attendees. For many people there is a sense of safety drawn from repetition and routines – the knowledge of what is coming next helps reduces stress.

**Tap three times**
An excellent exercise for memory, coordination, cross-lateral work, gross motor skills and physical exercise. Each participant has a shaker while the lead facilitator plays a bass drum using a mallet. I play a simple pulse and have the participants shake their instruments along to the pulse. I then call 'Tap on your hands' and they tap on their opposing hand three times then we go back to the pulse. I then call out 'Tap on your leg' and they tap on their legs with the shaker three times. I then put the two actions together so we tap on our hands followed by legs and continue to add various body parts until we have quite a few to remember and move through.

Variations

- After starting the game off with the hand tap, work around the group and have each member add a body part. If you run out of body parts suggest shaking in the air, tapping the floor or the chair, etc.

- Once you have started remind the group that they have to remember the order, because you will not be calling them out after each one is added.

- Start to speed up the calling of the body parts and see how fast the group can get until it reaches a rumble.

- Try and see how many times around the circle you can go without verbally mentioning the different body parts.

**'Oooo…Aaaahhh'**
As part of the drum warm up I have people play a very simple heartbeat rhythm (two bass pulses followed by two counts of silence) to bring everyone together. Then I explain to the group that in the space between the beats we are going to put in some words or noises. So, we then start to shout words in-between the beats. Then we move it along to the girls

singing one thing and the boys singing another thing, e.g., alternatively girls sing 'Ooooo' and the boys shout 'Aaaahhh'.

This is a totally inclusive activity that is fun and allows the use of voice and drums so those that are unable to drum are able to join in using their voices instead. We then continue with rumble games and then rhythm practice which gradually becomes more challenging as the session progresses until we have a small repertoire of rhythms intermingled with prolonged periods of improvised drumming that we can alternate between. I also use 'call and response' activities and rhythm games to engage my audience, with an overriding focus on fun.

### Who's on their own?

I often put a solo section into my circles, allowing individuals to shine in the spotlight. I will have the group in a groove and then count them down to a stop before calling out (in 4/4 time), 'Who's on their own, who's on their own? 1, 2, you're on your own', and gesture towards someone indicating that it is their turn to solo. Once they have finished, we all give them a big round of applause and I count everyone back in. I will sometimes use the PA system with a wireless microphone for those with poor muscle tone who play softly; using a wireless microphone amplifies their quiet contribution. This is an activity that celebrates everyone's contribution to the whole. Any solo is welcome, be it one note, many notes, a vocal expression, a smile or even silence.

### Clap your hands

In this game I teach the group a simple combination of 'Clap your hands, Stomp your feet, Wiggle your bum'. Playing a rhythm, I then count down from four to one and shout, 'Clap your hands' (Clap our hands three times), then 'Stomp your feet' (Stomp our feet three times) and then 'Wiggle your bum' and we wiggle three times. We then go back to the groove. Once this has become established by dropping into it a few times, we then go around the circle adding a new body movement onto the initial three, one person at a time. So, the initial three plus one then back to the groove, then add another one and so on. These movements can be subtle such as eye blinking, stretching fingers out, nodding of head, vocal sounds – anything over the count of three until we have gone around the whole group. Be aware it has to be the person's choice of movement and be patient while they make their mind up. Sometimes it is useful to have a support worker and client work as a team. The emphasis is always on simplicity and fun.

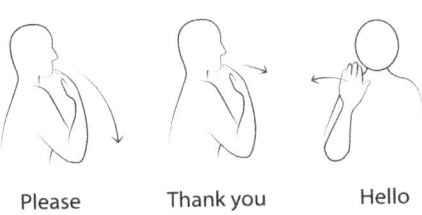

Please     Thank you     Hello

Something that is also important to be aware of, and something sometimes difficult to write about, is 'compassion fatigue'. A large number of consecutive sessions like these can take a toll on you. As much as you enjoy it, it is important to be aware and pay attention to what is going on for you. So be sure to build in suitable rests or break time away from these groups as working with them can be very demanding. You cannot give if you do not look after yourself.

## AUTHOR'S BIOGRAPHY
### Ray Watters, BA (History & Education), Fd.Sc (Counselling) MBASP

Ray is a full-time drum circle facilitator and humanistic counsellor with his own business – Drumwithus. Ray counsels people from all walks of life, but specializes in supporting adolescent boys in educational settings. He uses drumming in his counselling practice where he can, working with groups and one to one. As a drum circle facilitator, Ray works with a variety of audiences, but has been drawn to, and worked in the neurodiverse field for over 10 years. He also works regularly in well-elderly and mental health settings.

    Email: ray@drumwithus.com
    www.drumwithus.com
    Facebook: drumwithus

## RECOMMENDED READING

Rogers, N. (2011) *The Creative Connection for Groups, Person-Centred Expressive Arts for Healing and Social Change.* Palo Alto, CA: Science and Behaviour Books Inc.
Silberman, S. (2016) *Neurotribes: The Legacy of Autism and How to Think Smarter about People Who Think Differently.* London: Allen & Unwin.
Thaut, H.M. (2005) *Rhythm, Music and the Brain, Scientific Foundations and Clinical Applications.* London: Routledge.
Williams, D. (1996) *Autism, An Inside-Out Approach.* London: Jessica Kingsley Publishers.

# Working with Physical and Intellectual Disabilities

JORGE OCHOA AND JACQUI BARRETT

**OVERVIEW**

Working with individuals with physical and intellectual challenges may take you to a variety of settings. You may have the opportunity to work with individuals within the public, private, or homeschool education system, with organizations dedicated to the support and awareness of specific disabilities, at community events and for corporations, etc. Physical limitations may include, but not be limited to, those with conditions that affect strength, endurance, range of motion, loss of a limb and oral issues (drooling and/or mouthing of objects). Sensory limitations may also be present, such as difficulty with balance, vision, touch and hearing. Challenges faced by those with an intellectual disability include difficulties in understanding and processing of information. Many challenges may be faced, but the rewards and successes are priceless.

Over the years, one of the best things, among many others, that I have appreciated while working in this area is the sense of humour of an ongoing group that I facilitate with intellectual disabilities. With this particular group, I intentionally call individuals by a different name when doing solos. I love the laughter among the group. I love the breaking down of barriers as individuals come out of their shell and of course cannot say enough about the hugs! I have learned that everyone is truly an individual and that a person should not be judged by their disability. Two people with the same disability have their unique personal challenges and strengths. Most of all, make your sessions fun, this will be an important part of any healing or learning that takes places and will keep people motivated for more.

## POSITIVE OUTCOMES

A number of research studies have shown significant improvements from music-based programs, many of which included drumming within their activities, in both physical and psychological outcomes for people living with disabilities. A study by Pasiali, LaGasse and Penn (2014)[1] showed increases in focus, and attention for adolescents with neuro-developmental delays. In an earlier study, Pavelicevic and colleagues (2013)[2] demonstrated that active music-making increased social confidence, self-regard and the quality of inter-personal relationships.

Other research studies have showcased physical improvements in motor coordination that result from rhythm-based interventions.[3] Rhythm is now understood to serve as a timekeeper in the therapeutic application of music for motor rehabilitation goals and is foundational to auditory–motor synchronization. Research into the way drumming actively strengthens our immune system is also highly relevant to people with disabilities whose physical health is often compromised, making them more susceptible to illness and disease and more recently studies have shown drumming can also assist in pain reduction for people whose physical disabilities result in heightened levels of discomfort.[4]

---

1   Pasiali, V., LaGasse, A.B. & Penn, S.L. (2014) 'The effect of Music Attention Control Training (MACT) on attention skills of adolescents with neurodevelopmental delays: A pilot study.' *Journal of Music Therapy* 51, 4, 333–354.
2   Pavlicevic, M., O'Neil, N., Powell, H., Jones, O. & Sampathianaki, E. (2013) 'Making music, making friends: Long-term music therapy with young adults with severe learning disabilities.' *Journal of Intellectual Disabilities* 18, 1, 5–19.
3   Homayounpour, P., Kakavand, A. & Mohammadi, A.Z. (2016) 'The effects of drum music training (rhythm) on perceptual motor skills in children with developmental co-ordination disorder.' *International Journal of Humanities & Cultural Studies*, ISSN 2356-5926.
4   Dunbar, R., Kaskatis, K., MacDonald, I. & Barra, V. (2012) 'Performance of music elevates pain threshold and positive affect: Implications for the evolutionary function of music.' *Evolutionary Psychology: An International Journal of Evolutionary Approaches to Psychology and Behavior* 10, 688–702.

Sometimes, what may seem insignificant or a tiny step may actually be a life-changing experience for the client. After one session in the brain injury unit, a client handed me the following letter:

> I arrived at this rehabilitation centre following a severe fall which resulted in both a head injury and multiple fracture of my left thigh. For 3 weeks I have been depressed, stressed and afraid to move my leg. On joining the drumming session I immediately felt relaxed for the first time since my accident. Much to my surprise and delight I realised that I was tapping my left foot in time to the rhythms we were playing. Up until that moment I had been holding my leg stiffly and had no movement. Mentally and physically I felt better following the session and found the drumming extremely therapeutic. Thank you.

From this moment this client was able to start physical rehabilitation on her badly damaged leg. She was able to let go of the intense fear of moving her leg or having anyone touch it. She is a physiotherapist and was amazed at how she felt after just one session.

Other key outcomes I have noticed from my own experience include:

- improvements in communication ability
- improved sensory regulation
- improved teamwork skills, cooperation, and group cohesion
- the development of leadership skills
- positive changes in mood and emotional states
- a medium for the expression of individual creativity, both verbal and non-verbal.

## SETTING UP FOR SUCCESS

Having a broad understanding of the special needs and medical conditions of the individuals you are supporting is a key to success and an important responsibility in terms of your duty of care. Ask questions before an event or session to elicit the information you need to align your session appropriately. Have discussions with care staff and families about anticipated physical, cognitive, and behavioural challenges and how they are dealt with. Also inquire about the strengths of the group or an individual. During the session, ensure that you ask participants how comfortable they are with the different exercises and note their responses (verbal and non-verbal) in relation to different aspects of your program, so that you can adapt it where necessary to better suit their needs.

Considerations include:

- Provide instruments that include a variety of styles and sizes. Holding and playing smaller and lightweight instruments (usually synthetic) may be more suitable for those with a decreased range of motion, strength, and endurance. Drums made out of PVC or fibre are lightweight compared to wood or fibreglass. Some instruments to consider would include frame drums with soft-headed mallets, djembes, bongos, maracas and shakers. Look for shakers that are made of high impact plastic, so they do not break easily when dropped, and be wary of small shakers that can be choking hazards (e.g. egg shakers and other fruit shaped items). Bongos are a great drum to work with on mid-line crossing. Wrist jingle shakers may be used for those with limited grasp. Ankle shakers are also available.

- It is very important to check instruments for any cracks, broken or loose pieces and sharp edges prior to the session.

- Have mallets available for those with sensitive hands. Drums with synthetic heads are also easier on the hands than animal skins, and are more hygienic as they are able to be cleaned and sterilized between clients or groups.

- Shakers with handles may be easier for some to hold onto, especially for those whose hands are difficult to open.

- Provide seating with arms for those with balance issues and seating with a back for those with weak postural or core strength. It is important that individuals have a stable base of support when playing. If possible, feet should be planted on the ground. This will provide better balance and can improve endurance.

- Encourage people to take breaks from playing as needed.

- Provide simple and clear directions with simultaneous visual and verbal modelling.

- Have water readily available.

- Be aware of room temperature needs.

- Make space available for those in a wheelchair.

- Wipe all instruments before and after each session with a safe disinfectant.

## COMMON CHALLENGES AND HOW TO MINIMIZE THEM

On occasions, individuals may get out of their seat at an inappropriate time. Consider sitting these individuals near you. Calmly redirect as needed. Offering these individuals a large drum to play (positioned between their legs on the floor) may also deter them from getting out of their seat. Colourful tape on the ground around their chair can also be used to set boundaries for sitting and staying in place. If an individual wishes to stay standing, allow them to stand outside of the drum circle to reduce interference. Often you will have care assistants, but at the very least, it is advisable to also have at least one other person to assist you.

Allow a 'safe area' for an individual to go to if they are overstimulated by the sound. Allow them to withdraw from the circle and to join in when ready. Do not make an individual stay in the circle. Keeping an individual in the circle may cause sensory overload and meltdown. The use of noise-reducing headphones or earplugs can be of assistance. At the beginning of the session review what 'soft' and 'loud' sounds look and feel like. If you are made aware of individuals who are hypersensitive to sound, begin the session at a low volume and increase gradually. Hold the drum circle in a carpeted room whenever possible, as the carpet will assist with dampening the sound.

You may experience sessions where one or more individuals have oral motor difficulties (mouthing of objects and/or drooling). Have synthetic instruments for hygienic purposes. They can easily be disinfected afterwards. For those who place items inside their mouth, avoid using small instruments (e.g., egg shakers) as they can become a choking hazard. It is very important to check instruments for any cracks, broken or loose pieces and sharp edges. These individuals should be monitored closely and redirected to keep the item out of their mouth. Again, a helper is of great value to assist with this.

Communication can be challenging with different people in disability groups. For participants with hearing impairment, learning or cognitive disabilities, the use of visual aids can often be beneficial. Visual aids in the form of brightly coloured cards with pictures, numbers or words can be helpful in managing the musical output and behavioural actions of your group. You can make these cards very simply. I have found the following card messages useful:

- Stopping – 4, 3, 2, 1, Stop; Starting – 1, 2, Let's All Play
- I Play; You Play
- Louder; Softer (Quiet)
- Stop; Go
- Wait; Listen
- One at a time; All together.

Remember, *pictures often work better than words.*

## PRACTICAL APPLICATIONS OF THE DRUM CIRCLE
### Starting and stopping
I usually start a session with starts and stops. This builds a foundation of clients being aware of starting and stopping together. I will lead this exercise at first but then encourage clients to take the lead on this. This can be carried out verbally ('4, 3, 2, 1 and stop' and '1, 2, let's all play') or with signing or some other symbolic way that the participant can use to communicate.

### Playing soft and loud
Using standard drum circle facilitator techniques I show and explain to the participants that when I raise my arms high with my palm facing up, they are to play at a louder volume. When I bring my arms down with my palms facing the ground, they are to play at a lower volume. During the session, one should provide simultaneous verbal cues as the arms move. Keep in mind that mutisensory instructions are generally very important for those with special needs. This activity is good for helping participants gauge pressure/force as they alter their playing in response to changing volume.

### Listen to the bell
An exercise that I frequently use involves the 'Agogo' bell (a hand-held instrument with two bells, see following page). This bell is held in one hand

and played with a stick using the other. One bell has a high pitch (the smaller one) and the bigger bell has a low pitch. I instruct the women to play when the high bell is played. When the low bell is played, the men play. This provides both auditory and visual cueing which would benefit those with either impairment. This is an activity that addresses following directions, focus/attention, and impulse control from the group. It also builds leadership and confidence skills for the one playing the bell.

## Singing favourite songs

I ensure that the songs we sing together are age appropriate, and I often change the words to include the client's name and the instrument they are playing. As an example, when working with older population groups we will sing and play along to old favourites, e.g., 'Coming around the mountain'. This may morph into 'Mathew's playing on his drum (Boom, Boom, Boom)', etc. Find out the theme and function of the group or if there is anything special to celebrate or draw attention to. Is it a birthday, or an end of year or personal celebration? Choose songs appropriate to the theme. Find out what chants, songs and activities the participants already know and start with these.

## A typical session of around 50–60 mins
Let's begin

I always start my session by connecting with individual participants, through a handshake, a high five, a hug, a smile, a hello, or eye contact – whichever feels appropriate for that person.

### Hello song

Using an individual's name and the instrument they are playing. I use 'Hello (name), how are you, Hello, (name), how are you? Hello, (name), how are you? Let us play some music. Play your (instrument and sound) e.g. 1) frame drum, djembe – boom, boom, boom, 2) shaker, maraca – shake, shake, shake, 3) bell – ring, ring, ring. Let us play some music.' Make up your own hello song and tune.

### Starts and stops

Practice '1, 2, Let's all play' and '4, 3, 2, 1, Stop'. Use a simple rhythm. Do this a few times until everyone can stop and start together. This brings real focus and attention to the group.

### Brain gym game
A favourite in my groups is left finger on nose, right finger crosses over to touch left ear, then swap to right finger on nose and left finger to right ear. Repeat to the nursery rhyme 'Humpty Dumpty'. Add some claps or clicks in there to make it interesting, or try it in-between a simple heartbeat rhythm.

### Pass the beat and pass the rumble
One at a time around the circle each person plays something in order – first time a little rhythm phrase, next time a short rumble.

### Echo
Each person plays a short sequence on their instrument or body (clap or click fingers, verbal sounds, touch your head, touch your knees, etc.), then we all copy their rhythm a few times.

### Energizer
Use a rumble on your drum/shaker to answer a question. Ask the question – 'Rumble if you…(e.g., have a dog, a cat, a sister, a brother, have been on an aeroplane, ridden a horse, love ice cream, love spinach, etc)'. Get participants to come up with ideas, everyone rumbles if they identify with the statement.

### Singing and movement
Dancing and/or signing to a favourite song, e.g., (1) 'The Hokey Pokey'; (2) 'When the Saints go Marching In' (I often change the words to include the client's name and instrument, e.g., 'Oh, when Judy, she plays her drum', 'Oh when Matthew, he claps his hands'); (3) 'The farm song' (to the rhythm of 'Old MacDonald Has a Farm') using clients names and choice of animals, e.g., 'My friend Jason has a farm, oh yes he does. And on his farm he has 10 red chickens' or 'a grumpy big dinosaur' or 'a pride of lions'… encourage some creative suggestions; (4) teach and sing a simple chant (some favourites of mine are 'Zimbole', 'Che', 'Che Kule', 'Babala Gumbala'). There are lots of ideas on YouTube.

### Requests
Ask participants for their requests, it may be a game, a favourite song or leading a rhythm. This gives them a sense of control and ownership of the group.

### Time to finish
Close with some free play, a favourite game or a goodbye song of their choice. And perhaps a positive summarizing statement on their effort and achievement during the session. This completes the session.

## Working with blind and visually impaired people

I worked for seven years at a school for blind and visually impaired kids. The classes were small, with up to 10 students in a class and I knew them all well and which instruments they individually enjoyed.

Before starting, I would go around the group for introductions, learning their name and then asking them to play their instrument (and name and describe it). I recommend using a mix of percussion instruments (wood, bells, shakers and drums, djembe, ocean, dundun and frame drums). This allows each student to know where everyone is sitting and to identify the different sounds/instruments around them. I would also suggest dividing the class in two teams (they can choose the team name) so they can have a drum play off between the groups, which they love. A samba whistle is useful to get their attention.

Halfway through the session it is good to swap instruments. This may be done via student request or the facilitator may choose. Some of the kids maybe very musically talented and can be encouraged to suggest ideas to create new rhythms and games. You should also regularly introduce new instruments, focusing on their shape, sounds and texture – elements for them to explore.

In a session, singing a few songs and playing along is fun. You can teach a rhythm or two and encourage the group to freestyle, starting with the dundun or bass drum, then bringing in the instrument groups – shakers, wood, bells then other drums. Having the Samba whistle and a range of signals for different commands is helpful. Introduce lots of stops and starts, and highlight (solo) different combinations, e.g. instrument groups, boys/girls, the named groups (apples/pears, tigers/lions, etc.) or body percussion. It is recommended to always have a bass drum keeping the pulse throughout these arrangements – that might be the facilitator or one of the students who has a good sense of timing.

Focus on making the session fun with plenty of humour, laughing and as much input from students on what to do next, or the types of rhythms/games they like to play, as possible.

## Working with hearing impaired/deaf people

The vibration of the drum allows people with limited hearing to participate actively and enjoyably in a drum circle. If doing this work regularly it is recommended to learn some basic sign language – 'hello', 'go', 'stop', 'faster', 'slower', 'softer', 'louder', 'well done', 'thank you', and for the different instruments you are using.

Always try to sit where you can have eye contact with the group and use facial expressions, especially a happy and funny face. Instructions and rhythms are learned by sight so body movement needs to be clear and obvious to the student. Use your feet to show the timing. Wriggle your arm up in the air to get attention, wait, then give directions using your hand for stopping, starting or changing the rhythm. Use your whole body (without going overboard). Slightly exaggerate the rhythm you are playing so they can see the pattern your hands are making. Lift your hands off the drum. Choose an appropriate speed, not too fast.

I recommend starting with some body percussion, doing a couple of combinations and then getting some students to come up with some of their own. Then hand out instruments and teach a simple rhythm, then try a second rhythm, and, if the kids are into it, put the rhythms together. You might then allow these rhythms to morph into their own group rhythm. Often your role is simply to keep the pulse steady and do some facilitation when needed. You can use stops and starts with small groups to showcase different sections based on instruments or seating, and encourage individual participants to stop and start the group rhythm themselves. I have also found encouraging dancing for some students to be beneficial.

Use instruments with good vibrations and colour. Frame drums held against the body are great, also djembes, ocean drums, shakers, tambourines, rain sticks and anything with a vibration or that is interesting in shape and colour. *An important lesson I learned in my first session with a class of deaf high school students was that many of them are very noise sensitive. Don't use loud or high-pitched instruments that can hurt their ears.* Be aware of volume, there is no need to play loudly. Mid-range is good.

## ADDITIONAL ADVICE

I have had great pleasure in working with this population. I love to see the smiles and the bond that the drumming has created. It is very important that 'no player is left behind'. From a hand drum to a shaker everybody can have a part. Focus on the strengths and celebrate the successes, no matter how big or small. Respect the individual and look beyond the disability. Meeting the person where he or she is, instead of trying to fit them into a specific regimen of drumming allows for individuals with these needs to experience the enjoyment of making music at their own level and with great satisfaction.

And always remember, in order for learning to occur and skills to develop in this context, it is important that the experience be as fun and as consistent as possible. When there is a level of predictability, the participant becomes more at ease and therefore more receptive to the experience. Balance repeated exercises that develop core skills with new experiences so that the participant enjoys a high level of success, remains comfortable and confident, focused on the task and eager to learn new activities.

## AUTHOR BIOGRAPHIES
### Jorge Ochoa, OTR

Jorge is an occupational therapist and group drumming facilitator in San Antonio, TX. He is the founder of TamboRhythms, a company dedicated to promoting FUNctional living through rhythmic expression regardless of age or previous musical experience. He has facilitated events at schools/learning centres, worked with seniors and those with special needs, and has provided adult and community education programs.

> Email: tamborhythms@yahoo.com
> www.TamboRhythms.com

### Jaqui Barrett, MNZAC

Jaqui is a counsellor and family therapist, working for support agencies and in private practice in and around Auckland, New Zealand. In 2001 she set up her company RhythmDotCom and since then has run interactive music and drumming sessions throughout New Zealand in hospitals, rehabilitation units, prisons, aged care facilities, schools, community gatherings and in the corporate and mental health sectors.

> Email: jaquib1@gmail.com
> www.rhythmdotcom.com

## RECOMMENDED READING

Ratigan, S.L. (2009) *A Practical Guide to Hand Drumming and Drum Circles*. Self-published.
Sacks, O.W. (2007) *Musicophilia: Tales of Music and the Brain*. Toronto: Knopf.
Thomas, K. (n.d.) *Drum Circle Cookbook – Recipes for Group Drumming Fun*. www.kennethomas.com/book-DrumCircleCookbook.html (accessed 4 August 2020).
Thomas, D. & Woods, H. (2003) *Working with People with Learning Disabilities*. London: Jessica Kingsley Publishers.

# Working with Seniors

## LULU LEATHLEY

**OVERVIEW**

Improvisational music-making with seniors is recognized as an effective way to uplift and build community in a care facility or adult day centre. Often placed in a facility after a long and independent life, seniors can find it difficult to adapt to their new settings. Working with these people is especially gratifying because you can see their appreciation as they receive much-needed attention and pleasure from being able to participate with others.

The settings you will find yourself working in are many and varied, and include: community centres, adult day centres, drop-in respite facilities, assisted living facilities, intermediate and extended care homes. Populations vary as well, covering a broad range of needs, from well-elderly ('welderlies') to common diagnoses such as early-onset dementia, stroke, Parkinson's and other neurological conditions, as well as people at the end stage of their lives. The 'welderlies' are usually at an event on their own while the extended care patients are often mixed up together. End-of-life stage is hopefully with family members and in a private room.

Every situation is different, as is every participant, so it is important to be flexible and to be able to change direction with different activities that will suit the situation at hand.

## POSITIVE OUTCOMES

Working with seniors, facing different levels of physical and cognitive challenges, for over 20 years, I have found many positive benefits. Drumming with seniors creates a feeling of community and belonging that is often missing from their lives. It's evident on their faces and also the faces of care-givers and family members. Fortunately, over the last five to 10 years, there have been a number of well-validated research studies on the effectiveness of music-making using drumming. A wide range of studies, across multiple population types and environments, has found that improved 'feelings of belonging and social acceptance' are a common outcome from drum circle music making.[1] Dr Barry Bittman's (2001) study on the power of music-making is foundational.[2] He and his partners have consistently found an increase in social interaction and communication with these activities, and that the same modality can reduce burn-out for carers as well – hence my earlier recommendation to involve staff in these sessions.

Dr Bittman and others have shown that there is a reduction in anxiety and agitation with residents during these types of music-making sessions. And I have encountered this, many times over the years, most notably when my mother-in-law, at 98, suffered a fall, which resulted in a serious head injury. Her anxiety level was extremely high and when I brought in my instruments and played with her, she calmed right down. There was a dramatic difference in her demeanour. The improvement of mood, and how that enhances person-centred-care, is clearly evident in my sessions, exemplified by the fact that it brings families together in a happy and engaging way. Rates of depression and other depressive mood conditions are common across the aged care landscape and several studies have

---

1   Ascenso, S., Perkins, R., Atkins, L., Fancourt, D. & Williamon, A. (2018) 'Promoting well-being through group drumming with mental health service users and their carers.' *International Journal of Qualitative Studies on Health and Well-Being 13*, 1. https://doi.org/10.1080/174826 31.2018.1484219
2   Bittman, B., Bruhn, K.T., Lim, P.B., Neve, A., Stevens, C.K. & Knudsen, C. (2001) 'Testing the power of music-making: A study demonstrating the efficacy of recreational music-making as a means of inspiring creativity and helping long term care residents' bond.' *Focus on Caregiving*. www.themusictherapycenter.com/wp-content/uploads/2016/06/provider_magazine_article. pdf (accessed 21 August 2020).

pointed to the clear improvements that drum circles can make in relieving these conditions.[3]

Dr Daniel Levitin, a world-renowned neuroscientist has been at the forefront of researching music and the brain. In his book, *This Is Your Brain on Music: The Science of a Human Obsession*,[4] he states that music is fundamental to our species, perhaps even more so than language. He demonstrates that listening to music coordinates more disparate parts of the brain than almost any other activity and playing music extends this even more! The impact of rhythm on our lives begins in the womb and continues to have a fundamental impact on our physical and cognitive abilities. For older people this often equates to improvements in body movement, mental clarity and mood.

Over continued sessions in care facilities I have seen evidence of increased sensory stimulation, leading to improved cognitive function, including attention span, short-term memory and the ability to follow clues with participants. Reductions in anxiety and improvements in focus and memory have been found previously in research on drumming with people with dementia as well as those with mental health issues and their carers.[5] This same research also revealed an increase in residents' personal sense of autonomy after group music-making sessions. Within aged-care facilities there are many protocols and systems that often leave seniors feeling powerless and not heard. Playing a large drum or even a small shaker to a group song can provide an important sense of empowerment and autonomy.

Other benefits stemming from research into drumming include improvement in the immune response of individuals when engaging in weekly music-making sessions.[6] Seniors are always at great risk of catching

---

[3] Bittman, B., Bruhn, K.T., Stevens, C., Westengard, J. & Umbach, P.O. (2003) 'Recreational music-making: A cost-effective group interdisciplinary strategy for reducing burnout and improving mood states in long-term care workers.' *Advances in Mind-Body Medicine 19*, 3–4, 4–15.
Fancourt, D., Perkins, R., Ascenso, S., Carvalho, L.A., Steptoe, A. & Williamon, A. (2016) 'Effects of group drumming interventions on anxiety, depression, social resilience and inflammatory immune response among mental health service users.' *PloS one 11*, 3, e0151136.

[4] Levitin, D. (2008) *This Is Your Brain on Music*. Harmondsworth: Penguin.

[5] Ascenso, S., Perkins, R., Atkins, L., Fancourt, D. & Williamon, A. (2018) 'Promoting well-being through group drumming with mental health service users and their carers.' *International Journal of Qualitative Studies on Health and Well-Being 13*, 1. https://doi.org/10.1080/17482631.2018.1484219
Van de Winckel, A., Feys, H., & De Weerdt, W. (2004) 'Cognitive and behavioural effects of music-based exercises in patients with dementia.' *Clinical Rehabilitation, 18*, 253–258.

[6] Bittman, B.B., Berk, L.S., Felten, D.L., Westengard, J. Simonton, O.C., Pappas, J. & Ninehouser, M. (2001) 'Composite effects of group drumming music therapy on modulation of neuroendocrine-immune parameters in normal subjects.' *Alternative Therapies in Health and Medicine 7*, 1, 38–47.

any virus or bacterial infection that comes near, so building up their immunity through this form of exercise is a useful prevention strategy. Chronic pain is another debilitating condition commonly effecting seniors, and one that is a very difficult to treat. Studies have shown that there is a reduction in pain levels as a result of participation in music-making sessions.[7]

## SETTING UP FOR SUCCESS

It is important to visit the facility you will be working in before your event in order to identify appropriate parking and access to the workshop space, as well as to locate carts or trolleys and the assistants who will help get the instruments in the building. Arriving at least an hour before you start is helpful as well, to ensure no last-minute hiccups.

Prior to the day of your workshop get as much information about the abilities of your group as you can to help you gear your event to their specific needs. Often you may find people are limited to using one hand or have vision or hearing impediments so need a shaker instead of a loud drum or are in a wheelchair and can more easily play a 'Tubano' (large drum) beside them instead of a 'Buffalo drum' (small frame drum) on their lap. Having a wide range of instruments to select from will ensure that everyone can participate.

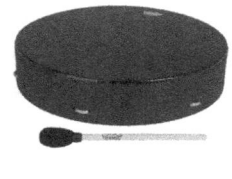

Often these care facilities don't have a central meeting area, so many of your events are likely to be in a dual-use space like the dining room or a small recreational room. Tables and chairs will often have to be moved to accommodate the instruments and the people. It is common for many people to be in wheelchairs so it is important to have enough space in the circle for them to be able to manoeuvre in and out. As I'm setting

---

[7] Dunbar, R., Kaskatis, K., MacDonald, I. & Barra, V. (2012) 'Performance of music elevates pain threshold and positive affect: Implications for the evolutionary function of music.' *Evolutionary Psychology: An International Journal of Evolutionary Approaches to Psychology and Behavior 10*, 688–702.

up the circle, and people are arriving, I will sing a song such as 'I've been working making music' (from 'I've been working on the railroad'). Often the participants are already sitting around the room waiting for me to begin; in that case I will play some music on a portable speaker and hand out instruments for them to play along with until we're ready to start our own routine.

## COMMON CHALLENGES AND HOW TO MINIMIZE THEM

Many people who hire you may initially view this work as 'entertainment or performance' and not appreciate its therapeutic nature or that it is a participatory event for the entire community, including the staff. A huge challenge for me has been watching the staff leave to have a break when I walk through the door. It is important to let the senior person that hired you know the benefits of having the staff participate, so that they can directly experience the therapeutic aspects of this work and gain awareness of their residents' ability and pleasure in participating. It is also a great way of residents and carers having fun together, reinforcing the personal nature of their connection while reducing the dependent aspect of their relationship.

Often a resident will not want to participate or will be very sensitive to the volume of the music. I always have a bag of foam earplugs to give out and will start my sessions with shakers and softer percussion instruments, a song, chant or story to get the 'naysayers' involved. Before you know it, they will have smiles on their faces and be playing away!

Limiting the number of participants is helpful. Many facilities want all their residents to be at the event which can mean numbers of up to 50 to 60 in some cases! You have to have a huge amount of energy to facilitate a group this big and give each person the attention they deserve. Where possible try to convince your contractor to allow you to run smaller groups. Many of these people get so little attention that it is much better to have a smaller group of 10 to 20, allowing you to look each one of them in the eye, take their hand and really get to know them as individuals.

At times I have encountered a resident who suddenly becomes anxious and agitated if the music gets too loud for them. Having your 'radar' turned up, and keeping an eye on everyone's body language is important so that you can react accordingly by changing the music to a slower more relaxed pace; giving out chimes, shakers and frogs (wood percussion) and perhaps starting a 'guided visualization' (see example of guided imagery below) to calm the person down.

## PRACTICAL APPLICATIONS OF THE DRUM CIRCLE

My sessions are usually an hour long but I am constantly reading the group to see if they are fatigued and need to take a breather or end the session a bit earlier. Often it will go over an hour as everyone is really enjoying singing and playing, but I am careful not to go too much over time. I have activities that I do every time so that the residents get to know them and join in with ease. I also have other activities up my sleeve so as to be able to inject them into the session when something arises in the moment, and we need a change of dynamic.

Here is an example of one of my programs that I have at the ready.

### Pre-session music

I bring a portable speaker with me and put on some music while the care-givers are bringing the residents into the room, which I have already arranged in a circle, leaving gaps for wheelchairs. I often put on Christine Steven's Drum Call from her excellent CD 'Drumming Up Spirit'.[8] It's so engaging that it draws people in. I also play uplifting music from the era of the residents or some music that I think appropriate to that particular residence.

### Introductions

I like to go around and welcome everyone into the session by singing or rapping their names and shaking hands with everyone. A wave would be fine but it's important to look each resident in the eye and be at their level, not standing above them.

### How do you do!

I extend my right hand to grasp the resident's hand, looking them straight in the eye, shaking their hand saying: 'How do you do and how do you do and how do you do again!'

I will go around the whole circle, and include any care-givers and family members who are there as well.

---

[8] Stevens, C. *Drumming up Spirit – Uplifting World Rhythms and Chants.* https://ubdrumcircles.com/product/drumming-up-spirit-play-along-cd

## Muscle up – warming up

We have 630 muscles in our bodies, so let's give them some attention. I count from one to eight as everyone lifts their arms up, then give a big sigh ('Aaaaaahhh') as we lower the arms down to the count of 8, 7, 6, 5, 4, 3, 2, 1. I then do the same with the shoulders, counting from one to eight as they raise their shoulders up and from eight down to one as they give a big sigh and lower their shoulders. You could do the same with the legs, elbows, even eyes!

## Hello Song

I sing this song to the tune of 'Skip to My Lou' giving out shakers to each person: 'Hello…how are you? Hello…how do you do! Hello…how are you? Let's all make some music!'

Find a similar song that is well known to the age and culture of the group you are working with.

## Shaker activities

### Shaker wave

Everyone shakes and waves at each other across the circle then I invite them to make a sound wave around the circle (like at a football game). I go around the circle with my hand extended to each person to invite them to shake a greeting to everyone.

### Shake to the beat

I play a steady beat on a drum and invite the residents to shake with the beat. I invite everyone to shake in a funny way. I will pick out someone with an interesting motion and ask everyone to copy that person for a few bars and then go back to their own way of shaking. Change the beat and repeat.

### Shakers in the air

Sing to the tune of 'If You're Happy and You Know It':

> *'Put your shakers in the air, in the air!'* (Shake three times)
> *'Put your shakers in the air, in the air!'* (Shake three times)
> *'Put your shakers in the air, leave them for about a year.'*
> *'Put your shakers in the air in the air.'* (Shake three times)

> 'Put your shakers by your knees, by your knees... if you please...'
> 'Shake your shakers near your nose...' etc.

## Passing out the drums

Sing or say:

> 'Passing out percussion to everyone, everyone, everyone.'

> 'Passing out the drums to everyone with a Boom Boom Boom Boom Boom!'

They can start playing along on their drums as they receive their instrument, especially on the Booms!

## Heartbeat story

I tell this story with every population that I work with. It brings people to stillness, as they listen.

> The sound that you are now hearing is the very first sound you ever heard.
> It's the sound of the first drummer, and the first drummer was a woman. That woman was your mother. We were all born drummers. We listened to our mother's heartbeat for nine months and after we were born, we were comforted just by lying on her chest and listening and feeling the sound of the drum inside her.
> It's the one thing that unites us on the planet. The Heartbeat.
> So much so that a Navaho elder once said that 'The drum is the Great Spirit's favourite instrument and that's why he gave us all a heartbeat.'
> So, if you would join me now in the heartbeat rhythm. Tap-Tap...Tap-Tap...Tap-Tap...Tap-Tap. Let's start to walk...we're going up a hill...(faster and faster to a rumble and Stop!)
> Give yourselves a big hand, you're all drummers now, so now let's all play!

## Rhythmic naming

This is one of the best activities for seniors of all sorts. Asking them their name and then playing it on their instrument (one beat for each syllable) draws them into the music-making through a personal connection. It also helps me learn the names of my group participants! Using their whole name and having everyone play it together is a great levelling activity that is fun and engages the whole group. Depending on their ability, I will often get two or sometimes even three names playing at once, creating a polyrhythmic song…John Bird, Sally Jones, Andrew Cassidy. This rhythmic naming activity works with every population.

## Story songs

One of my favourite activities is drawn from Heather MacTavish's story songs.[9] I have used these for the past 17 years with great success. I make up a story about something in my life or according to the participants' interest and infuse the story with suggestions for songs. As I tell the story the participants must try and figure out what song I am thinking of and whoever figures it out, calls it out or starts singing. An example would be my dog's story: I have a dog whose name is Millie. I first saw her in a store window and fell in love. I wondered how much that dog would cost…the song I'm searching for is? ('How much is that doggie in the window?').

This process of linking songs to memories is a great way to personalize a program, and has real cognitive benefits.

## If you can say it you can play it

Ya Ya Diablo, an African musician and teacher always said: 'If you can say it, you can play it.' The syllables of the words translate to beats on the drum. We say 'I like chocolate' (five beats) and then play it several times. We then say and play: 'I like strawberry' (four beats). Following this I will ask one half of the group to say and play 'I like chocolate' and then ask the other half to say and play 'I like strawberry'. Connecting both parts on the first note ('I'), we create a polyrhythmic song.

I will then ask if anyone has a favourite food. We say it and then play it. I may ask for a favourite colour and then a favourite animal and put them all together, saying and playing at the same time – for example, 'Purple rabbits eating pecan pie.' It can get quite hilarious and sometimes a bit naughty!

## Guided imagery

I slow things down at this point and ask the residents to put down their instruments, take a few big, deep breaths and sink into their chair or bed.

---

9  MacTavish, H. & Balsara, Z. (2011) *Songs, Science and Spirit: Musical Keys to Open Special Doors of Ability.* Cotati, CA: Provident Publishing.

I play a heartbeat on a large frame drum, or a steady tone on a metal singing bowl, a 'Hapi' drum or any instrument that sounds relaxing.

### Take the smile inside (guided imagery script)
I ask them to close their eyes if they feel comfortable and then put a smile on their faces. 'Take that smile into the mouth and swallow it down so your throat is smiling. Let that smile go into your lungs, both your left and right lungs, feel those lungs smiling. Now send that smile into your heart, every part of your heart is smiling. That smile is going into the kidneys and then the pancreas, the spleen, the digestive system, the bladder and the bowel all smiling.' Finally, I ask them to take a few deep breaths and wiggle their toes and fingers before opening their eyes.

## Closing
### Goodbye song
I always end my sessions singing to the tune of Woody Guthrie's 'It's Been Good To Know You.'[10]

I go around and look every Resident in the eye and shake their hand singing:

> 'So long, it's been great to drum with you
> So long, it's been great to sing with you
> So long, it's been great making music with you
> Keep singing and playing along.'

## EXERCISE ROUTINES
Keeping limber and mobile is a constant challenge for people as they age and many older citizens will have regular exercise classes or physiotherapy

---

10   See YouTube: www.youtube.com/watch?v=zqiblXFlZuk.

support as part of their weekly routines. Drum circles can be integrated into these programs by combining stretching routines with musical play. The simplest way to do this is to start a heartbeat rhythm and between the beats add a different stretch. For example:

- B, B – Clap your hands low
- B, B – Clap your hands high
- B, B – Twist to the left
- B, B – Twist to the right
- B, B – Chest out, shoulders back
- B, B – Lift your right knee
- B, B – Lift your left knee
- B, B – Stretch out your right leg
- B, B – Stretch out your left leg.

Each one is repeated several times.

Often, I will space these out by having periods of free play (improvised music) between each set.

## ADDITIONAL ADVICE

It can be good to get down to eye level with seniors, and one way to do this effectively is to use a mobile stool that you can sit on and roll around to different points of the circle – see the image below.

After working with many different populations in diverse situations over the past 20 years I can't tell you how much I love working with seniors of all backgrounds. They are so appreciative, they jump right to it, they don't complain and love the music-making! I feel I have made a valuable contribution to their day and the hugs and smiles I get are worth all the effort. There is a tsunami of this age group coming, so this work is going to be increasingly important, building community, lowering stress levels, building immune systems and bringing smiles to weary faces.

## AUTHOR'S BIOGRAPHY
### Lulu Leathley, BA

Lulu is an author, speaker and founder of 'LuluJam', based in Vancouver Canada. With over 35 years' experience, Lulu has designed music programs and drum circles for diverse populations from children and cancer patients to college students and seniors. She is the co-author of the recent book, *1, 2 Let's All Play*, with Mary Knysh.

With a BA from the University of Victoria, she also holds post-graduate diplomas, certificates and advanced training with Village Music Circles, Health Rhythms and Rhythm2Recovery. Her unique approach, which draws upon her background in Orff and Montessori, helps people from all abilities make music while receiving health, wellness and therapeutic benefits.

Email: lulu@lulujam.com
www.lulujam.com

## RECOMMENDED RESOURCES

*Alive Inside* (Netflix documentary on Alzheimer's) www.youtube.com/watch?v=IaB5Egej0TQ, accessed August 5 2020).

MacTavish, H. and Balsara, Z. (2011) *Songs, Science and Spirit: Musical Keys to Open Special Doors of Ability*. Cotati, CA: Provident Publishing.

Memmott, J. (2008) *Therapeutic Uses of Music with Older Adults*. Silver Spring, MD: American Music Therapy Association.

Music Alive! www.musicforpeople.org: A series of webinars with a group of international music educators and facilitators to assist the vulnerable populations in Care Facilities during the COVID-19 Pandemic. These webinars are filled with activities involving music and movement designed to bring calm and comfort to vulnerable individuals when distanced from their regular support group and families.

# Working with Dementia and Alzheimer's

JANA BRODER

**OVERVIEW**

It is quite common in today's world to find older adults with Alzheimer's and dementia in a variety of settings including retirement communities, senior day care facilities, nursing homes, residential memory centres and, of course, living within local communities. As a drum circle facilitator, I have chosen to bring the joy of drumming to these communities, where I have found the experience to be equally rewarding for me, the patients, their families and their care-givers.

Some drum circle facilitators may be resistant to working with this population because they believe the clients may not be able to respond or appreciate drumming or music activities. These older adults can be challenging and unpredictable, and often they appear as a 'normal' ageing adult. There are even some days, or times of the day, that a senior with Alzheimer's or dementia may be totally lucid and able to engage normally;

but this is soon followed by the progressive memory loss state that is the primary symptom of the illnesses.

However, in my experience, I find the above quandary is not a valid reason to eliminate this population from the fun experience of drumming. And I am backed by an increasing body of scientific research that says this population can benefit greatly from music, specifically, drumming, singing and movement, as part of their daily life. In bringing this musical activity into their experience, I have seen, and heard from their care-givers, that it helps them with many of the issues they battle with as they live with these progressive illnesses.

## POSITIVE OUTCOMES

It is not surprising to see that drumming is experienced as a positive event in so many ways for people with these degenerative issues. Studies show that despite decreased cognitive functioning, older adults' ability to enjoy and engage with music remains intact and that their fondness for music is present throughout the progression of dementia.[1] Many relatives report the strong connection their loved ones have with music, despite their memories of faces, family and friends disappearing altogether.

Across this population, research is showing us that listening and making music improves the quality of life for those who participate, with outcomes like feeling good, (improved mood), a sense of accomplishment and improved social wellbeing.[2] Research is also starting to show us that mental health issues such as depression and anxiety can benefit from a consistent drumming program.[3] This is particularly relevant for seniors who often suffer loneliness and isolation that has lead to chronic rates of these depressive symptoms. Rather than turning to medication, nursing homes may be better implementing drumming or more general music programs.

Additionally, significant research is being done with older adults that points to a positive impact on their cognitive abilities through involvement

---

1   McDermott, O., Orrell, M. & Ridder, H.M. (2014) 'The importance of music for people with dementia: The perspectives of people with dementia, family carers, staff and music therapists.' *Aging & Mental Health 18*, 6, 706–716.
2   Ascenso, S., Perkins, R., Atkins, L., Fancourt, D. & Williamon, A. (2018) 'Promoting well-being through group drumming with mental health service users and their carers.' *International Journal of Qualitative Studies on Health and Well-Being 13*, 1. https://doi.org/10.1080/17482631.2018.1484219
3   Fancourt, D., Perkins, R., Ascenso, S., Carvalho, L.A., Steptoe, A. & Williamon, A. (2016) 'Effects of group drumming interventions on anxiety, depression, social resilience and inflammatory immune response among mental health service users.' *PLoS ONE 11*, 3.

in musical activities, including drumming and singing.[4] This research showed improvements in both visual and verbal memory, similar to studies that have been done with music and children that lead to improved academic performance. And finally, though the selection is small, there is some research indicating that music activities with patients with dementia helped reduce their level of agitation.[5] As dementia progresses, behavioural disturbances such as agitation, aggressiveness, wandering and general confusion increase as well. This is can be very confronting for families and carers alike and often leads to further drug treatment. Musical interventions, like drumming, offer potential alternatives to reduce this issue.

## SETTING UP FOR SUCCESS

Sustained success comes from ensuring good communication prior to and at arrival to any facility, and making this a priority throughout the visit. Surprising seniors with Alzheimer's or dementia with a loud and unknown activity like a drum circle can induce anxiety and agitation. To have a profound and transforming impact on these older clients, facilitators should use a slowly paced, peaceful and compassionate approach.

Some of the techniques I use to build trust and rapport include:

- complimenting them (let them know how beautiful their hair looks or how much you love the sweater they are wearing)
- looking them directly in their eyes when speaking to them and make eye contact with every single participant (where culturally appropriate)
- touching their hands and placing them on the instrument
- allowing them to watch you tap on the drum and then inviting them to 'audition' for the new band that's about to form
- inviting them to dance and or sing
- telling them how great they sound and how much you enjoy making music with them
- listening to their stories about music in their lives (they love to share).

---

4   Degé, F. & Kerkovius, K. (2018) 'The effects of drumming on working memory in older adults.' *Annals of the New York Academy of Sciences*, 10.1111/nyas.13685. Advance online publication.
5   Choi, A.N., Lee, M.S., Cheong , K.J. & Lee, J.S. (2009) 'Effects of group music intervention on behavioral and psychological symptoms in patients with dementia: A pilot-controlled trial.' *International Journal of Neuroscience 119*, 4, 471–481.

## COMMON CHALLENGES AND HOW TO MINIMIZE THEM
One of the most common challenges in a memory loss community comes when the facilitator first arrives at a facility unaware of the surroundings and the specific tendencies or behaviours of the population. People with Alzheimer's often have a shortened fuse when it comes to their emotions and insecurities; little things can escalate quickly. Often the music itself brings up memories; tears may flow one moment, and uncontrollable laughter follows the next. It is important not to over-react and try and fix this phenomenon, but rather remain calm and empathetic.

Many of the patients have one common goal: to escape! This makes it especially important for the facilitator to be mindful of the exit doors when loading in and out of the building. When you start to play it is common to meet initial resistance to doing the activity. The most common excuse is 'my son is picking me up any minute', which is rarely the truth, but is often what they genuinely believe. I *never* argue the point; instead, I might suggest a seat in the drum circle that faces the door so that we can see when their son arrives.

It's also important to know that people with Alzheimer's can get physical in a variety of ways. It's always good to know in advance who has those tendencies. Care staff can sometimes help, but most of the time you won't know until it happens. In my time working with this population I been slapped, spanked, kissed, pinched and proposed to! I am often chased around the drum circle by a senior who is trying to spank my bottom…a *quite* common response!

A final challenge comes from people's reaction to volume. Some members of drumming groups are likely to be heavily medicated; they can have ringing ears as a side effect of a drug they are taking or a heightened sensitivity to loud noise that startles and disturbs them. It is best to begin the drum circle with clear instructions about keeping the volume low and it is helpful to demonstrate 'tapping'. I begin with a quiet beat and singing a gentle song. At about the halfway point, I bring up the volume and tempo slightly to get them moving and exercising a little. I bring it back down towards the end, and eventually finish by going up to each participant and holding their hands and thanking them for being in the band.

## PRACTICAL APPLICATIONS OF THE DRUM CIRCLE
I have found the following activities work well with this population, as they provide enjoyment as well as potential therapeutic benefits.

## Singing and drumming cultural songs

Singing and drumming cultural songs together encourages mental stimulation and awakens memories, as well as activating movement of their bodies and the use of their voices. Each participant is given their instrument and their hands are placed gently onto their drums. I have adapted my drum circles by including singing; in my case, I frequently sing African folk songs. (Any cultural songs will do.) While singing, I lead them into rhythmic drumming to the songs. Soon, drums, shakers and tambourines are beating along with the singing and participants add their own body movement to the rhythm. The facilitator should maintain awareness of the volume level and the energy level while also ensuring that those participants who are sensitive to loud sounds are comfortable. The positive outcomes are immediate as everybody in the circle 'wakes up' with the energy and joins in, 'remembering' how to use their voices, hands, and bodies in unison.

## Synchronize heartbeats

Synchronizing each participant's heartbeat with the group helps to calm the agitation some participants bring to the group. I begin by modelling the heartbeat sound through the drum; first I produce a very faint double deep bass sound, followed by the sound of 'whoosh'. Participants are encouraged to join in, and after a minute or so of this, we change the 'whoosh' sound to a single clap. With continued practice, the group develops their own group heartbeat rhythm. As the group becomes comfortable with this, their soothing and grounding heartbeat, I add new challenges between the drum beats, including activities such as clapping twice, scratching the drum, snapping their fingers and singing. It is important that you, as the facilitator, be clear with your instructions and model the heartbeat during the activity from start to finish. To end the activity, I always count backwards from eight until we all end together in a silent moment.

These are variations of the heartbeat rhythm and, if done slowly and deliberately, are effective in bringing the group into harmony. An important outcome from this unified heartbeat exercise can be seen in a general reduction in group stress. There is often a clear transition from physical and emotional agitation to a sense of group calm and belonging.

## Solos

Individual solos are a great way to reduce participants' sense of loneliness and isolation with their acceptance into this friendly group activity; it also encourages their inner 'rock star' to appear! I start by encouraging a light and easy groove with the group. As this activity progresses, the whole room is tapping their drums or their feet and, often, moving their bodies a bit too. I complicate their participation by adding stops and starts which they view as a huge accomplishment. In my experience, they are capable of rising to the challenge every time with a little practice.

After we have practised and mastered stops and starts, I explain that on the next stop, one person will jump in and play all by themselves, whatever they want to play, for as long as they want to play until I count the group back in. It is important that the facilitator enthusiastically celebrate each solo as a model for the whole group. I encourage the group to celebrate each participant's 'success' after each solo is complete and with this intention in mind, we go around the room until each person has taken a solo and is celebrated, no matter how big or small their contribution was. The positive outcomes from this exercise include the attention and recognition often missing from their lives – creating the sense of being a 'star performer' with the appreciative energy coming back to them in the form of applause and compliments.

## ADDITIONAL ADVICE

*Don't be afraid to work with this population.* Many facilitators avoid memory centres and people with Alzheimer's and dementia, thinking they are too hard to engage. My experience is quite different, and with practice this could become a favourite group to drum with. They love to be noticed and complimented!

*Come with an open mind and be prepared to be pleasantly surprised.* A story comes to mind that changed my perceptions about judging what is going on in my drum circles. I was facilitating a drum circle in a memory centre with a group of participants and their nurses and care-givers. I began with the instructions that all hands should simply be placed on their drums. As they waited, I began to sing one of my African songs and started to drum lightly. I noticed a frail-looking participant sitting in a wheelchair near her nurse; she had begun to cry. Of course, my immediate internal process was to question my own activity. I asked myself: 'Should I stop?', 'Am I too loud?', 'Does she want to leave the session?' I made the decision to continue to sing and play with the larger, engaged group through the 40-minute session, meanwhile, noting that the woman wept and seemed distraught throughout the program. When we finished, I walked over to the distraught patient's nurse to check-in and make sure everything was alright. I asked the nurse if she was aware of any reason her patient might feel sad and seem so upset. Her response was unexpected since I had already prejudged the situation as 'bad'. It was revealed by the nurse that this 93-year-old patient with Alzheimer's had been in Africa as a missionary for many years earlier in her life and the songs I sang brought those long-forgotten memories to the forefront of her mind. Her tears were 'happy tears' and she was remembering pleasant pastimes as the group was singing and playing along with me.

I had completely misinterpreted the situation: a good lesson indeed!

## AUTHOR'S BIOGRAPHY
### Jana Broder
Jana Broder is the owner and director of the firm 'Drum Magic' in Florida and has been actively facilitating drum circles since 2002. She has won several small-business awards and teaches classes in how to run a professional drum circle business. She has worked with a wide range of populations using drums but has increasingly focused her work in the area of 'seniors', an area which has grown very fast and has proven to be the most positively affected group that she drums with.

>Email: Janabroder@drummagic.net
>www.drummagic.net or www.drummagic.com
>Facebook: Drum Magic, LLC

## RECOMMENDED RESOURCE
Aldridge, D. (ed.) (2000) *Music Therapy in dementia care*. London: Jessica Kingsley Publishers.

*Alive Inside* (Netflix documentary on Alzheimer's) www.youtube.com/watch?v=IaB5Egej0TQ, accessed 5 August 2020).

Richards, C. (ed.) (2020) *Living well with dementia through music: A resource book for activity providers and care staff*. London: Jessica Kingsley Publishers.

Rio, R. (2009) *Connecting through music with people with dementia: A guide for caregivers*. London: Jessica Kingsley Publishers.

# Grief and Loss

## CAROLYN KOEBEL AND LAURA PAWUK

**OVERVIEW**

The therapeutic benefits of drumming for people's mental health and well-being have been well documented, and its application and use as a powerful tool for transforming grief is expanding. Many drum circle facilitators are increasingly called on to create experiences for bereavement camps and grief groups involving diverse groups of participants. Traditional cultures have long-standing practices of communal grieving involving drumming, dancing and vocalizing/singing; I have personally experienced this in my study of the Ewe in Ghana, the Garifuna cultures of Belize, the cremation rituals in Bali and even in the Second Line funerals of New Orleans. West African traditional healer Sobonfu Somé states:

Communal grieving offers something that we cannot get when we grieve by ourselves. Through validation, acknowledgement and witnessing, communal grieving allows us to experience a level of healing that is deeply and profoundly freeing. We experience a collective sharing, so that an individual doesn't need to bear all the weight of the suffering.[1]

One of the most deeply profound moments I have borne witness to involved my community drumming ensemble of adults with developmental disabilities offering a performance at the memorial service for one of my hospice clients, who was a member of their peer group. Not only did this prove deeply meaningful for the family who had lost their loved one, but it provided a forum for public grieving for her friends and peers, a community that is often discriminated against in terms of their perceived ability to feel and process things on the same emotional level as their neurotypical peers. Drumming and sharing sacred songs amid streaming tears was a powerful collective ritual for everyone in that room that day. It was when I looked out and saw her peers swaying and signing the words to the song that my own tears joined the collective waterfall.

## POSITIVE OUTCOMES

Since the early 2000s, researchers have avidly sought to document the beneficial impact of group drumming on our psychological, neurological, physiological, emotional and spiritual wellbeing. Tina Maschi and her colleagues (2010)[2] found, in consecutive studies, that consistent feelings of calmness, energy, empowerment, and connectedness emerged after group drumming sessions

---

1   Somé, S. (n.d.) 'Embracing grief: Surrendering to your sorrow has the power to heal the deepest wounds.' www.sobonfu.com/articles/writings-by-sobonfu-2/embracing-grief (accessed 5 August 2020).
2   Maschi, T. & Bradley C. (2010) 'Recreational drumming: A creative arts intervention strategy for social work teaching and practice.' *Journal of Baccalaureate Social Work 15*, 53–66.
    MacMillan, T., Maschi, T. & Tseng, Y.F. (2012) 'Measuring perceived well-being after recreational drumming: An exploratory factor analysis.' *Families in Society: The Journal of Contemporary Social Services 93*, 1, 74–79.
    Maschi, T., Macmillan, T. & Viola, D. (2013) 'Group drumming and well-being: A promising self-care strategy for social workers.' *Arts & Health: An International Journal for Research, Policy, and Practice 5*, 2, 142–151.

with social work students. And Bittman[3] led several studies that showed that engagement in group drumming positively enhances mood-elevating neuroendocrines and decreases the body's stress response, all of which can be powerful antidotes to positively counteract the body's physiological response to grief.

The effects of group drumming on people undergoing mental health treatment are the focus of a number of recent and ongoing studies. Adults undergoing mental health treatment who engaged in group drumming showed significant decreases in depression and anxiety while improving social resilience.[4] Additionally, this study showed positive modulation of immune factors from a pro-inflammatory toward an anti-inflammatory immune profile. Bensimon, Amir and Wolf (2009)[5] looked at the positive impact of drumming on post-traumatic stress disorder (PTSD) with soldiers. Their findings showed that 'a reduction in PTSD symptoms was observed following drumming, especially an increased sense of openness, togetherness, belonging, sharing, closeness, connectedness and intimacy, as well as achieving a non-intimidating access to traumatic memories, facilitating an outlet for rage and regaining a sense of self-control'.

The benefits of group drumming on youth have been demonstrated in a number of studies. Stone[6] further discusses the benefits of group drumming for connecting with self and others, while increasing feelings of groundedness and peace. In his youth, family and community drum circles, he found that drumming transcended and often erased barriers between group members.

---

[3] Bittman, B.B., Berk, L.S., Felten, D.L., Westengard, J. et al. (2001) 'Composite effects of group drumming music therapy on modulation of neuroendocrine-immune parameters in normal subjects.' *Alternative Therapies in Health and Medicine 7*, 1, 38–47.
Bittman, B.B., Berk, L., Shannon, M.., Sharaf, M. et al. (2005) 'Recreational music-making modulates the human stress responses: A preliminary individualized gene expression strategy.' *Medical Science Monitor 11*, 2, 31–40.
Bittman, B.B., Bruhn, K.T., Stevens, C., Westengard, J. & Umbach, P.O. (2003) 'Recreational music-making: A cost-effective group interdisciplinary strategy for reducing burnout and improving mood states in long-term care workers.' *Advances in Mind-Body Medicine 19*, 3–4, 4–15.
Bittman, B.B., Snyder, C., Bruhn, K.T., Liebfreid, F. et al. (2004) 'Recreational music-making: An integrative group intervention for reducing burnout and improving mood states in first year associate degree nursing students: Insights and economic impact.' *International Journal of Nursing Education Scholarship 1*, article 12.

[4] Fancourt, D., Perkins, R., Ascenso, S., Carvalho, L.A., Steptoe, A. & Williamon, A. (2016) 'Effects of group drumming interventions on anxiety, depression, social resilience and inflammatory immune response among mental health service users.' *PLoS ONE 11*, 3.

[5] Bensimon, M., Amir, D. & Wolf, Y. (2008) 'Drumming through trauma: Music therapy with post-traumatic soldiers.' *The Arts in Psychotherapy 35*, 34–48.

[6] Stone, N.N. (2005) 'Hand-drumming to build community: The story of the Whittier Drum Project.' *New Directions for Youth Development 106*, 73–83.

His work was informed by Winnicott's[7] theories on transitional objects, leading Stone to assert that drumming creates safe transitional space, and drums become transitional objects that connect youth to youth, youth to adults, youth to ancestors, and youth to community. In the 'Whittier Drum Project', hand drumming is creating community, facilitating healing and, as one participant put it, building a collective self-esteem. Young people indicated that they felt free to express themselves because they knew that their playing would not elicit negative feedback. They also reported feeling understood and connected with others who shared the grief experience.[8] Certainly, these concepts can support people of all ages who are engaged in drumming at a time of loss.

Hilliard's (2005)[9] review of existing research about the effects of music for people in end-of-life care revealed positive changes in physical issues such as pain and low energy as well as in the areas of emotions, spirituality, and quality of life. The benefits of engaging in music at a time of loss extend to those who are grieving as well. Drumming facilitators can glean concepts from the findings of Katrina McFerran's music therapy work with grieving adolescents. She notes that unstructured improvisation provides a sense of fun and relief from the challenging focus on grief and that participants valued the opportunity to release in this way.[10] It is important to note her recommendation to couple unstructured improvisations with structured experiences. Structure provides a strong container through which challenging emotions can be expressed. When balanced with unstructured improvisation, participants can freely release the intensity they are holding.

## SETTING UP FOR SUCCESS

When conversing with agencies and collaborators about utilizing group drumming and drum circle modalities in end-of-life or bereavement settings, it is important to understand the goals for the experience and needs of the participants.

---

7   Winnicott, D.W. (1953) 'Transitional objects and transitional phenomena.' *International Journal of Psycho-Analysis 34*, 1–26.
    Winnicott, D.W. (1971) *Playing and Reality.* London: Tavistock/Routledge.
8   McFerran, K., Roberts, M. & O'Grady, L. (2010) 'Music therapy with bereaved teenagers: A mixed methods perspective.' *Death Studies 34*, 541–565.
9   Hilliard, R. (2005) 'Music therapy in hospice and palliative care: A review of the empirical data.' *Evidence-Based Complementary and Alternative Medicine: eCAM. 2*, 2, 173–178.
10  McFerran, K., Roberts, M. & O'Grady, L. (2010) 'Music therapy with bereaved teenagers: A mixed methods perspective.' *Death Studies 34*, 541–565.
    McFerran, K. (2011) 'Music therapy with bereaved youth: Expressing grief and feeling better.' *Prevention Researcher 18*, 3, 17–20.

- What is the purpose of the drumming?
- What precautions must be taken?
- Do any participants have sensitivity to sound?
- Will group members need assistance or accommodations?
- How will assistance or accommodations be provided?
- Who else will be present if help is needed?

In many cases, event organizers are interested in including this experience as part of a broader profile of experiences during a day-long, weekend or even week-long experience. In some cases, we may be called upon to help open up the tender emotional spaces that the participants are guarding, while in others, we may be invited there to bring lightness – smiles, relief, stress reduction, a sense of playfulness and joy. And, we may be called on to create rituals like a playful morning warm-up, an opening or closing event, a candlelight remembrance ceremony, or a relaxation experience.

The drum circle is an inviting and accepting environment where all emotions are welcome – withdrawal, anger, depression, numbness, denial, etc., and as such, we should ensure a safe and confidential space with access to tissues, water and support staff. Since we will not likely know the individual stories of loss that our participants are carrying, we may also want to inquire in advance if there are any potential 'triggers' we should be mindful of as we design our experience.

## COMMON CHALLENGES AND HOW TO MINIMIZE THEM

In her book, *The Ethics of Caring*, Kylea Taylor[11] clearly reveals that our own vulnerabilities have the potential to unknowingly and adversely affect us and our clients unless we become aware of them. This is especially true for work in this area. The powerful energies created through group drumming can create an altered state of consciousness that naturally illuminates our own fears and desires.

Before entering this work, it is important to examine our own vulnerable contexts. Doing so strengthens our competence for facilitating supportive experiences. We may experience an over-identification with a participant's experience if it closely mirrors an event in our own life story. We want to prepare in advance for this possibility so we are able to

---

11　Taylor, K. (2017) *The Ethics of Caring: Honouring the Web of Life in Our Professional Caring Relationships*. Santa Cruz, CA: Hanford Meade.

maintain our own groundedness and leadership capacity to hold space for others on their grief journey. Also, becoming aware of the shadows of our psyches that are universal can help us navigate confusion that will inevitably arise so that we can enter into a higher capacity for care.

Examining your own awareness of death is vital when working with people who are grieving. Consider viewing a film such as *Being Mortal*[12] or otherwise sitting with your own feelings about death and mortality. In addition, it is also important to process the losses and grief that we have experienced throughout our lives. When working in the grief environment, it is important to recognize the likelihood that some of your participants may have experienced a traumatic loss similar to ones you have experienced.

In addition, becoming aware of the unique needs of the people who are grieving is just as important. One of my favourite collaborators for bereavement drumming groups is my grief counsellor. As you move more deeply into the transformational capacity of the drum circle, it is highly advisable to partner with co-leaders who have advanced training in grief counselling to help ensure the safety of all participants. In most cases, these individuals will know the background of each participant, including the type of loss that they have sustained.

It is also important to recognize that denial can be a very effective coping strategy for protecting a person from the emotional trauma of losing a loved one. One study designed for children to cope with parent loss caused adverse reactions.[13] Researchers learned that whilst music-making experiences were welcomed before the parent's death, attempts at continuing afterwards caused emotional stress because the music experiences were focused on processing what they needed to deny. I have encountered many people who, though they expressed an interest in engaging in music, chose not to do so. They indicated that they needed to stay composed and that the music would open the floodgate of grief.

Ensuring that a professionally trained mental health clinician is present and/or available may increase clients' willingness to participate. Knowing that someone is available if needed can decrease the stress and anxiety that may accompany someone when drumming. Having this person on hand can be a resource to both you and any client should you not know how to respond. They can be approached if you have questions or concerns.

---

12  *Being Mortal* (2015) Directed by Thomas Jennings & Nisha Pahuja. https://youtu.be/lQhI3Jb7vMg
13  Saldinger, A., Cain, A., Porterfield, K. & Lohnes, K. (2004) 'Facilitating attachment between school-aged children and a dying parent.' *Death Studies 28*, 10, 915–940.

## PRACTICAL APPLICATIONS OF THE DRUM CIRCLE (AND VIGNETTES)

A great deal of my work has revolved around the use of drums and percussion one on one with an individual who is at end-of-life. In some cases, this has involved a receptive environment in which I was offering the music for the client to receive. In other cases, we were creating the music together. In each case, knowing what would be most meaningful to each client, based on their history and life story, allowed me to access a deeper exchange by including drumming in our encounters.

Perhaps the greatest confirmation of the power of this work I received was in an individual session with an older African-American male, near end-of-life, who identified as Pentecostal. For my first couple of visits I shared spiritual music with him, accompanied by guitar, while I presented him with drums to join me (in which he did not engage). When I changed my approach on our third visit and accompanied myself on a lively frame drum groove, singing the client's preferred musical content, the client became highly animated, announcing 'That's what I'm talkin' about!'

I have found that many older adults have a deep affinity for the music (and dancing) of the Big Band Era. As such, I do not find it surprising that they love the drums – some have even affectionately likened me to Gene Krupa. Several female hospice clients have stated that they always wanted to play the drums, but were never allowed to do so as girls growing up during an era when it was highly discouraged. For many of them, it is an ecstatic and joyful experience to finally have the opportunity to cut loose and express these long-held desires. In some of my memory care groups, the clients become particularly enlivened and engaged when the drums are introduced into the environment, as evidenced by tapping, patsching, clapping, moving rhythmically and drumming when presented with an instrument.

Drums and percussion occupy a prominent role in a variety of multicultural and spiritual traditions. As such, I have found wide receptivity to the frame drum for individuals who connect with yogic practices and traditions, as well as with Hindi and Sikh clients for whom kirtan and bhajans are preferred devotional chant styles. In these scenarios, I may accompany while they sing, we may both drum together, we may both drum and sing together, or they may simply receive the music. With some individuals, they may have well-established meditation practices in which they merely request that I play a slow (frame) drum meditation for them. In a group bereavement setting, I may invite all participants to join me on frame drums, sharing a simple technique for doum (the bass sound) and pah (a touch/press), and cha (a brush stroke). We may engage in a guided group relaxation exercise, a mindfulness practice, or a memorial remembrance and time of sharing. In one such group, I created an honour chant (see Figure 20.1) that I initially sang, and invited participants to join with me as they became familiar with the words. Most of them joined in on their frame drums, quietly at first, but growing in solidarity as the intervention progressed. I used the chant as a way to invite the participants to share the name of their loved one and their relationship to the deceased. We sang the song in-between each person's time of sharing, and continued to drum throughout to ground the experience.

*Figure 20.1: In Our Hearts*

In one improvisational drumming bereavement group, we incorporated the ocean drum. As Hilliard[14] states '...the use of the ocean drum to emulate the waves of grief, sometimes subtle, sometimes strong' can be a powerful tool in grief work. Indeed, it was the first instrument my bereavement counsellor fell in love with, for precisely this reason. As such, it can be a wonderful instrument to pass around in a drum circle environment, from one person to the next, to let them individually explore it as an audible expression of their grief, receiving the underlying rhythmic support of the entire group.

On another occasion, my hospice client asked me to facilitate a family drumming session when her grandson was due to come to town for the weekend with her daughter. She was particularly concerned that he not be caught up in the sadness of the occasion, and wanted to cultivate a time of joy and positive memory-building for him. As such, I came with a wide selection of drums and percussion instruments, such that everyone present could participate. By the time we got to the end of our musical jamboree, he had collected all of the instruments for himself and surrounded himself

---

14  Hilliard, R. (2001) 'The effects of music therapy-based bereavement groups on mood and behavior of grieving children.' *Journal of Music Therapy* 38, 4, 291–306.

with this new drum-set, and proceeded to solo and entertain us all. His grandmother could not have been more delighted by the entire experience.

As a facilitator, it can be very significant to recognize the different energies that are invoked by the djembe as compared to the frame drum, and to consider when you may wish to choose one over the other, depending on the type of experience you are hoping to cultivate. In general, my participants have often commented that the energy of the frame drum tends to feel more introspective/introverted, while the energy of the djembe feels more extrospective/extroverted. In this context, we may wish to explore this intentionally, depending on whether we are hoping to help the individual move more deeply into the emotional interior of their grief, or to move into a place of reclamation and joyfulness.

One of the themes we used in our drum circle at our 'partner-loss' group, was that of 'sounding our grief'. On this occasion, I brought a wide variety of drums and percussion instruments in an attempt to offer the most expressive palette I could to participants. The goal of this group was to connect deeply to our feelings and tenderness for our departed loved ones – in this case, our chosen life partners. The intensity of grief in this particular group can be quite profound. The most masculine-looking male in the group chose the sweetest of instruments, a bell tree of graduated brass bells, to represent his love. When participants were asked to share why they had chosen their particular instruments, he said that none of the instruments in the collection could accurately capture the sweetness of his wife, but he chose that one because it came the closest. This musical improvisation was deeply connecting and deeply stirring for all the individuals.

A possible extension of this concept is playing our emotions on the drums, which can be incredibly validating for participants to witness and be witnessed. Drumming provides a safe way for people to process their emotions. The sense of shared social empathy allows for normalization of the grief response and decreased feelings of isolation and disconnection.

Another collaboration was at a day-long grief group. On this occasion, we chose to focus on reclaiming our power after a significant loss. This is a theme that was prominent in the work of Ruth Bright, a pioneer in grief and loss music therapy.[15] This drum circle was composed of primarily cone drums (djembe and tubano) in order to engage the participants in a more energetic style of play than frame drums might facilitate. In the centre, I placed a dun dun (a double-headed, cylindrical West African drum) that

---

15  Bright, R. (1996) *Grief and Powerlessness: Helping People Regain Control of Their Lives.* London: Jessica Kingsley Publishers.

was to be played with sticks. We started out exploring sounds. I gave a very brief instruction on how to hold the drum and how to use both bass and tone technique to access more of the sound and expressive capacity of the instruments. I explained to each participant that the goal of this session was to focus on reclaiming our power after being knocked down by the heavy blow of our personal losses. The group began to entrain and gain steam in the improvisation, and as there was more sound filling the room, I invited participants to come up one at a time to pick up the drumsticks, assuring them that we would be here to sustain and support them in this endeavour. After each person had entered the centre and explored this space, we slowly lowered the volume and moved into silence. The grief counsellor and I asked participants to share how that experience was for them, and group members gave one another beautifully supportive feedback. One of the things I am always mindful of is the safety of the participants, seeking ways to give them the fullest range of musical expression without causing injury to themselves or others. As such, placing the drum with sticks in the centre gave them space from those around them, as well as a way to generate a much bigger sound, with bigger gestures, without the added concern of bruising or injuring their hands if they were playing with similar intensity on a cone drum.

## Children and grief

During a weekend-long family bereavement camp, eight school-aged children engaged in a drumming experience. Each of them held an 8-inch diameter paddle drum and mallet. I've found that when structure is needed, it can be created with uniformity of instruments. When children play the same instrument, they more easily focus on the intended experience. The children played an emotion on their drum which was then played together with everyone. They also identified their coping skills and how their coping skills made them feel. The tenderness with which they supported each other and the enthusiasm they shared were palpable. When one boy randomly picked 'in trouble' from a hat, he sank in his chair with sad eyes and gently tapped the drum. The others slouched and made small sounds with their drums, too. Some children leapt from their seats into the middle of the circle shouting and drumming what helped them feel better. 'Playing soccer!' Everyone joined in the wild drumming.

Several years ago, four area hospices in my region collaborated to create a collective bereavement camp weekend in which staff and resources were shared among the agencies. Staff shared universal enthusiasm for an evening bonfire and drum circle event. It was clear that the goal for this gathering was to uplift everyone's spirits, and to come together to reconnect to life-giving energy, playfulness and joy. The participants were doing emotionally heavy work during the daytime, so we wanted to offer an experience of release and unification. This circle was an intergenerational gathering of individuals and families who had experienced a wide range of losses. There was a broad mixture of instrumentation, with plenty of portable percussion for those who wanted to dance and move while musicking. We left plenty of space for individual creativity, and inserted facilitation techniques if and as needed to shape the energy. Participants enjoyed dancing, moving and lots of singing. Some of the participants led songs, some requests were made and facilitators included songs that would fit the energy of the circle. Many staff were involved as well, and it was very meaningful for them to see the participants access joy and release.

A variety of recreational drum circle techniques can be applied and modified for this setting. One potential application to grief settings is to have the group members create a rhythmic pattern to represent the name of their (deceased) loved one on the drums. This concept can be used to generate ensemble patterns or sequences or even 'song forms' in which you can create a shared 'chorus' phrase that thematically unifies the experience. Group members can each individually play their unique pattern at the same time to create a composite groove, or group members can support each other one at a time, and play the individual names in unison as a gesture of solidarity and support to the individual sharing about their loved one.

Another beautiful application of the drum circle is to create a circle of remembrance. This can be approached in a wide variety of ways. This may also be incorporated as part of a candlelight remembrance ceremony. One method I like is to anchor the experience in a chant and a unifying rhythm, such as a heartbeat. Depending on who my participants are (and who they are grieving the loss of), I sometimes introduce an ancestral honour chant shared by African healer/wisdom teacher Malidoma Somé, entitled 'Poorah Mamineh'.[16]

'Poorah Mamineh' is honouring and welcoming in the spirits of all your grandmothers, mothers and all female ancestors, while Poorah Samineh' is honouring and welcoming in the spirits of your grandfathers, fathers and all male ancestors. I use the song as a way to create a holding container in which individuals can come up to the centre, one at a time, to place memory objects or pictures of their loved ones, or to light a candle for their

---

16 A recording of it can be heard here: https://carolynkoebel.bandcamp.com/track/poorah-mamineh-2.

loved one. Any number of songs/chants/or phrases can be substituted, according to the needs of your group.

I would also consider incorporating a handpan, sansula-type kalimba, or cedar flute into this environment to induce a more reflective musical mood. If possible, adjust the lighting in the space to be gentle and inviting. Consider utilizing one of these warm, melodic instruments as a visual and auditory cue to the group that we are fading away  from the drums, and coming into a time of closure and re-integration of this present experience.

Music therapists James Borling, and Robert Miller contributed a beautiful piece on 'Conscious Drumming: Drumming from the Heart'[17] in *Tataku: The Use of Percussion in Music Therapy*. Conscious drumming 'unifies the organizational, social, and internal benefits of group drumming with the group support, sacredness, and ritual of the talking stick'. This format creates a healing ritual for a grieving community. The technique alternates periods of group drumming with individual sharing while maintaining a constant pulse throughout. An individual comes to the centre of the circle with the talking stick to speak while the group maintains a gentle heartbeat pulse. As the speaker finishes and places the talking stick back on the centre altar, the group returns to collective rhythmic play. This pattern continues until everyone who wants to speak has had the opportunity to do so.

This approach has widespread potential for grief work. For example, we may invite individuals to come to the centre one at a time, or even in family units, to share a memory, a piece of poetry, or possibly a song that represents their relationship to their deceased loved one. Ultimately, the decision to incorporate ritual in your gathering will depend on the community you are serving and the ways in which you introduce and facilitate the sacred inside of this type of healing circle.

## ADDITIONAL ADVICE

In general, we want to use our facilitation tools to build empathy and rapport with participants, and to establish a sense of trust and safety. I strongly recommend that you develop your musical flexibility, knowledge, repertoire of grooves and playing techniques. I have found it invaluable to

---

17  Borling, J. & Miller, R. (2008) 'Conscious Drumming: Drumming from the Heart.' In B.B. Matney (ed.) *Tataku: The Use of Percussion in Music Therapy*. Denton, TX: Sarsen Pub, p.231.

study the frame drum, djembe, conga, and auxiliary percussion instruments in depth, so that I can model diverse techniques, and help shape a rich musical experience for the participants. In many instances, when I am drumming with culturally diverse participants, I consciously insert culturally specific rhythmic patterns that I hope the participant might recognize, as a way to communicate, non-verbally, that I recognize their presence in the circle.

Again, to reiterate, exploring your own death awareness, grief experiences and trauma is essential for working successfully with those dealing with grief and loss. Identifying ethical vulnerabilities outlined by Taylor (2017)[18] and taking steps to ensure that they do not interfere with clients' experiences are paramount. Further, understanding differences in cultural and religious perspectives around death and dying is essential if you serve diverse communities of grievers.

One final area of edification may be to familiarize yourself with the universal tasks of mourning. Doing so can provide an understanding of the context of the group itself. Worden (2009)[19] identifies the following tasks: (1) accept the reality of the loss, (2) work through the pain of grief, (3) adjust to an environment in which the deceased is missing and (4) discover a lasting and healthy way to feel connected with the deceased whilst moving forward into a new life.

## AUTHOR BIOGRAPHIES
### Carolyn Koebel, MM, MT-BC

Carolyn has been leading community rhythm events and facilitating therapeutic and transformational group drumming events for the past 24 years. She is a board-certified music therapist, having earned the Hospice and Palliative Care music therapy certification, and is a world percussionist, performer and educator at Western Michigan University, Kalamazoo College and St. Mary-of-the-Woods College. She has worked in hospice care for the past 15 years, interweaving drums and percussion into her individual, family and group work. In 2014 she produced the 3-CD collection *Honoring the Passage: Voices from Hospice Music Therapy & Beyond* and in 2019 *Honoring the Passage II: More Voices from Hospice Music Therapy*.

---

18  Taylor, K. (2017) *The Ethics of Caring: Honouring the Web of Life in Our Professional Caring Relationships*. Santa Cruz, CA: Hanford Meade.
19  Worden, J. (2009) *Grief Counseling and Grief Therapy: A Handbook for the Mental Health Practitioner*. New York: Springer Publishing Company.

Email: carolyn.koebel@gmail.com
https://carolynkoebel.com/music-therapy and www.carolynkoebel.com; https://carolynkoebel.bandcamp.com/album/honoring-the-passage-ii-more-voices-from-hospice-music-therapy
Facebook: www.facebook.com/carolyn.koebel

## Laura Pawuk, MM, MT-BC, Certified Music Imagery Specialist

Laura is a board-certified music therapist. For over 20 years, she has cared for the mental health needs of children and adults in hospice and palliative care, and those who are grieving the loss of a loved one. She has facilitated individual and group bereavement experiences for families, young children, middle-age adults, and those from marginalized communities such as young adult partner loss, the GLBTQ community, and those with dementia and Alzheimer's disease.

Laura taught courses about Music Medicine at Northwestern University and the University of Illinois-Chicago. She is an Assistant Professor of Music Therapy at Eastern Michigan University and is training to become a fellow in the Bonny Method of Guided Imagery and Music.

Laura and Carolyn recently contributed to, edited and published *Honoring the Passage: Selected Songs from Hospice Music Therapy*, a songbook released by the music therapy community for end-of-life and bereavement care.

Email: lpawuk@emich.edu

## RECOMMENDED READING

Brooke, S. & Miraglia, D. (2015) *Using the Creative Therapies to Cope with Grief and Loss*. Springfield, IL: Charles C. Thomas Books.

Irish, D., Lundquist, K. & Nelson, V.J. (1993) *Ethnic Variations in Dying, Death, and Grief*. Washington, DC: Taylor & Francis.

Levine, S. (1991) Guided Meditations, Explorations, and Healings. New York: Anchor Books.

Parry, J. & Ryan, A.S. (eds) (1995) *A Cross Cultural Look at Death, Dying, and Religion*. Chicago, IL: Nelson Hall Press.

Pavlicevic, M. (ed.) (2005) *Music Therapy in Children's Hospices, Jessie's Fund in Action*. London, UK & Philadelphia, PN: Jessica Kingsley Publishers.

Taylor, K. (2017) *The Ethics of Caring: Honouring the Web of Life in Our Professional Caring Relationships*. Santa Cruz, CA: Hanford Meade.

Weller, F. (2015) *The Wild Edge of Sorrow: Rituals of Renewal and the Sacred Work of Grief*. Berkley, CA: North Atlantic Books.

# Living with Cancer

RUFUS GLASSCO

## OVERVIEW

Many cancer patients and survivors know of the importance of complementary alternative therapies to supplement their course of treatment and improve their health and resiliency. More and more cancer support services are now offering group drumming classes as part of their patient welfare service. Existing support services that offer yoga, meditation, nutrition classes, reiki, chi gong and sound healing, art and narrative therapy, etc. are often well suited to offer these types of therapeutic, group hand drumming classes.

This demographic is best served in places that provide support to those people specifically dealing with cancer, as many are dealing with challenges that others have experienced before them. This allows people to become experts at navigating these issues and supporting others with their knowledge and experience. In these places they can feel more comfortable dealing with and talking about the many different aspects of managing a cancer diagnosis. Such challenges include the side effects of chemotherapy and radiation (nausea, brain fog, hair loss), the challenges of negotiating the health system, the anxiety and fears surrounding tests and waiting for results, what to expect from upcoming tests and procedures, the difficulties with communicating with colleagues and loved ones, and being abandoned by many close friends and family. And the tumult of emotions that often makes life a roller coaster ride.

## POSITIVE OUTCOMES

Among the most common issues confronting people living with cancer and their friends and families, is the stress and worry of an unknown future and the loss and grief that accompanies this period of their lives. A wide range of studies has shown that drumming helps relieve anxiety and leads to improved mood.[1] A Canadian pilot study on children hospitalized with cancer that included active music-making with drums found that participation led to significant improvements in mood.[2] Patients at cancer support drum circles often report being less conscious of the worries that dominate their lives after these sessions – at the Leonard P. Zakim Center for Integrative Therapies and Healthy Living in Boston, patient Zeynep Aytekin reported, 'It has made me feel lighter and happier... It has also helped me to forget about my radiation treatments, negative thoughts or any discomforts I had'.[3]

Another important research finding, highly relevant to cancer patients, is the impact of group drumming on the immune system health of participants. A recent systematic research review points to the central role of stress pathways in linking music to an immune response.[4] According to this review, by Daisy Fancourt and her colleagues (2014), a group drumming intervention had a positive effect on the dehydroepiandrosterone-to-cortisol (DHEA/Cort) ratio and an increase of natural killer cell (NK) activity. Additionally, Dr Barry Bittman and his team showed how group drumming has immuno-enhancing and stress hormone (cortisol)

---

1   Ascenso, S., Perkins, R., Atkins, L., Fancourt, D. & Williamon, A. (2018) 'Promoting well-being through group drumming with mental health service users and their carers.' *International Journal of Qualitative Studies on Health and Well-Being 13*, 1. https://doi.org/10.1080/17482631.2018.1484219
    Fancourt, D., Perkins, R., Ascenso, S., Carvalho, L.A., Steptoe, A. & Williamon, A. (2016) 'Effects of group drumming interventions on anxiety, depression, social resilience and inflammatory immune response among mental health service users.' *PLoS ONE 11*, 3.
2   Barrera, M.E., Rykov, M.H. & Doyle, S.L. (2002) 'The effects of interactive music therapy on hospitalised children with cancer: A pilot study.' *Journal of Psycho-Oncology 11*, 379–388.
3   Dana Faber Cancer Institute (2017) 'Rhythm therapy: How drum circles help patients cope with cancer.' https://blog.dana-farber.org/insight/2015/07/rhythm-therapy-how-drum-circles-help-patients-cope-with-cancer (accessed 5 August 2020).
4   Fancourt, D., Ockelford, A. & Belai, A. (2014) 'The psychoneuroimmunological effects of music: A systematic review and a new model.' *Brain Behaviour & Immunity 36*, 15–26.

decreasing effects.[5] Stress is linked to many degenerative and negative health outcomes like cancer, and receiving a diagnosis of cancer is, ironically, even more stressful. This research is significant not just because it proved what people already expected – that group drumming reduced stress, but that group drumming also increases the activity of cells that perform important immune-sustaining functions (NK and LAK). For cancer patients living with compromised immune systems these benefits cannot be overstated. The Fancourt-led review also reported on one study that established increasing CD4+ T cell counts among older adults who participated in group drumming workshops. In that group, lymphocyte and memory T cell counts increased as well.

Additional impacts, well supported by research, are the feelings of group belonging and support that accompany participation in group drumming and the reductions in pain and fatigue that accompany these interventions.[6] New friendships and strong camaraderie develop in these circles where connection is made through the alignment of individual rhythms and people can release their feelings in safety through the instrument. The powerful cathartic nature of drumming contrasts dramatically with the confused and often overwhelming effort of expressing these emotions and feelings in words.

Other outcomes that I have noticed in my work in this field include:

- new percussive skills and a greater openness towards learning new things and being optimistic about the future

- a greater appreciation for healthy, group activities that are fun

- an uplift in mood – endorphins are released by aerobic activity

- a feeling of greater acceptance – being heard and understood

- the giving and receiving of empathy

- a growing understanding and appreciation that they are not victims of cancer, but experts in resilience and recovery who have valuable skills and expertise to offer that can benefit others.

---

5 Bittman, B.B., Berk, L.S., Felten, D.L., Westengard, J., Simonton, O.C., Pappas, J. & Ninehouser, M. (2001) 'Composite effects of group drumming music therapy on modulation of neuroendocrine-immune parameters in normal subjects.' *Journal of Alternative Therapies* 7, 1, 38–47.
6 Bradt, J., Dileo, C., Magill, L. & Teague, A. (2016) 'Music interventions for improving psychological and physical outcomes in cancer patients.' *Cochrane Database of Systematic Reviews 8*, CD006911.

## SETTING UP FOR SUCCESS
Here are some of the key factors that I have found make for a successful program.

### Location and timing
- Daytime classes in an accessible location with reasonable parking rates and, ideally, community transport support.
- A location far from people who are working (office workers, doctors and nurses diagnosing patients) and who might be bothered or disrupted by the sounds coming from a recreational drum circle.
- Ten to 15 participants ideally committed to coming every week for six to eight weeks, with the understanding that some will miss classes for a variety of reasons – feeling ill, medical appointments, returning to work, no energy, no transport.

### Mutual respect within the circle
- Confidentiality – what happens in the circle stays in the circle – get everyone to agree.
- Come to every class if you can, understanding that each class is self-contained, and that if you miss a class or two, you won't be left behind. Remind participants not to come if ill with something contagious, as others may have compromised immune systems.
- Regular attendance is important in order for a socially cohesive and mutually supportive group to develop.
- No perfumes or cologne, as some people have very high sensitivity to smells.

## COMMON CHALLENGES AND HOW TO MINIMIZE THEM
One of the common challenges is helping people who don't know each other to relax and get comfortable in the group. I start my groups with a series of 'ice-breakers'; getting them to share a bit about themselves and their knowledge, using a name game and inspirational beats (see the practical example section on the following pages). Missed classes are also common as people struggle with their health and other priorities. Ensure your minimum group size is large enough to accommodate significant absenteeism.

Another common challenge is the group member who needs more attention and often dominates the conversations. As a facilitator you need strategies to manage a dominant group member – I find it is best to focus on group needs and return quickly to new activities, or to reflect on the dominant member's comments and ask the group their opinion on the same issue. This may include asking other group members to share their strategies for dealing with a similar issue or challenge – defaulting to the wisdom and abilities of the group is better than the facilitator feeling responsible for resolving every situation. It is important to follow up with these members afterwards (but in private), and offer to give more detail or answer more questions. As classes go on, the group will often spend more time talking, bonding and sharing, and less time playing. This is a sign of trust building and progress.

Many people going through cancer treatment experience 'brain fog' also known as 'chemo-brain' – a decrease in mental sharpness, clarity and focus. Avoid teaching tricky rhythms, and as much as possible go back to the same rhythms week after week and reinforce them. If you teach rhythms, write them down in simple notation to give to the participants. They may want to remember them but can feel anxious about the class ending, and not having the opportunity to practise the rhythms so they can remember them more easily. Teach people how to improvise effectively, and help them by providing a strong pulse. I often start by playing different rhythms and games and allow these to evolve into improvisational jamming.

During your program some members will likely receive potentially devastating diagnoses or prognoses. It's important to check in with each other before and after each class, and to acknowledge what is shared between group members, and emphasize the support they can offer each other. I also include opportunities in my drum circles for the group to send extra love and support, through the power of their drum, to anyone who needs it.

## PRACTICAL APPLICATIONS OF THE DRUM CIRCLE
### Guided imagery

I use a small portable rechargeable speaker to provide soothing background music for a variety of different journeys that take people to different places in nature to be healed – we walk along a beautiful forest path, or swim in a buoyant sea next to a favourite beach or visit a mountain-top temple with giant healing crystals hanging in the air, emitting healing sounds and different colours of light. I take people on a different journey each class, to be healed (or activate their innate healing abilities) in nature by sound, by water, by rhythm, by vibration, by being in community, and through our connection to mother earth and her ability to draw out our toxins and cleanse them.

It's important to ground people first by getting them to sit comfortably and concentrate on deepening their breathing and letting go of distracting thoughts. The music will help to bring them along on a journey that can either be to a place that you as the facilitator may describe, or you can provide general details and ask them to use their imagination to visit a place they are familiar with and comfortable in. Frequently remind them that they are safe in this place and that others who are there are like them, at peace and happy to be receiving healing energy/releasing/connecting with others. There are many guided imagery and guided meditation journeys available on CD or iTunes and for free on YouTube. I recommend using them for inspiration, and then creating your own journeys using your own favourite music, so you don't have to rely on notes, and just tell a familiar story instead.

Guided imagery is a form of guided meditation, which is much more accessible for people who have never meditated before, or meditated on their own. Research has proven that transcendental meditators, compared to a control group, have 70 per cent fewer inpatient and outpatient medical visits (for older adults), and 55 per cent fewer cancer admissions.[7]

## Rhythmic naming

This is a familiar game for many drum circle facilitators, which often starts with the question 'What's the rhythm of your name?'

- Teach the group to say and play this question, playing along to each syllable on their drums.
- Demonstrate how to answer by saying your first name, your nickname, or your superhero name: I chant my first name, percussively ('RU-FUS!') and say, 'Say it everyone.' The group echoes my name verbally.
- Then I say, 'Play it everyone' and everyone says and plays my name on their drum: 'RU-FUS!'
- Then I chant: '1, 2, Let's hear from you!' and look to the person next to me.

---

[7] Orme-Johnson, D. (1987) 'Medical care utilization and the transcendental meditation program.' *Psychosomatic Medicine* 49, 493–507.

- The group repeats the question, 'What's the rhythm of your name?' The next person says their name, and the facilitator commands the group: 'Say it everyone!' and so on…

### Extension
This is also a great way to get the group to share strategies for resilience and wellness. Subsequent questions can be: What are you grateful for? What's your favourite way to stay healthy? What do you love to do? What's your favourite way to have fun? What's the name of someone you love (include pets)? How do you like to help others? This leads to great conversations, as participants discover new things they have in common, new strategies for wellness and coping, new resources and new ideas.

## Inspirational beats (From the HealthRhythms© Protocol)
This exercise invites participants to use the drum as a canvas for emotional expression, by asking participants to answer questions without words, followed by an interpretation by other group members. The most remarkable thing about this exercise is that, before words have been used to explain a participant's answer to a question, group members are able with 95 per cent accuracy to guess what the person playing was actually feeling. This creates powerful bonds of empathy, and because the person expressing their feelings didn't actually have to say anything, others are encouraged to express bottled-up emotions in a safe way, knowing they will be heard and understood by the group.

Here are some examples of how I use this in my work.

We begin by examining how our voices can convey different emotions, such as nervousness or sadness. We then offer participants an opportunity to experiment with playing different emotions on the drum. What would anger sound like? When someone demonstrates what anger sounds like to them, ask for their permission to ask the group what they heard. Then encourage others to share what they felt and thought when they heard the anger expressed on the drum. Then ask the person who drummed how accurate the interpretations were, and if we missed anything. Ask the group if they would express anger in the same way, or would it come out differently if they were communicating anger? Then ask for someone to demonstrate what sadness might sound like on the drum. What is the quality of the sound that was created? What made it sound sad? Then ask someone to experiment creating the sound of happiness on their drum – always end on a good note. Ask others what they heard that made the drum sound happy?

In your next session you might pick up where you left off and ask if anyone can express the anger they have experienced at any stage on their journey through cancer; perhaps to express how the modern medical system has made them feel, or the reaction of certain loved ones, or friends or employers. Many will want to express their anger about a surprising variety of scenarios and realities they have had to face; leave extra time for this.

After people share their feelings, it's important to honour their courage and their willingness to express themselves and share difficult feelings. It's also good to thank those who offer interpretations, and to offer them initially yourself if you feel like the group is not able to interpret or hear something that you feel is important. Be sure, however, not to jump in with your own interpretations – leave lots of time for people to drum, and lots of time for people to interpret. It's also very important to ask the group how they deal with similar situations and emotions, how they get past them and how they learn to let them go. The wisdom of the group is far greater than the facilitators.

In the first session we explore the many ways of expressing different emotions on the drum. This gives them the emotional literacy to express themselves emotionally in a variety of ways, and encourages others to participate in this kind of expression in subsequent classes (some will need further encouragement, and not all wish to participate – and shouldn't be forced). Each week after that, I prepare 'Inspirational beats' questions that are tied to the different theme of that week's workshop: e.g. 'How does it feel when after letting your family and friends know about your diagnosis, some of those people completely disappear from your lives, almost like they think your cancer could be contagious and has to be avoided? How does that make you feel, and what might that feeling sound like on the drum?'

After delving into some of these difficult issues (based on research and input from participants about the challenges and difficulties of living with cancer), always make sure to ask a more positive question, to finish off on a good note: e.g., 'How does it feel when someone you least expect shows up and offers to bring you a meal, or help you run some errands, or help in the garden, or do something really nice for you? How does that make you feel, and what might that sound like on the drum?'

## Losing your foundation (Rhythm2Recovery)

Sometimes things change unpredictably in life and the foundations that have supported us previously start to wobble. A diagnosis of cancer for you or someone close can have this effect. In these times we have to avoid panic and work towards finding a new source of stability, a new rhythm.

This may not come quickly, but will appear with time. How do we manage that transition and find our way through that period of uncertainty to a more stable future?

Start with the facilitator/s playing a steady pulse in 4/4 and layer everyone in.

After allowing the grove to solidify, the facilitator/s purposely loses consistency and destabilizes the rhythm – the group must then adapt themselves to either steady the rhythm or transition into a new rhythm. This is similar to the challenges of a transition in an Arthurian drum circle.

Discuss with the group the feelings they encountered when the stable bass died away. What strategies did they call on to help find their feet once more?

How important was it for people to listen to each other and work together to find their way forward? How do these concepts relate to how you manage after a diagnosis of cancer?

## Improvisational play

It is important to teach participants how to play their own rhythms, but within a common rhythmic structure or framework to keep the groove, or the pulse, of the music strong, and to avoid rhythmic chaos. Begin by telling them that in order to improvise, we first have to turn off a part of our brain, otherwise we can't do it. The part of their brain they are required to turn off to enable improvisational play is the part responsible for self-criticism. We can't tell ourselves we're not any good at improvising whilst we improvise at the same time. To turn that around, it is implied that a great way to take a vacation from that nagging, naysayer voice most of us have inside out heads is to drum in an improvisational way!

To teach a group of people to improvise on the drum in a fun and easy way:

- Begin by playing two bass notes on the first two beats of a four-beat rhythm (4/4) phrase. I teach them the bass note is often played on the first beat, (1), as it gives us a clear idea of where the musical phrase begins. You might use the analogy from the Rhythm2Recovery model, that the bass provides safety in drumming – if we get lost, all we need to do is listen for the bass drum, or the pulse, to find out way back to playing in sync with the music again.[8] In between those two bass notes we have two more beats, where we can experiment with improvisation.

---

8   Faulkner, S. (2016) *Rhythm to Recovery.* London: Jessica Kingsley Publishers.

- Play two bass notes and rub the drum skin on the third and fourth beats, before going back to two bass notes on the first and second beats. Get participants to copy, or mirror what you're doing in real time.
- Rub the drum in different ways each time – demonstrating that there is no right or wrong way to do it.
- Then replace the rubbing with scratching the drum skin: bass, bass, scratch! Demonstrate scratching in a different, random way each time (one long scratch over two beats, then two or three or four scratches after that, always followed by two bass notes). Participants do the same thing, randomly changing the number of scratches each time. (*Note*: some people find the scratching sound irritating.)
- Then replace the scratches with claps, again demonstrating different ways of clapping, and different numbers of claps. The participants follow suit.
- Finally replace the clapping with tone notes on the edge of the drum, again playing a variety of tone rhythms and number of tone notes in between two bass notes.
- Then it's time to get the class to try improving, so begin randomly playing any number of rubs, or scratches, or claps, or tone notes, between the two bass notes that everyone plays together, at the same time.
- After a few seconds of this, instruct them: '1, 2, Make up your own!', and remind them that there is no right or wrong way to do this. Sometimes people will forget to play the two bass notes, or may shift their pattern so they are playing the two bass notes when others are improvising, and I remind the group (without singling anyone out) to play two bass notes together, while I play the bass notes louder and chant: 'Bass, bass, make up your own, bass, bass, no right or wrong' a few times.
- Sculpt the group, and end with a big rumble.

## High five on the drum
I usually do this right after the group effectively improvises for the first time. People are so surprised how good they sound, and how easy, almost effortless, it was to make up music on the fly. They now feel like they're part

of a band, and they've just aced their first performance or exam, and that demands some recognition and celebration!

- Right after the group finishes drumming; ended with either a stop cut or a drum roll, instruct the drummers to turn to their neighbour, offer them a high five, and say 'You're an awesome drummer!'
- Normally you don't have to tell them to do this, but sometimes you can remind them to turn to their other neighbour and offer them a high five too, and tell them they're an awesome drummer. That can lead to more air-high fives around the circle.

Participants usually do this enthusiastically, and it produces huge smiles and lots of laughter – a great group bonding game for fostering greater cohesion and connection.

### Jump right in. Adapted from Dave Holland[9]

1. The facilitator invites people to play a game: 'When I say "Jump right in!" play three bass notes.' DEMO: 'Boom Boom Boom!'
2. 'Then when I say: "Slide to the groove!" Slide your nails across the drum, followed by two Tones, and repeat.' DEMO: 'Scratch, tap tap, Scratch, tap tap.'
3. Facilitator: 'Jump right in!' (Class responds: 'Boom Boom Boom!') 'Slide to the groove!' (Class responds: 'Scratch, tap tap, Scratch, tap tap.' JUST TWICE.)
4. 'Excellent. The third step is "Don't forget to breathe!" How can you forget to breathe? Fortunately, it's automatic, but we've also been given control over our breathing. And when we remember to slow down our breathing, we reduce our stress and release endorphins!' The facilitator models breathing in deeply, and letting out a big sigh, relaxing the shoulders and doing it again.
5. Facilitator: 'Jump right in!' (Class responds: 'Boom boom boom!') 'Slide to the Groove!' (Class responds: 'Scratch, tap tap, scratch, tap tap.' JUST TWICE.) 'Don't forget to breathe!' (Class responds with two deep breaths and sighs.)
6. 'Wonderful – the final stage is to "Make a connection!" Look across

---

9   Holland, D. (2007) *Drumagination: A Rhythmic Play Book for Music Teachers, Music Therapists and Drum Circle Facilitators*. Dave Holland & Beatin' Path. www.interactiverhythm.com

the room and make eye contact with someone, and then smile at them, and then say "One, two, I see you!" and point at them, but not with an outstretched finger, but with the "Disney Point". (Demonstrate the 'Disney Point': pointing with upturned palm.)

7. The facilitator goes through each of the four commands, allowing the class to respond each time.

8. The facilitator goes through each of the four again, slightly faster, ending with 'Make a new connection.' This encourages people to make a connection with a different person.

This game does a few things – it's a great ice-breaker that helps people to relax, to de-stress even more, to look deeply at each other, to laugh, and it reminds them of how good it feels to breathe deeply. We go back to this game a few times, and I'll also shout out 'Don't forget to breathe!' a couple of times each class, as many people fall back into poor habits of shallow breathing.

### Give a little to yourself! Adapted from Dave Holland[10]

1. The facilitator shouts out 'Give a little to yourself!' asking the drummers to give themselves some credit for all they are doing. Instead of patting themselves on the back they play three bass notes on their drum: 'Boom Boom Boom!'

2. The facilitator then shouts out 'Give a little to your neighbour!' and the drummers lean over to one of their neighbours' drums and play three bass notes on it: 'Boom Boom Boom!' Not telling people which way to go adds to the confusion and the fun!

3. The facilitator then shouts out 'Give a little to your *other* neighbour!' and the drummers lean over to their other neighbour's drum and play three bass notes on it: 'Boom Boom Boom!'

4. The facilitator then says 'What about the family?' Explaining that we have to give a shout out on our drums to all our extended family – our family members and close friends we consider family – the ones who support us – to honour them for doing so much for us. The drummers respond by playing a double bass ('BOOM!') with both hands, then raising their hands to the sky as they shout: 'Hey!'

---

10 Holland, D. (2007) *Drumagination: A Rhythmic Play Book for Music Teachers, Music Therapists and Drum Circle Facilitators.* Dave Holland & Beatin' Path. www.interactiverhythm.com

## DRUM CIRCLES FOR SPECIFIC POPULATION GROUPS

5. Repeat steps 1–4 a little faster.
6. Repeat steps 1–4 even faster, ending in a big, celebratory rumble.

This game helps bring the group together, to support each other, in gratitude, and also to remember and honour the wider communities that support them. People really enjoy shouting 'Hey!' and the speeding up part – it's a simple way to show how much people appreciate the support they receive. And it reminds us that we all can use a little help sometimes, and that's OK.

### 'By the numbers' – using tonal chimes[11]

1. Demonstrate how tonal chimes (see following page) work by dropping the hand, and snapping back the wrist to provide a clean strike.
2. Ask everyone to pick a favourite number between one and eight. Then ask them to play one note when I say their number. The facilitator offers to play on the one, to show everyone where we begin. The facilitator then counts out loud from one to eight, repeating this cycle a few times, and ending by getting softer each time. A unique melody is created using people's favourite numbers; a song that has never been heard before.
3. Ask everyone to pick a second number between one and eight. It can be next to the first number or far apart – it doesn't matter – just try to remember to play one note on the same two numbers each time around. The facilitator offers to play on the one and the five, at the start and the middle of the phrase. The facilitator counts out loud from one to eight, as before, and repeat the cycle a few times, ending by getting softer each time.
4. Now ask people to play two quick notes on one of their numbers, and one note on the other, for a total of three notes. They can play two notes on their first number, followed by a single note, or vice versa. The facilitator counts out loud from one to eight, and the cycle is repeated as before.

Participants are genuinely surprised at how they can spontaneously create a song that sounds beautiful, in just a few minutes. This is the magic of

---

[11] This game is best played on a pentatonic set of tonal chimes or resonator bells (Rhythmband or Suzuki), but can also be played with drums and percussion.

the pentatonic scale, but also proof of the synergy of the group – another wonderful example that the group is far more able and wise than any individual.

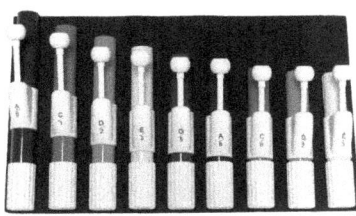

### The one word share
I always finish my workshops with a 'one word share': a way of checking in with everyone to see how they are feeling, or what they thought of the drumming session. I always inform people that if someone else says the same word they were thinking of saying, before they have a chance to, that they don't need to come up with a new word – we've had a shared experience, so it's very normal to hear the same words spoken again and again (e.g., relaxed, peaceful, grateful, connected, calm). One day a woman said the word 'distracted', a word I hadn't heard before. A few eyebrows were raised in the group. I wanted to ask her about it, but she came up to me before I had the chance to approach her, and she said, 'Ever since I was diagnosed with cancer, I haven't been able to stop thinking about it. For the last hour and a half, I wasn't thinking at all about cancer – thank you so much!'

## ADDITIONAL ADVICE
I begin each workshop by mentioning a theme, and why I think it's important, perhaps sharing how embracing this concept has been of personal benefit. I like to share a pertinent quote or two by famous sages on the subject and tie the inspirational beats questions or intentional drumming (asking participants to create a chant or mantra of something positive they intend to do in the future and have them drum out the syllables as they chant) into the theme. Some of the themes we explore include the importance of play, of forgiveness and letting go, of helping others, of living in the moment, and of self-care of mind, body and spirit.

## AUTHOR'S BIOGRAPHY
### Rufus Glassco

Rufus has been working for Wellspring Cancer Support Centres in the Greater Toronto Area since 2010. He now works at three Wellspring Centres and has also worked for Gilda's and Ronald McDonald House. Rufus does other work in healthcare centres working with people with addiction, depression, schizophrenia, bipolar disorder and other mental health issues, as well as people with dementia and Alzheimer's and their care-givers.

He also provides wellness and stress reduction workshops to doctors, nurses, social workers and other community healthcare providers. 'While the work I do with cancer patients doesn't pay very well, it is the most rewarding work that I do. When prospective corporate, school or government clients ask why my rates are high, I explain the work I do with them helps to subsidise the work I do to support people with cancer and their care-givers. Just about everyone has known someone who has been diagnosed with cancer.'

Email: rufusglassco@gmail.com
www.soundbenefits.ca
Facebook: www.facebook.com/soundbenefits.ca
YouTube: www.youtube.com/user/consumowrestler

## RECOMMENDED READING

Cunningham, A.J. (2010) *The Healing Journey*. USA: Healing Journey Books. Download a free copy here: www.wellspring.ca/wp-content/uploads/2015/05/healing_journey.pdf.

Nagarsheth, N. (2009) *Music & Cancer: A Prescription for Healing*. Burlington, MA: Jones & Bartlett Learning.

Popkin, K. (2015) 'The role of music therapy in cancer care.' *American Society of Clinical Oncology Post 5*, 15. www.ascopost.com/issues/september-25-2016/the-role-of-music-therapy-in-cancer-care (accessed 5 August 2020).

# Prisoners

## SIMON FAULKNER

**OVERVIEW**

Working in the prison system means working across a very diverse group of institutions –some modern, some ancient, some private, some public – with different rules, philosophies and intentions. It also means working with a very diverse group of detainees, some of whom have committed crimes that challenge our ability to remain non-judgemental, and who may be confrontational and sometimes intimidating. In prisons, family breakdown, economic disadvantage, low levels of education, trauma, mental health issues and drug addiction commonly underlie the lives of inmates, and some knowledge of working with these issues can be useful.

Group activities, like a drum circle, can be greatly appreciated by prisoners and staff alike and incorporated into recreational and rehabilitation programs, with a range of different benefits. They can also create significant security risks that need to be managed carefully, as prisoners are brought together. Prisons are full of decent people who for a range of reasons took a wrong turn in their lives, but they also harbour serious criminals with little empathy for outsiders, who are constantly alert for opportunity and advantage. Women need to be particularly alert when working in male prisons. Complacency is one of the biggest dangers of prison work.

## POSITIVE OUTCOMES

Research studies of drumming interventions in prison contexts have shown positive benefits across a range of social and emotional areas. One significant study[1] conducted in Australia across seven separate institutions and involving 114 male and female prisoners in minimum-, medium- and maximum-security units concluded that drumming when combined with reflective practice had a positive impact on:

- emotions and emotional regulation
- positive feelings
- capacity to talk with others
- self-worth
- learning about themselves
- feeling part of a team
- self-confidence and social skills
- relationship-building abilities
- emotional barriers, connecting with others and forming friendships, and behaviour.

This same study showed significant reductions in levels of prisoner anxiety and depression and similar results have been showcased in studies in the mental health field.[2] It is widely recognized that a high percentage of prisoners have co-occurring mental health and trauma-related symptoms.[3]

---

[1] Faulkner, S. & Bartleet, B.L. (2019) 'Drumming Interventions in Australian Prisons: Insights from the Rhythm2 Recovery Model.' In M. Balfour, B.L. Bartleet, L. Davey, J. Rynne & H. Schippers (eds) *Performing Arts in Prisons*. Bristol: Intellect.

[2] Ascenso, S., Perkins, R., Atkins, L., Fancourt, D. & Williamon, A. (2018) 'Promoting well-being through group drumming with mental health service users and their carers.' *International Journal of Qualitative Studies on Health and Well-Being 13*, 1. https://doi.org/10.1080/17482631.2018.1484219
Fancourt, D., Perkins, R., Ascenso, S., Carvalho, L.A., Steptoe, A. & Williamon, A. (2016) 'Effects of group drumming interventions on anxiety, depression, social resilience and inflammatory immune response among mental health service users.' *PLoS ONE 11*, 3.

[3] Fazel, S., Hayes, A.J., Bartellas, K., Clerici, M. & Trestman, R. (2016) 'Mental health of prisoners: Prevalence, adverse outcomes, and interventions.' *The Lancet. Psychiatry 3*, 9, 871–881.

And there are a growing number of practitioners using drumming interventions successfully in forensic mental health facilities based on this evidence. Additional outcomes noted by prisoners themselves and drawn from qualitative feedback include:

- reductions in the stress associated with incarceration
- a safe form for expressing and releasing the tensions and other emotions that build up inside prison
- a humanizing experience that counters the de-humanizing prison norm
- a process that can be used to reduce or reconcile differences between prison population groups, ethnicities, gangs, etc.
- improved staff/prisoner relationships, and, by association, prison security.

This last point is one that resonates particularly favourably with prison authorities if you need a persuasive argument for the benefits of such a program when pitching to correctional management. Additionally, it is important to be able to align the benefits of your work to the evidence around prisoner recidivism. Evidence shows clear links between prisoners' social and emotional health and the likelihood of a quick re-entry into the prison system. Programs that focus on psycho-social education, healthy relationships, inter-personal skills and emotional regulation all address the key determinants of a successful transition back into the community.[4]

A final benefit of bringing drumming programs with a therapeutic focus into the prison system is the fact that many prisoners have low levels of literacy. Yet, in most prisons, the rehabilitation programs available often require reasonably high standards of reading and writing skills. This discriminates against many prisoners, forcing them to abandon these programs, increasing the level of shame associated with their illiteracy, and sometimes leading to their inability to complete programs needed for parole. Expressive therapies, like drumming, that have less focus on reading and writing, often have higher rates of engagement, participant enjoyment and consequently better outcomes.[5]

---

4   UK Ministry of Justice (2015) 'What works in reducing reoffending – a rapid evidence assessment.' https://assets.publishing.service.gov.uk/government/uploads/system/uploads/attachment_data/file/449347/reducing-reoffending-in-adults.pdf (accessed 5 August 2020).
5   Schippers, H., Balfour, M., Bartleet, B.L. & Rhynne, J. (2014) *Captive Audiences – Creative Arts in Prisons*. Queensland Conservatorium Research Centre, Griffith University.

## SETTING UP FOR SUCCESS

One of the common challenges of working in prison environments is moving your equipment in and out through security – a process that may take 15 minutes one day and an hour on another occasion depending on the security level of the institution at the time, as well as your standing with the security team. Prison staff are notorious for making it difficult for contractors who they disrespect or who for some reason get on the wrong side of them – respect and good manners go a long way with prison staff; complaints can be highly counterproductive even when they are well justified.

Another important consideration is an appropriate space. Sadly, many jails are full to overflowing and recreational space is often very limited or just not available at all. Prior to taking up any contract visit the prison, meet the staff and identify a suitable space – don't leave this to chance. It can be useful to set up a preliminary visit and offer a team building session for the staff prior to working with the prisoners – if you are in the 'good books' with management and staff before you start, you are halfway to a successful program, and they may even prioritize a suitable space for you to work in.

## COMMON CHALLENGES AND HOW TO MINIMIZE THEM

Among the most challenging issues when it comes to introducing a drum circle program into a prison community is the negativity of those in power towards arts-based programs and their rehabilitative potential. Many prison staff hold strong, and generally negative, views on prisoners and their potential to improve their lives. Arts programs are often seen as unjustified rewards and purposefully sabotaged. The idea that music has an intrinsic value for both individuals and the community is not understood; nor that it can be a means of assisting people to develop important skills; or that creativity can change and heal people. Involving staff and educating them with a hands-on experience or showcasing some of the research that supports your work can help reduce this bias.

Group make-up is particularly important when considering working in prisons. Prisons are hierarchies, and have a very clear pecking order that starts with the prison officers on top, although this can be challenged by some prison gangs, and usually places sex offenders at the bottom. In-between these extremes there are often violent battles for influence. When choosing who will be allowed to participate in your drum circle, it pays to have someone deciding that for you who has a clear understanding of this issue and how it relates to their population, so that power rivalries, with the potential to be violent, do not surface in your group.

Disruptions to your program are very common in prison scenarios as changes in security arrangements, and other demands on prisoners and staff, will generally take priority over your work – this is something you need to accept and learn to accommodate. Prison programs are usually contracted by a division head and calling them in advance to ascertain whether any changes in scheduling are happening that may impact your program is always important; in my early prison days, I would often turn up after a long drive to find the whole session had had to be cancelled, and there was nothing that could be done about it.

## PRACTICAL APPLICATIONS OF THE DRUM CIRCLE

Among the most useful exercises I use in prisons are versions of 'call and response' connected to reflective discussions, where an individual sends out a rhythmic phrase on their drum and it is answered by the group. I use this exercise to look at how people respond to different scenarios in life. The call can represent an infinite number of possibilities – 'What calls you to anger?', 'What calls you to anxiety?' And the response is ours for the choosing – 'How do you respond to aggression' for instance? 'How do you respond to kindness?'

### Managing aggression

In another variation I represent aggression with a sharp rumble and play 'call and response' normally with the group members echoing back my calls unless they hear the aggressive phrase. They must learn to recognize how aggression sneaks up on them and to respond with control – in this game when the aggressive phrase is called out by the facilitator the group responds very quietly (using their fingertips). This is in part a regulatory exercise, as they learn how not to get drawn into other people's anger and exercise self-restraint.

### Examining values

It is well understood that shared values are essential to harmonious relationships, families and communities, and that many of the core values we hold dear are those that revolve around trust (e.g., honesty, respect, loyalty, kindness). For many prisoners, trust is in short supply and as well as abusing the trust of others, they have often had their own trust abused from a young age. Introducing exercises that allow for explorations of trust and healthy values can impact their behaviour and help them develop better relationships. Ask each group member to think of one thing that is important to them in their relationships with other people and then one by one around the circle have each person say, 'Rumble on your drum if you believe [insert their value] is important in a relationship.' This can lead into group discussions on why these things are important and the challenges of living up to them.

### A trust exercise
Form a maze of drums scattered across the room and then ask for two volunteers to work together to negotiate that maze. One of the two will have their eyes closed, and the other will lead them by playing different sounds on the drum they carry, no talking is allowed. Before they start they need to agree on different sounds on the drums which will indicate which direction to proceed in. After this exercise is completed, you can often open a good discussion on trust, looking at how it relies on good communication and how it needs to be correlated to the risk involved. Other important questions revolve around rebuilding trust and what happens when people lead you astray.

### Peer pressure and social influence
This is a major issue for many prisoners, both because of the strong power hierarchy among inmates and because of the strong impact a peer group can have on influencing a recently released individual back into a life of crime when they may be considering changing their ways. A good drumming exercise to address this and open up a conversation is to have an individual play a drum rhythm that represents a positive behavioural example and the group try to influence that person by playing a different rhythm together that represents a less honest option. Or vice versa – it can be equally useful to look at the positives of helping an individual move away from a problem behaviour towards something more honourable.

The difficulty of holding onto your rhythm in the face of your friends (or family) advocating another rhythm is significant and the skills and commitment necessary to do so can be examined in a subsequent group discussion. *Note there is no dishonour in losing your rhythm in this exercise as all of us are vulnerable to peer influence.*

### Community connection
Another core drum circle exercise that can be linked to useful reflection for prisoners is the 'Layering in' game, where one person starts a rhythm

(usually with a strong bass pulse) and one at a time each member of the group layer in with their own rhythmic contribution on drums or percussion (or even voice). This exercise can be used to look at the skills needed for community connection – listening, patience, compromise, tolerance, etc. It can also draw attention to the benefits of diversity in a community, reducing intolerance, discrimination and fear of people who are different. In this exercise each person contributes to the whole and their differences enrich the music. You can also layer out the rhythm to close – one person stopping at a time until there is only the bass pulse left.

## ADDITIONAL ADVICE
Some of the most pleasurable experiences of my career have been working in jails, where I have learnt as much as I have given. Though the environments are harsh, the people are often desperate for interaction and generally welcoming. It is also a place where many people are keen to learn. The drum circle is always a highlight for them. The creativity that comes from musical expression is also a pathway for thinking creatively on how to move their lives forward, and many people in prison, especially adults, make significant changes – it is often a place for contemplation and reassessment. Enjoy your work, but remain vigilant and keep yourself safe.

## AUTHOR'S BIOGRAPHY
### Simon Faulkner BSocSc (Psychology & Addiction), MCouns.
Simon is the director of the therapeutic service 'Rhythm2Recovery' and has worked in multiple prison environments, including juvenile detention centres, women's prisons, specialist Aboriginal prisoner wings, maximum-security jails, and forensic mental health. Simon trains professionals internationally in a model of therapy based on his book *Rhythm to Recovery*, which combines rhythmic music with cognitive reflection.

> Email: simon@rhythm2recovery.com
> www.rhythm2recovery.com
> Facebook: www.facebook.com/rhythm2recovery

## RECOMMENDED READING
Balfour, M., Bartleet, M.L., Davey, L., Rynne, J. & Schippers, H. (eds) (2019) *Performing Arts in Prisons*. Bristol: Intellect.

# Veterans

## TERRIE KING AND KEVIN CALLO

### OVERVIEW

The veteran population is a cultural group that is found throughout many communities. Over the past decade, much focus has been placed on the importance of recognizing how culture affects a person's lived experience. By definition, a culture has unique customs, values and traditions. One only needs to be within a drum circle whose members are veterans to clearly recognize the power of the veteran culture. Included are a common language, code of manners, norms of behaviour, belief system, dress and rituals.[1] It is this powerful culture that supports and directs the engagement process within the veteran drum circle.

Belonging, acceptance and purpose are all factors of the veteran culture and when the military service experience ends through factors such as discharge, retirement or disability, there is often a strong sense of loneliness which can lead to depression. The drum circle provides an opportunity

---

1  Moore, B.A., Penk, W. & Friedman, M.J. (2019) *Treating PTSD in Military Personnel: A Clinical Handbook.* New York: Guilford Press.

for veterans to come together once again, enjoying the social connection, camaraderie and brotherhood that is so strong in the military culture.[2]

Organizations that may have particular interest in a veteran drum circle include Veteran Affairs (VA) health clinics, organizations that serve the homeless, faith organizations, social clubs for veterans, colleges/universities and community service agencies. Small consistent groups of no more than 8–12 seem to be best suited for this population and a closed group (same, stable membership) is preferred. The veteran drum circle can provide social connection and therapeutic benefits within a safe and structured environment.

## POSITIVE OUTCOMES

When working with the veteran group, it is important to have a guiding framework or model of practice to support the therapeutic process. One model of practice that can be supportive in a therapeutic drum circle program is the 'PEO model' (see Figure 23.1) which was developed by occupational therapist, Mary Law, PhD, OT (C).[3] This model guides the practitioner's ability to consider all aspects of the **P**erson (veteran), within an **E**nvironment (drum circle) while engaging in an **O**ccupational experience (drumming). Culture guides the experience and the person's ability to fully engage is dependent on these three factors.

If the facilitator is aware of this process, the key factors that support the person's ability to fully engage are managing the environment and the drumming activities in order for the drum circle to be the change agent for the veteran's occupational experience. Though very seldom is there a perfect balance in all three factors, once in a while 'flow' will show up and time stands still.[4]

The shared 'mission' of creating music together provides an opportunity for leadership, commitment to the team, loyalty and perseverance, all values of the veteran population. Because sharing feelings is not an easy task for a veteran, the use of the drum to convey emotions is especially supportive to the group members – the drum is their voice. Often for the

---

2   Richman, M. (2018) 'The loneliness factor: How much does it drive depression in veterans?' www.research.va.gov/currents/0218-The-loneliness-factor-in-depression.cfm (accessed 6 August 2020).
3   Law, M., Cooper, B., Strong, S., Stewart, D., Rigby, P. & Letts, L. (1996) 'The Person-Environment-Occupation Model: A transactive approach to occupational performance.' *Canadian Journal of Occupational Therapy 63*, 9–23.
4   Oppland, M. (2020) 'Eight ways to create flow according to Mihaly Csikszentmihalyi.' *Positive Psychology*. https://positivepsychology.com/mihaly-csikszentmihalyi-father-of-flow (accessed 22 August 2020).

first time in civilian life, the veterans experience a place of 'belonging' and the ability to give 'voice' to their unspoken emotions.

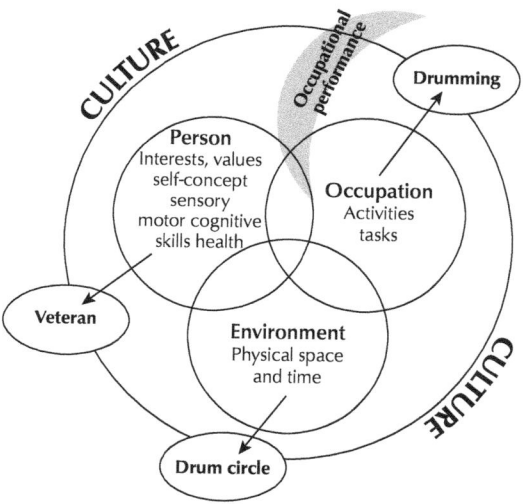

*Figure 23.1: The PEO model*

A shared connection begins with the *drill*. The first team building exercise taught in boot camp is *drill*. Also known as marching in detailed formation, drill develops uniformity and a sense of cohesion as recruits march in unison to a cadence. A military cadence is a call and response where chants are exchanged between a platoon leader and the rest of the platoon. The sound of shoes or boots beating on the ground helps keep the tempo. Cadence is also used in physical training (PT) as military servicemen and women jog in formation while in step. In addition, cadence is used in the field while soldiers hike up and down miles of difficult terrain.

Veterans have been trained to associate rhythmic synchrony to elements of team building including trust and camaraderie. In many cases, camaraderie is what veterans miss the most as they transition from military service to civilian life. Drum circles can provide a close-knit support system, reduce stigma associated with receiving psychotherapy, and help veterans understand that they are not alone in their journey towards post-traumatic growth and healing.

Drum circles provide a platform for individuals to communicate anger, pain, guilt, etc., through the volume and accents of their palms striking the drum. The experience becomes more powerful when the group drums in unison, echoing each other's emotions. Veterans have described the experience as 'spiritual', 'peaceful', and giving them a 'heightened sense of awareness'. These profound experiences are what keep veterans engaged in drum therapy as they develop lasting relationships with fellow veterans.[5]

Veterans thrive in a safe, bonded, task-oriented group, focused on a goal-directed mission. The drum circle creates a therapeutically rich environment that invites social connection whilst meeting a goal. Each week the level of trust deepens and the level of honesty expands. The veteran has the ability to voice thoughts and struggles with like-minded individuals that share a common culture and style of inter-personal interactions.

In the USA the Department of Veterans Affairs has adopted a philosophy called 'The circle of health' for aligning mental health interventions to the needs of veterans. A therapeutic drum circle program can promote each of these elements – see Figure 23.2 below.[6]

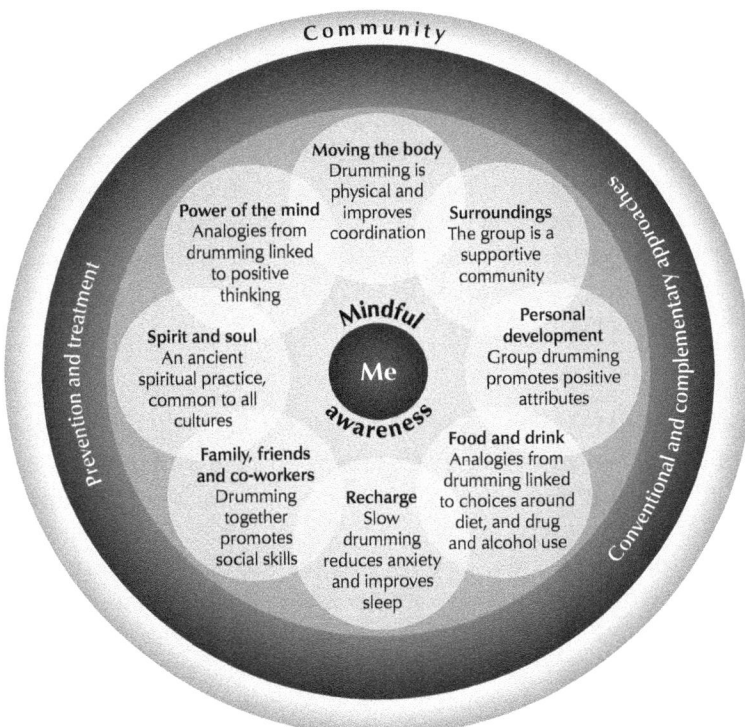

*Figure 23.2: Circle of health and drumming*

---

5   Bensimon, M., Amir, D. & Wolf, Y. (2008) 'Drumming through trauma: Music therapy with post-traumatic soldiers.' *The Arts in Psychotherapy 35*, 1, 34–48.
    Richmond, J.H. (2019) 'Drumming up harmony: How rhythmic synchronisation fosters pro-sociality.' Unpublished Doctoral Dissertation, The University of Melbourne.
6   Veterans Affairs (2019) 'The circle of health.' www.va.gov/WHOLEHEALTH/circle-of-health/index.asp (accessed 6 August 2020).

## SETTING UP FOR SUCCESS

It is very important to have a committed administrative group if offering the program in an organization – one that understands and values the work. Ensure a consistent, safe and secure environment where the drum circle can meet each week. Veterans have been trained to 'recon' and will arrive early to assess the environment and determine the level of security of the setting – arrive early yourself for set-up. Give time for settling into the environment. Give plenty of time and don't rush, especially through the initial sessions. Veterans function optimally with structure and routine. Therefore, keeping the drum circles consistently on the same day and at the same location and time is important. Beginning each session with simple breathing exercises and light stretching may help participants feel present, aware, and prepared for any physical and mental demands that occur during the drum circle.

Refreshments tend to ease tension and often the group will linger after the drum circle is over to socialize with a cup of coffee. If you can, it helps to have a co-leader who is a veteran or at least take steps to understand the veteran population better yourself. Be direct and clear with your expectations as veterans want to succeed and need a clear mission and definition of what 'success' looks like for each session. Include opportunities for physicality as part of the drumming experience – veterans love physical challenges. Don't be afraid to use a secure outdoor space as nature is quite supportive for emotional safety and healing.

## COMMON CHALLENGES AND HOW TO MINIMIZE THEM

A significant challenge you may face when working with this population is the initial 'buy in' phase. Veterans often are looking for logical methods for ending struggles and can be very frustrated with a system that seems to be less than supportive. Veterans may not see the purpose of a drum circle in light of the severity of their needs. The facilitator should be very clear and set good boundaries when first establishing the group. Veterans prefer 'rank and order' and are quite willing to follow a system if well established. There may be benefits in holding different specialized groups for the veterans, their partners and their children. Each select group has specific concerns that can be better addressed through separately focused group formats. Dependents (family members of a veteran) need to share their unique needs and often go unnoticed with most of the attention going to the person of service. The dedication and struggles of living with a veteran can be exhausting and contribute significantly to the overall burden of care.

Another challenge that may surface is the 'let me tell you how the system has failed me' discussion by a member who can dominate if not supported. This can become a difficult slope to climb out of, if allowed free reign. Recognize the struggle and then move the group to solution finding as it pertains to how the circle can support the member. Veterans do not want to share 'war stories' and do not like to show weakness – emotions are usually kept quiet. Realize that shared silence is often more powerful than tears.

Veterans may be reluctant to engage in these forms of expressive therapies because they may feel vulnerable expressing themselves to others, specifically male veterans who have been immersed in masculine military culture where emotional expression is a sign of weakness. Also, some may feel that they lack the musical abilities to contribute to the group.[7] Therefore, it is essential to emphasize that previous music experience is *not* necessary. It may be helpful to explain that drumming in the context of therapy is not intended to develop technical musicianship skills; instead its therapeutic benefits stem from participation, connection, cathartic expression and fun. It is important for the group to know that the drum circle is a safe, supportive space: 'what happens in the drum circle stays in the drum circle'.

## PRACTICAL APPLICATIONS OF THE DRUM CIRCLE
### Jam session

A 'jam session' may be applied at the beginning of each session as a warm up. This helps break the ice and relieve tension whilst using an informal and inviting approach. A warm-up jam also sets the tone for each session. Note that loud noises may trigger symptoms associated with post-traumatic stress disorder (PTSD). However, in a supportive, musical setting veterans will often learn to accommodate the sounds of drums (exposure therapy) and begin to recognize drums as a non-threatening mode of expression. One simple, yet effective and highly popular, rhythmic pattern that can be used as a warm-up jam session is the drumbeat used by Queen in their song, 'We Will Rock You' – two bass notes followed by one tone or a clap. This rhythmic pattern is distinctly familiar and fairly easy to play, even for those that are new to drumming. A group leader or a volunteer can initiate the drumbeat and the rest of the circle can join in. (In the military, it is not uncommon for soldiers to take turns leading a cadence.) Once the drum

---

7   Lobban, J. (2018) *Art Therapy with Military Veterans: Trauma and the Image.* Abingdon: Routledge.

pattern is established and everyone begins to feel comfortable, individuals can take turns improvising simple variations around the original beat. The group leader may wish to go around the circle and designate participants to take short rhythmic solos. Remember that the drum circle is a no-pressure zone so individuals may take a solo only if they feel comfortable. As the jam session comes to a close, the group leader may gradually *decrescendo* or decrease the volume as the rest of the circle follows. The drumming fades out until silence is achieved as a group.

## Physical Training (PT)

This is usually done after about the third gathering when some connection has formed. Sit in close circle formation with knees almost touching and drums in position for play. The goal is to reach with right hand across our personal drum to our neighbour on the left striking a bass note on their drum followed by reaching with left hand across our personal drum to our neighbour on the right, striking a bass note on their drum. Each member moves in synchrony, gradually increasing speed and movement. *I've never seen such focus and determination to keep the entire group following for a set time period.* This exercise promotes crossing the mid-line, which is associated with improvements in cognitive function.[8]

## Cadence

Cadence is used to organize and collect a group towards a goal. This activity begins with one person as the lead tempo keeper, and gradually every member adds a simple beat to the rhythm. The 'tempo keeper' then starts a chant that is used to make a statement of some kind – the chants can get rather 'colourful', so be ready, but the level of joy is also amazing and very helpful as a closing activity if the session has been a bit heavy and emotional. This is a good way to send them home supported and remembering the positive.

---

8   Buchele Harris, H., Cortina, K.S., Templin, T., Colabianchi, N. & Chen, W. (2018) 'Impact of coordinated-bilateral physical activities on attention and concentration in school-aged children.' *BioMed Research International*, 2018, 2539748.

## Mindfulness

Dr Shari Geller provides a deep work around therapeutic drumming and mindfulness.[9] Mindfulness is purposely paying attention. Drumming provides a way for group members to focus and purposely pay attention to sound, patterns and space. One practice to support mindfulness is to begin with a grounding exercise through the use of a simple bell chime. This exercise is supportive at the beginning of group to help members actively be ready for the experience and then again at the end as a transitioning practice for closing the group. The exercise introduces the participants to the chime and the practice of quiet focused attention. Opening practice is used once members are seated in the drum circle. Members are asked to close their eyes or gaze to the floor, the chime is struck and once members are unable to hear the tone, the member opens their eyes and raises their hand. Group members watch quietly until all members have raised hands. Group discussions focus on changes noted in mind, body and breath. Group members share the experience of the stillness created and the beauty of the silence. As a closing activity, members are asked to focus on the chime sound considering a thought of gratitude. The members are invited to share one or two gratitude thoughts if desired.

*Note*: Mindfulness needs to become a regular practice to be successful and many therapists use it as a regular part of their practice.

## Emotional regulation

Drumming is a natural body/brain regulator providing a way for group members to recognize body/brain states such as being out of control, escalating, just right and low energy. Through a series of drum rhythms, there are opportunities to move the body/brain purposely into fast, slow, wild and erratic tempos. The facilitator leads the changes with members copying the new patterns as they flow from one to the other. After a series of tempo changes, the facilitator begins a slower rhythm (60 bpm) and encourages members to feel free to add improvisation – finding space for their own rhythm and flow, matching the tempo and flow of the facilitator. Discussion follows about the group members' body/brain experiences for each tempo and secondary effects noticed. Connections are made about life situations that create chaos, calmness, excitement, anger, fear, etc. Group members learn to understand misdirected energy and power, increasing

---

9  Geller, S. (2009) 'Cultivation of therapeutic drumming and mindfulness practices.' *Dutch Tijdschrift Clientgerichte Psychotherapie (Journal for Client-Centered Psychotherapy)* 47, 4, 273–287.

self-awareness. Strategies are discussed for each life situation that support a regulated state.[10]

## Social integration

This social integration exercise creates a lot of laughter that breaks down social isolation and distancing. Modified from a Jim Donovan drum circle video exercise, group members divide into smaller groups and each creates a group drumming pattern that is maintained and linked to the group facilitator who is simultaneously holding a stable tempo rhythm. Each group continues their unique rhythm as a team until the signal is given to switch one member to the next group clockwise. The new member is assimilated into the new group without words. This continues for several rounds until the groups return to their original member format. Discussion follows regarding what supported and hindered their ability to find the new rhythm in the new group and the similarities to finding a new rhythm in civilian life are examined.[11]

## Tension and release exercise for anger management

Veterans may experience fluctuating levels of stress and anger compared to civilian populations. They are accustomed to high-stress environments where they are constantly on alert. On the battlefield, anger helps soldiers increase focus to confront immediate enemy threats. Anger also aids in developing camaraderie as soldiers collectively harbour anger in their quest to defeat an enemy. As veterans transition back to civilian life, they may experience difficulties managing anger. Being aware of specific triggers, feelings and physical reactions helps individuals respond to anger rationally. Anger may influence impulsive behaviours that can lead to negative consequences and create problems in relationships at home or work. Managing triggers and feelings takes time and requires conscious practice. Combining mindfulness strategies with drumming not only improves awareness but increases individuals' ability to de-escalate intense situations and achieve relaxation.

Progressive muscle relaxation is an effective mindfulness strategy where tension is applied to specific body parts by tightly clenching muscles together, followed by relaxing the muscles. Mentally scanning

---

10  Burt, J.W. (1995) 'Distant thunder: Drumming with Vietnam Veterans.' *Music Therapy Perspectives 13*, 2, 110–112.
11  Donovan, J. (2019) Social Connection Exercise Example. https://youtu.be/86Wqez1yn-0, (accessed 6 August 2020).

our body and focusing on the tension and relaxation helps bring forth awareness of how much stress we carry and how much control we have in releasing that tension. In terms of anger management, progressive muscle relaxation helps individuals regain control of their emotions and make thoughtful decisions. In music theory, tension and release are used to draw the listener into an intense musical passage using artistic devices such as increased volume and dissonant chords. The tension is then resolved with decreased volume and soothing chords.

In a drum circle setting, veterans can use the increased volume of hands striking drums to represent anger. The drum circle can begin playing a simple rhythm such as: 'boom-boom-chicka-chicka-boom-boom-chick.' As the rhythm is being played, the facilitator can gradually increase the volume until it reaches *fff* (or very loud in musical terms). Playing at *fff* represents the tension which allows participants to exert feelings of rage as they strike their drums. While playing in unison at *fff* for a few moments, the facilitator can lead the drum circle to begin the release and gradually decrease the volume. The release is where participants can grasp their sense of control in easing tension and de-escalating an intense moment. The facilitator can continue to gradually bring the volume down to a very soft level until the drumming feels soothing, and then fade out to silence. After the activity, the facilitator can ask participants how the experience made them feel, how it relates to real-life scenarios, and what strategies they use now to manage their anger, etc.

## ADDITIONAL ADVICE

Learn all you can about trauma-informed care and the neuroscience related to a brain that has experienced trauma. Attend military peer gatherings and have a veteran mentor to support your growth. Stay current with veteran population needs and keep up with the trends.

## AUTHOR BIOGRAPHIES
### Kevin Callo, BA

Kevin served six years in the United States Marine Corps. He has been a counsellor since 2005 and has experience working with military veterans, incarcerated populations, at-risk youth, and homeless populations. Kevin is a US State Department Music Ambassador and has promoted cultural diplomacy through music education in the Middle East, Asia, and Eastern Europe. He has also toured with Armed Forces Entertainment where he performed for US military servicemen and women in the Middle East-

Persian Gulf region. Kevin holds a BA in sociology from the University of Miami and is currently an MS in Marriage and Family Therapy candidate at the University of Southern California.

Email: kevintcallo@gmail.com

## Terrie King, OTR, LPC

Terrie has been an occupational therapy practitioner since 1989 and a professional counsellor since 2005. She has been leading drum circles since 2013 with individuals across the lifespan. In 1999, she helped to create a nonprofit, New Destinations, Inc. whose purpose is to support individuals with all abilities to live fully engaged lives. Seeing a gap in veteran services that support emotional needs, Terrie received a grant to provide therapeutic drum circles through a program called Circle of Courage. During the time of the grant, Terrie was able to provide drum circles to over 50 veterans and their families. In addition, four veteran group members were trained in drum circle facilitation to continue the work as peer mentors.

Email: terriekot@gmail.com
http://newdestinations.net

## RECOMMENDED READING

Balfour, M. (2018) 'Music projects with veteran and military communities.' In Bartleet, B.L. (ed.) *The Oxford Handbook of Community Music*. https://doi.org/10.1093/oxfordhb/9780190219505.013.2

Hoge, C.W. (2010). *Once a Warrior, Always a Warrior: Navigating the Transition from Combat to Home – Including Combat Stress, PTSD, and mTBI*. Guilford, CT: GPP Life.

Siegel, D.J. (2007) *The Mindful Brain: Reflection and Attunement in the Cultivation of Well-Being*. New York: W.W. Norton.

Vijay Iyer and Mike Ladd, featuring Maurice Decaul and Lynn Hill. *Holding It Down: The Veterans' Dreams Project* (music CD).

# Survivors of Natural Disasters

## JUDY GUTHRIE AND MICHELLE TAYLOR

**OVERVIEW**

Natural disasters, which seem to be occurring more frequently worldwide, have a huge impact on the location in which they occur and the devastation they cause affects millions of people annually. The survivors of tsunamis, volcanic eruptions, tornadoes, floods, blizzards, heatwaves, hurricanes, earthquakes, bush/wild/forest fires have lived through a life-altering experience. They have likely experienced extreme stress, anxiety, fear or terror. At the least, they will have observed significant damage to their property and in their community, and some will have lost their homes and possessions. At the worst, the survivors have witnessed human injury and loss of life.

In the immediate aftermath of a natural disaster, life is totally disrupted; nothing is as it was, and people can feel lost, vulnerable or numb. As the extent of the devastation becomes more apparent and real, many people start to rally and help themselves and each other to recover. It is an exhausting time and outside support is crucial. As we write this, the world is managing the COVID-19 pandemic and drum circle facilitators around the world are supporting individuals and communities by adapting to online technologies while planning community connection and resilience programs for the post-isolation period. The qualities inherent in a drum circle of safe connection, emotional expression through music and uplifting spirit are all essential to recovery from these types of incidents.

While traumatic and life-altering for adults, these events can literally change the neural connections in the brains of younger children who experience them,[1] both as a result of the direct traumatic event itself and also from the impact natural disasters have on the child's relational web. Thus, we often see greater levels of stress response reactivity in young people who experienced these types of events early in their childhood. It is imperative then that we are able to access communities and families at times of natural disaster and ongoing thereafter to mitigate against and minimize the impact such traumatic events can have on the community, the families and, in turn, the developing child.

Natural disasters, such as fires, floods, hurricanes and the like, certainly cause disruption and have significant impacts on individuals, families and communities. That said, times of natural disaster and threats to community tend also to bring about remarkable examples of resilience, cohesion and community-based collaboration. Out of the rubble we regularly see heroic acts and kindness that serve as a buffer to the tragedy of events. As a recent example of this the 2019–2020 Black Summer bushfires in Australia saw remarkable acts of kindness and generosity from the Australian and International community. Millions of dollars were raised for victims, donations of food and clothes were so great that services had to request they cease, and all around the world people began campaigns to support Australian wildlife devastated by the fires.

It is common to see music and the creative arts featuring centrally in community resilience; for example, in the aftermath of the Black Saturday fires in Australia in 2009, local choir groups and musicians worked together to express and heal, with the Whittlesea Community Choir producing a song 'Out of the Ashes'. Examples of this resilience and community spirit at times of disaster are evident all over the world and throughout history.[2]

---

1   Perry, B.D. (2001) 'The Neuroarcheology of Childhood Maltreatment: The Neurodevelopmental Costs of Adverse Childhood Events.' In K. Franey, R. Geffner & R. Falconer (eds) *The Cost of Maltreatment: Who Pays? We All Do.* San Diego, CA: Family Violence and Sexual Assault Institute.
    Perry, B.D., Pollard, R., Blakely, T., Baker, W. & Vigilante, D. (1995) 'Childhood trauma, the neurobiology of adaptation and "use-dependent" development of the brain: How "states" become "traits".' *Infant Mental Health Journal 16,* 4, 271–291.
2   Solnit, R. (2010) *A Paradise Built in Hell.* Harmondsworth: Penguin Books.

## POSITIVE OUTCOMES

Music has been a source of healing and connection for centuries. When words fail or are inaccessible, music can serve as a powerful form of communication. Survivors of natural disasters often struggle to create a language-based narrative of their experiences.[3] Creative or expressive therapies, such as music and drumming, serve to form connections between implicit (sensory) memory and explicit (declarative) memory.[4]

Research from the field of neuroscience reveals that somatosensory and rhythmically-based interventions provide regulatory effects in the face of emotional challenges or dysregulation. The work of Dr Bruce Perry[5] and Dr Stephen Porges,[6] among others, indicates that sensory and rhythmic input are initially experienced in the lower parts of the brain and travel upward through the emotional parts of the brain before reaching the cortex, our thought and memory centre. We know that our stress response system originates low in the brain and when activated in the face of perceived and/or actual threat can render our cortex inaccessible.[7] As such, we know that attempts to use insight or thought-based interventions to regulate our threat response are often ineffective. Interventions such as drumming provide the rhythmic and sensory-based regulation to calm and/or settle the activation of the stress response in the lower parts of the brain.[8] Neuroscience has provided us with a clear roadmap to regulate the stress response system via sensory and rhythmic input. Sensory and rhythmic regulation then in turn enables participants to have access to their higher order cortical functions to process and understand the impact of traumatic events.[9]

In an Australian study exploring music interventions with young people after the 2009 Black Saturday fires in Victoria, McFerran and Teggelove

---

3   Malchiodi, C.A. (2015) 'Neurobiology, Creative Interventions and Childhood Trauma.' In C.A. Malchiodi (ed.) *Creative Interventions with Traumatized Children*. New York: Guilford Press.
4   Malchiodi, C.A. (2015) 'Neurobiology, Creative Interventions and Childhood Trauma.' In C.A. Malchiodi (ed.) *Creative Interventions with Traumatized Children*. New York: Guilford Press.
5   Perry, B.D. (2009) 'Examining child maltreatment through a neurodevelopmental lens: Clinical applications of the neurosequential model of therapeutics.' *Journal of Loss and Trauma 14*, 240–255.
6   Porges, S. (2011) *The Polyvagal Theory: Neurophysiologial Foundations of Emotions, Attachment, Communication, and Self-Regulation*. New York: W.W. Norton & Company.
7   Perry, B.D. (2009) 'Examining child maltreatment through a neurodevelopmental lens: Clinical applications of the neurosequential model of therapeutics.' *Journal of Loss and Trauma 14*, 240–255.
8   van der Kolk, B. (2014) *The Body Keeps the Score: Brain, Mind and Body in the Healing of Trauma*. Harmondsworth: Penguin Books.
9   Perry, B.D. (1994) 'Neurobiological Sequelae of Childhood Trauma: Post Traumatic Stress Disorders in Children.' In M. Murburg (ed.) *Catecholamine Function in Post Traumatic Stress Disorder: Emerging Concepts*. Washington, DC: American Psychiatric Press.

(2011)[10] found that participants experienced more social cohesion. In fact, participants reported that playing music with others who had been through similar experiences and who understood them was important. Other reported benefits included impacts on mood (having fun) and a medium for them to freely and safely express their feelings related to the traumatic experience. My own experience running drumming groups with colleagues from 'Berry Street' Trauma services for Year Seven and Year Eight students who were child victims of the Black Saturday fires revealed similar outcomes. Participants in the groups were nine and 10 years old at the time of the fires. These drumming circles ran for 10 consecutive weeks, culminating in the students putting on a performance at the conclusion of the groups.

The children in these sessions reported:

- reduced hyper-vigilance
- increased capacity for attention
- presence of playfulness not otherwise observed
- increase in happiness
- sense of connection to others in the group through discovery of shared experiences, struggles and successes
- overall improvements in self-esteem and psychological wellbeing
- parental reports of improved behaviour.

Similar outcomes were experienced by my co-author Judy Guthrie, subsequent to Hurricane Irma, with the value and comfort of sharing the experience with others who had been through the same event strongly evident. The cathartic nature of the physical act of drumming with others provided a lift in mood and an exhilarating opportunity for releasing feelings and emotions. People relayed that these sessions left them full of gratitude and hope.

## SETTING UP FOR SUCCESS

It is even more important than usual to have a good contact person who can give lots of information about the group in order to plan appropriate activities: how many people are likely to attend and, particularly, who they are.

---

10  Mcferran, K. & Teggelove, K.(2011) 'Music therapy with young people in schools: After the Black Saturday fires.' *Voices: A World Forum for Music Therapy 11*, 10, 15845/voices.v11i1.285.

For example: if this is a circle for government officials after days of Disaster Management meetings, then this is a group who are continually making tough, stressful decisions. Their circle might emphasize personal and mutual support, relaxation and opportunities for reflection. If it's a circle for the staff of a primary school, then these people are holding together some semblance of order for the youngest survivors. They need support, empowerment, relaxation, fun. If it's a circle for families after a church service, this will be a circle from baby to Grandma and a celebration of family fun and faith. If the facilitator understands who the group is and the challenges they are facing, it is a great help in being able to read the group, adapting the flow of activities to suit their needs.

## COMMON CHALLENGES AND HOW TO MINIMIZE THEM

As many buildings may no longer exist, it can be a challenge to find an appropriate venue but hopefully the organizer has this worked out. Otherwise if the weather is conducive, outdoor locations may be more appropriate. Having chairs for the participants and other basic necessities cannot be taken for granted, and it is important to discuss your needs, however simple, with the organizer. The chairs create the circle from the very beginning, giving a sense of form, purpose, normality and dignity. It is also useful to think about transport and how you and the group attendees will get to the drum circle location, when roads and public transport infrastructure may have been compromised.

Survivors will have likely felt some level of trauma around the disaster and unfortunately most of us are not music therapists. We are, however, experienced drum circle facilitators with sensitive and compassionate spirits. The goal is, as always, to provide fun and relaxation through making music in an emotionally safe environment. We acknowledge that we are not trained to delve into the emotional depths of the trauma, but because the nature of the drum circle can create an emotional response in people, we need an especially heightened awareness to tread gently, being mindful of how the experience is unfolding for people. If someone is feeling overwhelmed emotionally, it is kind to acknowledge and support them and there will very likely be others in the circle who will do so as well. Following up afterwards, to ensure that person can get more support if needed, is important.

Working with children in group settings comes with an array of natural challenges that may well be exacerbated by the trauma of a natural disaster; in particular, the increased stress response reactivity of young people caused by such events. The coping mechanisms that ensue can lead to highly distractible, avoidant, and at times disruptive members of the group.

Establishment of collaborative group rules and affording young people a sense of ownership over these can go a long way in ensuring adherence to them, while keeping each other accountable and ensuring that people feel safe. That said, children who've experienced traumatic events can really struggle to remain regulated. The beauty of a drum circle is the flexibility it allows, whereby participants can drum through their dysregulation and in turn settle themselves down so as to rejoin the group structure. As such, facilitators need to always remain understanding and flexible and be prepared to alter their 'plan' for the session in a given moment to support the needs of an individual within the group or the group as a whole.

## PRACTICAL APPLICATIONS OF THE DRUM CIRCLE
### 'Rumble if…'

This is an easy, non-threatening way to involve participants right after the initial warm-up. Each participant asks a question using the question 'Rumble on your drum if…?'

This exercise can be used to ask generalized or quite personalized questions in a safe and fun way. It can be a way of the group recognizing that they share common feelings or dilemmas, a way for the facilitator to monitor individuals who may need more support, and often a way to have fun and evoke laughter as people will ask all sorts of different questions. This is also a valuable game for the facilitator to get a sense of the group's mood and spirit.

- 'Rumble if you have current (electricity) at your house yet', and only 1 or 2 out of 30 will rumble…but everyone laughs.

- 'Rumble if you have someone you can talk to about how you are managing at the moment?' If someone doesn't rumble you may need to offer additional follow-up.

- 'Rumble if you are feeling a little anxious about the future.'

The potential questions are endless and it is always good to have the group members make up their own. As the group rumbles together, tension is released, mood lifts and people recognize their common thoughts, feelings and experiences, binding them together in community.

### Fears, hopes and dreams

In this exercise we pass an imaginary ball using a rumble (rumble ball) between players and when it is caught, the rumble stops and the catcher has a choice of:

- sharing a fear or worry you are thinking about a lot – sharing your fears is a way of lessening their burden
- sharing a dream for the future – something positive you hope will come out from the disaster.

After sharing the speaker chooses another person in the circle and the imaginary ball is passed onwards. The rumble prior to speaking helps release any nervousness associated with talking and sharing within the group.

## The bass note: finding your way home (Rhythm2Recovery)

In working with child survivors of the 2009 Victorian Black Saturday fires the use of the bass note and the 'finding your way home' exercise served initially as a grounding technique for the group. Finding your way home is essentially a simple technique of teaching young people the bass note and the imperative role it plays in holding a rhythm together. The focus of the exercise is to show participants how to rejoin a rhythm when they get lost or fall out of sync.

This exercise is often done at the very beginning of group formation. The bass note is introduced with conversations about it being 'the anchor of the rhythm'. Conversations at this point can be drawn out about the bass note as a way of finding your place in the rhythm and can be likened to the role of home or family. We can be lost, we can be confused, we can be scared but we can always come home for connection. It is important to be mindful when working with children of any additional family or relational-based trauma they might carry in addition to that of the natural disaster. This is where having a good sense of the group ahead of time is important. Discussions about family or home being a safe place to come back to can be triggering and dysregulating for children who experience or have experienced trauma in the context of their home and/or family. If the home is no longer standing, what other things might we turn to, to give us a sense of security or stability?

When we were putting the group structure together for the child survivors of the 'Black Saturday' bushfires, we envisaged this exercise as a way of creating a safe base for the children and young people to come back to when lost in the rhythms and to establish initial group cohesion and safety. The outcome of this exercise however was far more powerful. In setting up the exercise with the children and talking about the importance of the bass note in finding our way back to connection and rhythm in the group, we inadvertently opened up a discussion we had not anticipated. The older group of children particularly reflected on the rhythms we have in our lives and the connections we have that we can keep and hold onto irrespective of a natural disaster like a bushfire. In among drumming, the children engaged in discussions about the importance of family, pets, friends, school and the everyday routines of life as being essential to the heart and soul of survival for them. What seemed a simple exercise to teach young people how to find their way back to a rhythm when lost became a rich discussion about the value of the familiar and key relationships and rhythms in overcoming the dislocation and trauma that natural disasters can bring.

## Heartbeat rhythms

Teaching the heartbeat rhythm and some extensions was a wonderful way to enable the children to express and demonstrate the different ways stress, anxiety and fear presented within them preceding, during, and at varying times after the 'Black Saturday' fires. The ability to express oneself without having to talk and to act it out in some way is exceptionally powerful and liberating for trauma survivors who often don't have capacity to discuss their experience in narrative.[11]

To set up the heartbeat exercise participants are taught the basic notes and commence with playing a heartbeat rhythm consistent with typical resting heart-rates.

| Timing | 1 2 3 4 | 1 2 3 4 | 1 2 3 4 | 1 2 3 4 |
|---|---|---|---|---|
| **Heartbeat rhythm** | B B - - | B B - - | B B - - | B B - - |

Then faster heartbeat rhythms and extensions are introduced such as:

| Timing | 1 2 3 4 | 1 2 3 4 | 1 2 3 4 | 1 2 3 4 |
|---|---|---|---|---|
| Heartbeat Extensions | B B Clap - | B B Clap - | B B Clap - | B B Clap - |
| | B B Rub your drum | B B Rub your drum | B B Rub your drum | B B Rub your drum |
| | B B T - | B B T - | B B T - | B B T - |
| | B B T T | B B T T | B B T T | B B T T |
| | B B T t T | B B T t T | B B T t T | B B T t T |

B – Bass note (centre of drum), T – Tone note (edge of drum). Uppercase – Dominant hand, Lowercase – Non-dominant hand.

After playing with these rhythms, participants were asked to think about their heartbeat before the fires, on a 'normal' day when going to school, on a 'normal' day at home. Then the activity moved to direct reflection of the

---
11 van der Kolk, B. (2014) *The Body Keeps the Score: Brain, Mind and Body in the Healing of Trauma*; Malchiodi, C. (2012) 'Art Therapy and the Brain.' In C Malchiodi (ed.), *Handbook of Art Therapy*. New York: Guilford Press.

experience of the fires, asking the children to drum the heartbeat rhythm to portray their experience of hearing the fires were coming, if they saw the fires, fleeing the fires and their family homes, waiting as the fires passed, being at the community centres waiting to know what happened to their homes, going back to their homes, going back to 'normal' life, like school. Children were also asked to reflect on how their heartbeat rhythm sounded on that day when they thought back to the fires as a way for facilitators to get a sense of ongoing traumatic impact on the students from 'Black Saturday'.

The children in the group reported finding it helpful to be able to 'show' how their hearts raced and what their fear sounded like through the use of the drum. Interestingly the groups were taken by the similarity of their experiences and were able to reflect on what they could see as a shared experience. Trauma can leave people feeling isolated and while the local communities worked tremendously post Black Saturday in healing and recovery, the responses of these children demonstrated the ongoing power such events have in leaving people feeling that their experience is different from others. To find such visceral connection through demonstrated drumbeats was a very powerful experience for these students.

The other way we used the heartbeat exercise was to re-create regulation post-activation of the student's stress responses by having them recount their fear via drumming. Given that we had taken these children back into trauma memory and activated their stress response systems it was imperative that we re-regulated them. As such we engaged in the use of a heartbeat rhythm more consistent with regulatory rhythms of 60–80 bpm, akin to resting heart-rates.[12] In doing so we were able to assist and demonstrate the regulatory power of the drum in calming the heart and settling arousal.

### 'Giving thanks' (Rhythm2Recovery)

As previously mentioned, times of natural disasters often bring out the best in people. In this exercise discuss with the group whether there are some people in your community you would like to thank and acknowledge after the disaster for the help and support they provided to you (e.g., firefighters), or perhaps you just wish to offer thanks to a higher power for your survival or some other positive you take from your situation.

In this exercise we teach a rhythm 'break' (accent piece) that goes as below, symbolizing the words, 'Thank you, Thank you, Thank you very much!'

---

12  Perry, B.D. & Pollard, R. (1998) 'Homeostatis, stress trauma and adaptation: A neurodevelopmental view of childhood trauma.' *Child and Adolescent Psychiatric Clinics of North America* 7, 33–51.

| Timing | 1 2 3 4 | 1 2 3 4 | 1 2 3 4 | 1 2 3 4 |
|---|---|---|---|---|
| Break | T t - T t | T t T t T | T t - T t | T t T t T |
| Words | Thank you, Thank you | Thank you very much | Thank you, Thank you | Thank you very much |

After practising the break, the group play a simple rhythm and then the facilitator counts that down to stop (4, 3, 2, 1, Stop) before adding the break. Then back to the rhythm – repeat several times and before the last time let everyone know that this last time, we will yell out our thanks on top of the break before we finish. Finish playing the break and shouting out our thanks together.

## Change (Rhythm2Recovery)

This is an exercise designed to help people adapt to and discuss the implications of the substantial change that is occurring in their lives post-disaster, as well as look at how to lead change. One person is asked to lead a rhythm and the rest of the group follow. After around 20 seconds a new leader with a new rhythm leads the group. Repeat this process four or five times. At the end the facilitator leads a group discussion looking at:

- Which changes were easiest to follow and why?
- What helped people transition between the changing rhythms?
- What helped people adapt to the changing rhythms?
- How important was it to have some rhythms that were consistent?

## Mindfulness – managing uncertainty (Rhythm2Recovery)

*Note*: To be effective mindfulness needs to become a regular activity – many facilitators incorporate a mindfulness routine into every session.

To the beat of a slow bass pulse (60–80 bpm – replicating the mother's heartbeat at rest). Pause between each bullet point.

- Notice your natural breath and breathe gently, slowly and in time with the pulse. Chest rising and falling, slowly and comfortably, feeling comfortably connected to the earth, grounded by the breath.
- Find the rhythm of your soothing breath.
- And allow all the weight of the world to fall from your shoulders,

stepping away from your worries and fears and finding a sense of calm.

- Bring your mind slowly to the concept of impermanence and change; recognizing the truth that these are constants in our lives and that control and permanence are fleeting and largely illusions.
- Just as we may recognize that change can move us from contentment to discontent, so we must also recognize that the ongoing nature of change will bring us back again.
- Now call to mind an aspect of your life that is undergoing great change, recognize the feelings that are associated with this thought and try to make room for these feelings without being overwhelmed by them – accepting and breathing around them.
- Breathe slowly, comfortably and naturally.
- Let us now reflect on the many times we have experienced change and uncertainty in the past and how we have managed to work through these previously – recognizing our own abilities to learn and grow through these challenges, no matter how unnerving or uncomfortable.
- Breath slowly, comfortably and naturally – trusting yourself.
- Allow yourself to release the bond of certainty and attachment that leads to fear and replace this with an acceptance and recognition of those things we cannot undo.
- Let us then picture the opportunities brought from change.
- Bring to mind the wonder and hope of new beginnings that stem from this time of uncertainty – picture this as a new light shining through a doorway, offering a new pathway to happiness and fulfillment.
- Breathe slowly, comfortably and naturally.
- Finally, let us offer thoughts of loving kindness towards those who are struggling with uncertainty, fear and doubt. Breathe gently and slowly, and in time with your breath make individual statements of support.
- In your own time, slowly move your focus back to the bass note.

Adapt this script and make it your own.

### Celebration circle (Christine Stevens)
This is a wonderful way to start bringing the circle to a close as it gives any participant the opportunity to express what they are feeling. I start by having everyone practise a big 'stop cut' in their chairs: 'Make a big X holding your hands above your head and now bring your hands down to your sides…with attitude!' I also add that it feels very powerful when you can silence a whole group with that simple action! Then the group rumbles and one at a time whoever has something to say can come to the middle of the circle, stop the group, say their piece, start the rumble again, take a seat…the next person comes up. End with a big rumble with dynamics. This can be a very positive and emotionally touching exercise as people express their gratitude for the joy of music, for life.

## ADDITIONAL ADVICE
The opportunity to drum with survivors doesn't present itself to all of us. If it does come your way, fear not and know that you have a gift that can make a huge difference to people who really need it. I have always ended all my circles with a short, guided meditation – a gentle heartbeat rhythm on one drum, an affirming story about the goodness in all of us and in the world, a turn of the rain stick or some notes on a native flute, then silence. And then around the circle, each can share how they feel in 'one word'. After much thought about whether this might be too emotional for survivors, I decided to go gently and see how it went. It is right up there with the richest of my drum circle experiences.

Children especially relish the opportunity to drum and with the regulation it provides to the central nervous system it is such a wonderful delight to watch reflective and developmentally appropriate conversations and discussions occur as a result.

## AUTHOR BIOGRAPHIES
### Judy Guthrie
Judy has been facilitating drum circles in Anguilla and Canada for 15 years and has experience leading circles with children, teens, elders, inmates and the general community. Judy has completed trainings with Arthur Hull, Christine Stevens and Simon Faulkner. She currently works between Calgary and Toronto in Canada during the Canadian summer, and Anguilla in the Caribbean during the remainder of the year.

On September 6, 2017, Hurricane Irma directly hit the tiny island of Anguilla as well as other nearby islands in the Caribbean. It was the most powerful storm ever recorded in the Atlantic with sustained winds of 300km/hour. Judy returned to her home there as soon as flights were available. The devastation was enormous and shocking. It was obvious that people were deeply affected and emotionally, traumatized by what they had lived through and yet the resilience of spirit and commitment to recover was also very evident. In the next two months, Judy facilitated 20 circles in makeshift schools with students and teachers, in cramped offices with government and Unicef officials, in roofless churches covered with tarps, with teams of electrical workers sent from around the world under a starry sky. There was much joy in those circles and such gratitude for a reprieve from the relentless work of recovery. It was a privilege to be able to bring this brief respite to the lives of those in her community.

Email: judycraigguthrie@gmail.com

## Michelle Taylor, BA (Hons), MPsych

Michelle Taylor is a clinical psychologist with a speciality in neurodevelopment, infant, child and adolescent trauma and attachment disruption. Michelle is the Co-Director of Blossomtree Psychology, an infant, child, adolescent and family private practice in Ballarat Victoria. In 2013 Michelle was recipient of a Creswick Foundation Fellowship exploring the impact of neurodevelopmentally-informed interventions in child trauma treatment. In 2019 Michelle became a Fellow of the Child Trauma Academy.

Michelle has over 22 years' experience working in government departments and community service organizations in remote rural and regional centres in Western Australia and Victoria. Michelle specializes in the provision of therapy to infants, children, adolescents and families who have experienced disruption in the development of attachment in the primary care relationship and/or developmental trauma. Michelle lives in Victoria, Australia and has lived through several of that country's worst bushfire disasters including 'Black Saturday' from 2009, in which 173 people were killed, and the recent devastating fires of 2020 that razed several towns and blackened over 17 million hectares (40 million acres). In the recovery period Michelle worked closely with children from bushfire-impacted communities using drumming activities as part of her psychological practice.

Email: chelle@blossomtreepsychology.com.au
www.blossomtreepsychology.com.au

## RECOMMENDED READING
Solnit, R. (2010) *A Paradise Built in Hell.* New York: Penguin Books.

# Aboriginal or First Nations Groups

SIMON FAULKNER

**OVERVIEW**

This advice is given for those who are non-Indigenous and are asked to work with Indigenous groups using the drum circle. This has been a big part of my working life and amongst the most rewarding groups I have had the honour to work with and support using drumming. However, as an individual far removed from my own Indigenous heritage, I am conscious of the limits of my cultural understanding and do not wish to give an impression that I speak on behalf of indigenous peoples.

I have worked with Indigenous people on several continents, across different age groups, and with people with different needs and expectations; some with very strong cultural traditions, others less so. It is my experience that music is a wonderful way of connecting with people generally and that this is particularly true for our Indigenous brothers and sisters. Equally true is that many of the Indigenous people we have worked with are still suffering from the dispossession, violence and ongoing prejudice that accompanied the colonization of their lands; an inter generational trauma that has left a lasting legacy. The drum circle can act as a tool for healing from these hurts and support reconciliation between the past, the present and the future.

When working with Indigenous peoples it is important to recognize the different worldviews that orientate our thinking, and how we see the world. Western thought has been dominated by reductionist thinking, where we have isolated different elements of the world around us in order to study and understand them. Our knowledge base, and therapeutic understanding, are dominated by a scientific/medical model which relies on being able to describe and quantify observations in order to accept them. Traditional Indigenous worldviews are based on the universal nature of relationship, with all things being connected and impacting on each other – it is a holistic knowledge that does not look to isolate variables. In traditional drumming, the drum itself is animate with physical, psychological, emotional and spiritual qualities.[1] Drumming in these communities comes with traditional protocols and responsibilities and it is essential to have the guidance and support of a respected elder or knowledge keeper before venturing into this area.

The use of music and the arts in general as a healing modality is embraced by Indigenous cultures. Art is central to the identity and expression of culture. Rhythm is a central aspect of most Indigenous music and the work we are doing with the drum circle is an extension of age-old traditions and understandings that sadly have been broken, lost and undervalued. We are now part of a movement to revisit and reintegrate this knowledge from the past.

In my own work the distinction between universal improvised drumming, and an Indigenous cultural drumming tradition is critical. And it may or may not be accepted by the cultural guardians in the community. If we come with open hearts, there is much for us to learn from this cross-cultural exposure, though we must always walk slowly and respectfully.

## POSITIVE OUTCOMES

Much of the work done by support services working with Aboriginal or First Nations peoples is focused on reducing the impact of the injustices they have experienced from the dominant culture. We are often working with the symptoms of intergenerational trauma derived from the abusive

---

1   Heinonen, T., Halonen, D. & Krahn, E. (2018) *Expressive Arts for Social Work and Social Change*. Oxford: Oxford University Press.

impact of colonization and dispossession. Indigenous people suffer grossly disproportionate rates of disadvantage against all measures of socioeconomic status. One of the many outcomes of this situation is high levels of problematic addiction and the associated problems it creates for individuals and their families and communities. Two studies by Dickerson and colleagues (2012, 2014) showed the potential for drumming initiatives in this area,[2] with positive engagement and maintenance of abstinence across the course of the interventions.

My own research has demonstrated that drumming interventions with Indigenous adolescents can reduce a wide range of 'risk factors' known to increase the likelihood of addiction and other anti-social outcomes, including contact with the criminal justice system.[3] These included improving a student's connection to the school community, reducing school absences and reducing behavioural issues. In the same study, student's self-esteem increased significantly and these levels were maintained 12 months after the program finished.

Other positive outcomes that have been recognized by colleagues who have witnessed the impact of these types of programs and self-reports from the participants themselves include:

- an increased feeling of safety
- a feeling of connection and belonging
- spiritual awakening
- bonding with community
- the cathartic release of feelings
- celebration
- connection to culture – when learning cultural drumming practice from respected elders.

---

2   Dickerson, D.L., Venner, K.L., Duran, B., Annon, J.J. Hale, B. & Funmaker, G. (2014) 'Drum-assisted recovery therapy for Native Americans (DARTNA): Results from a pretest and focus groups.' *American Indian and Alaska native mental health research (Online) 21*, 1, 35–58.
    Dickerson, D.L., Robichaud, F., Teruya, C., Nagaran, K. & Yih-Ing, M.S. (2012) 'Untilizing drumming for American Indians/Alaska Natives with substance abuse disorders: A focus group study.' *American Journal of Drug & Alcohol Abuse 38*, 5, 505–510.
3   Faulkner, S., Ivery, P., Wood, L. & Donovan, R. (2010) 'Drumbeat – Music as a toll for social learning and improved educational outcomes.' *Journal of Indigenous Education 39*, 98–108.
    Faulkner, S. (2018) 'Therapeutic applications for rhythm and reflection in support of people with co-occurring drug and alcohol and mental health issues.' *Journal of Dual Diagnosis 3*, 2, 5.

## SETTING UP FOR SUCCESS

Among the most important things we can do as drum circle facilitators working with Indigenous groups is to get to know the history and cultural traditions of the people we are about to work with. There are many excellent books available on the cultural traditions and histories of different Indigenous peoples, and often local health services have published guides to working in a sensitive and respectful way with these groups. This sort of familiarization can help you understand, appreciate and accommodate any cultural differences that might impact your ability to develop a working partnership.

Another thing that I find particularly important when working with Indigenous groups is to have one local Indigenous person as a liaison, and ideally a co-facilitator, who can help me negotiate the cross-cultural sensitivities, and build a bridge between me, my work and the needs of the participants. This is particularly important in traditional communities where inter-personal relationships follow strict protocols and where language differences can lead to misunderstandings. For instance, I recently did a group in a desert community in central Australia where there had been a spate of suicides. It was critical for me to have someone local inform me of their traditions as mention of any of the deceased names was taboo, and I could easily have acted inappropriately and undermined any trust without that knowledge.

## COMMON CHALLENGES AND HOW TO MINIMIZE THEM

The most serious issue that I have encountered in my work using drums and the drum circle with Indigenous groups is the issue of cultural appropriation, where there is resentment at the use of traditional drums and sometimes traditional rhythms from a specific cultural tradition, without the appropriate authority, by people outside the culture. This is a very sensitive area for some people stemming from the, relatively recent, cultural dispossession of many Indigenous peoples at the hand of their oppressors. In my own work I shy away from using specific cultural rhythms (and where possible use non- cultural drums like the Remo Versa range) and focus instead on universal patterns and improvisation. I also enlist the help of local respected elders to ensure attendees know that I am not trespassing into traditional drumming practices and ensure their support for my own form of community drumming prior to beginning.

Another common challenge when working with Indigenous groups is differing cultural norms and differing understandings of time that can impact the organization of events. Linear time is a foreign concept to many Indigenous societies who see all life as infinite and regenerative – a creative timeline that cycles endlessly. Non-linear concepts of time often challenge western concepts of punctuality. Punctuality is often interpreted in a more relaxed manner, and events will often start and finish when people are ready, rather than on a set schedule. It is critical to meet with local representatives of the contracting service to discuss issues such as these prior to beginning. In many Indigenous communities, kinship rules and boundaries will impact who can be in your circle. Often adolescents of different genders are unable to socialize, and other 'kinship' rules can restrict different members of a community from playing music together, e.g., mother-in-law and son-in-law.

Many Indigenous people are over-represented in the statistics of those with mental health issues, or those in prison or juvenile detention, those in child protection and those battling drug and alcohol addiction. The cause of much of this harm stems from the intergenerational trauma of colonization. It is thus likely that a drum circle you convene may include specific populations dealing with these issues or at least some people facing significant social and emotional issues. In supporting people working with these challenges, the safety and trust you can build in your circle becomes vital.

## PRACTICAL APPLICATIONS OF THE DRUM CIRCLE

In my work with adults in Indigenous communities, I tend to restrict the amount of free improvisation in favour of the unity and grounding nature of simple universal patterns focused on the pulse, like the heartbeat rhythm played in unison.

> The pulse is constantly changing, being affected by any and every alteration in the individual's physiology and psychology.
>
> Feel it change now with your breathing, with your thoughts. It is alive. It is nature. The pulse is the waveform that transports the life blood throughout the body. And the pulse of the music is the rhythmically recurrent undulations that are the life force that propels the music, emanating from its very heart.[4]

### Yarning time[5]

It is common for me to break the drumming process into different rounds or sections where I intersperse an integrative and calming rhythm with

---

[4] Diamond, J. (1999) *The Way of the Pulse – Drumming with Spirit*. Enhancement Books, p.29.
[5] Yarning is an Aboriginal way of conversing, sharing stories and cultivating knowledge.

opportunities for reflection and dialogue on a chosen theme, sometimes using a 'talking stick'. A change in the dynamic of the playing – getting softer and returning to a simple pulse – serves as a marker for a shift to dialogue and reflection. Sometimes the 'Yarning' theme takes the form of individual hopes, prayers or intentions, and other times it may be about honouring or remembering cultural values, stories or specific individuals. During the speaker's time the drum pulse remains steady and soft, before re-awakening into group improvisation with new energy and volume once they have finished.

Another useful practice, dependent on the approval of the community elders, is to integrate cultural instruments and chants into your circle. In Australia it is common in my work with Aboriginal communities to have a didgeridoo player and other community members playing traditional tapping sticks (clave). In my work with the coastal Salish in Canada there has often been an opportunity for local songs and chants accompanied by the frame drum to be incorporated into our work. Similarly, in many other countries where there is a local tradition of drumming, it is always empowering to connect this to your circle by inviting people to play their traditional rhythms, and sing or dance when they feel comfortable.

## Affirmations in language

Indigenous languages are a vital element in keeping people connected to culture and this strengthens feelings of pride and self-worth. Cultural knowledge, kinship, songlines and stories are reliant on language in order to be passed on from generation to generation. Many of these understandings are only visible through the traditional language, and imposing the language of the dominant culture has been a time-honoured practice of colonial imperialism.

Bringing Indigenous language into your drum circle is a sign of respect, and will generally make the process much more meaningful for those involved.

I often build in breaks (accent pieces) to a rhythm that we compose of local words. For children's games, these may be the names of local fauna or flora in their native tongue. For adults the themes maybe ones of cultural values or law. A simple 'four bass break' is where you count down a rhythm and hit the bass note four times – one time each on the first note of the bar across four bars, leaving the other three notes of the bar clear. And then add the selected words, one after each bass note – sung out by the group. This can be a great way to remind people of these types of specific themes and embed them rhythmically.

## Musical chairs – cultural perspectives

Another game I like to play is musical chairs, where we count down a rhythm to Stop (4, 3, 2, 1, Stop), and then have a break of silence where people change positions in the circle. In the silence you leave your instrument on or by your chair and move to a new place before starting the rhythm again. *Note*: this is not a competitive exercise – don't remove chairs!

We play this game for fun, and also sometimes to examine different cultural perspectives, recognizing that each time we move position we see, hear and feel things differently. In this form of the game when we change position, we ask people to reflect on how we might view a local issue through the lens of different cultures with respect and understanding.

## Using cultural symbols

Music therapist Jessica Shaller-Gerweck, MM, MT-BC, QMHP-C, utilized culturally meaningful symbology in her drumming and grief work with youth. The 'Strength of a Bear' and 'Wisdom of an Owl' chants came out of working with American Indian (AI) and Alaskan Native (AN) youth, ages 14–17, participating in a music therapy treatment group at a behavioural health clinic.

> 'Got the strength of a bear inside me, nothings gonna get in my way,
> Got the freedom of an eagle rising, life goes on goes on today.'
> 'Got the wisdom of an owl inside me, nothings gonna get in my way,
> Got the purpose of a wolf arising, life goes on goes on today.'

Many of the AI/AN youth in the group had experienced significant grief and loss events that profoundly impacted them, such as the death of a parent, sibling or friend. Losing a loved one to death by suicide was a common experience shared by the group members. 'Strength of a Bear' and 'Wisdom of an Owl' were written based on the importance and symbolism of Power Animals in the AI/AN culture. The chants were designed to be a culturally relevant source of empowerment and a reflection of hope. The lyrics were sung in conjunction with a heartbeat or a simple, steady beat so that the group members could join in participating as they were comfortable.

Group members were offered non-traditional drums to play along with the music therapist. Instruments commonly used in AI/AN rituals, such as the hand drum and Gathering Drum, were not used as group members represented various AI/AN tribes with different rules related to drumming with others. Also, the music therapist found it important to clearly separate the music experience in group therapy from other music ritual experiences of the AI/AN community, as a means of communicating respect and promoting comfort for group members.

This culturally sensitive approach was chosen following a group discussion about the role of music in the lives of the group members, their music experiences, and their feelings about the use of instruments they associated with AI/AN rituals by non-Native individuals in group drumming. The chants were presented in a fill-in-the-blank format so that each group member could select their own Power Animal and its related characteristic that they desired to embody. The chants were revisited at various times over the course of group treatment to promote full integration of the experience into the minds and bodies of the participants so they would be able to play and sing this chant in the future as needed. These chants were successfully applied to child and adolescent music therapy bereavement groups with an explanation of the term 'Power Animal' and its use as a metaphor. In this context, paddle drums and hand drums were available for use in addition to drums such as the djembe.[6]

## ADDITIONAL ADVICE

In work with Indigenous groups it is easy to unknowingly replicate patterns of cultural domination, particularly given the power dynamic inherent in leading or facilitating others through a new experience or process. As much as possible reduce your profile and refer to participants for their knowledge and leadership.

In his book, *Sand Talk* (2019),[7] Tyson Yunkaporta talks with Aboriginal elder Doris Shillingsworth on the way to work with Indigenous peoples. She has seen countless western-based interventions come and go, in her community, most of which are delivered from a patronising attitude of superiority. In her, and many other Aboriginal people's, experience, these programs come in with their own agenda and intention and fail to respect or connect to local people and their knowledge, which deems them bound to fail. Doris and Tyson recommend a new protocol of 'Respect, Connect, Reflect and then Direct' for those wishing to work alongside their people:

- Respect – the values, rules and boundaries of the people

- Connect – forge strong relationships and means of exchange that are equal for all

---

6   Recordings available at https://carolynkoebel.bandcamp.com/track/strength-of-a-bear.
7   Yunkaporta, T. (2019) *Sand Talk*. Melbourne: Text Publishing.

- Reflect – thinking as part of the group and a collective knowledge; available as your guide for action
- Direct – acting on the knowledge through shared negotiation.

Finally, *don't forget to laugh* and don't take yourself too seriously! Humour – particularly self-depreciating humour is a great way to forge links with Indigenous people of all ages and backgrounds and is probably the quickest way of putting people at ease and building trust.

## AUTHOR'S BIOGRAPHY
### Simon Faulkner, BSocSc (Psychology & Addiction) MCouns.

Simon has worked closely with Aboriginal and First Nations communities in Australia, New Zealand, Canada and the USA. In Australia, Simon's original program 'DRUMBEAT®' was recognized as one of only two programs making a positive impact on youth suicide in Aboriginal communities in the Kimberley region of Australia. Simon continues to train many indigenous health and education workers in the Rhythm2Recovery model, including teachers from the British Columbia Indigenous Education Unit, Counsellors from Yorgum Aboriginal Counselling Service and workers from the Kimberley Aboriginal Drug and Alcohol and Mental Health Service.

>Email: simon@rhythm2recovery.com
>www.rhythm2recovery.com
>Facebook: www.facebook.com/rhythm2recovery

## RECOMMENDED READING

Coates, K.S. (2004) *A Global History of Indigenous Peoples – Struggle and Survival.* London: Palgrave Macmillan.

Kenny, C. (2006) *Music and Life in the Field of Play: An Anthology.* Gilsum, NH: Barcelona Publishers.

Yunkaporta, T. (2019) *Sand Talk.* Melbourne: Text Publishing

# Wellness and Personal Growth

CHRISTINE STEVENS

## OVERVIEW

Group drumming for wellness and personal growth highlights the integration of spirituality and science. Wellness may be defined as the active pursuit of health; being of sound mind, body, and spirit. Since ancient times, drum circles were used for ceremony, healing, tribal gathering and rites of passage. We probably all hold some image of drumming around a fire buried in our DNA. From a scientific perspective, drum circles incorporate proven health strategies, including exercise, camaraderie and support, expression, spirituality, and creative music-making.

Much of my work in the wellness sector has been based on the HealthRHYTHMS® group drumming program. When asked why drumming is good for wellness, we found a composite response that includes seven evidence-based components: exercise, group support, camaraderie, self-expression, spirituality, visualization and music-making. This research, that was done with adults with no previous drumming experience, showed that this approach, which included specific activities such as breathing, laughing, guided imagery drumming, rhythmic naming, ice-breakers, rhythm games, and a wellness exercise, helped to modulate the immune system in a positive direction, and reduced the biological markers of stress.[1]

Drumming for wellness differs from shamanism and sound therapy by incorporating the active engagement of people playing together. In 2005, I created 'The Healing Drum Kit', which includes 24 rhythms. Ten years later, I partnered with Lakota elder, Uncle Manny Sandoval, to create a protocol and training program that combines the improvisational nature of drum circles with these healing rhythms. Three main components of this wellness approach included in 'The Healing Drum Learning Program' include intention, posture and expression – see Figure 26.1.

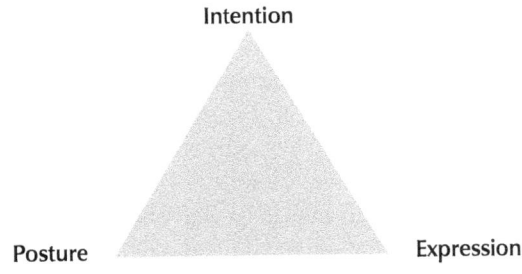

*Figure 26.1: Components of healing rhythms*

## POSITIVE OUTCOMES
### Mind

Drumming can be considered a form of active meditation. Early studies in music therapy drumming with Alzheimer's patients at the Veterans Affairs Hospital in Lawrence, Kansas by Clair and colleagues[2] showed that clients had more positive experiences in drumming compared to sing-along activities. Over time, they learned more complex rhythms and their level of entrainment improved, demonstrating that rhythm is processed in the lower and motor areas of the brain, and the mind-benefits of drumming are maintained regardless of higher cerebral neural damage that is common in stroke, Parkinson's disease and organic brain disease (OBD).

Drumming is a very accessible tool for music participation and self-expression; it has been found to improve social-emotional skills in schools

---

1  Bittman, B., Bruhn, K.T., Stevens, C., Westengard, J. & Umbach, P.O. (2003) 'Recreational music-making: A cost-effective group interdisciplinary strategy for reducing burnout and improving mood states in long-term care workers.' *Advances in Mind-Body Medicine 19*, 3–4, 4–15.
2  Clair, A., Bernstein, B. & Johnson, G. (1995) 'Rhythm playing characteristics in persons with severe dementia including those with probable Alzheimer's type.' *Journal of Music Therapy 32*, 113–131.

and also improve mental health with both patients and their care-givers.[3] In the wellness sector, there is wide scientific support for the benefits of meditation in its many forms.[4] Drumming is a mindfulness tool that allows people to breathe more rhythmically and in a more relaxed way. It is also beneficial because it engages the experiencing network, overriding the default neural network of self-absorbed and ruminating thoughts.[5] According to simultaneous state theory, the mind cannot think about problems or self-critical thoughts when engaged in drumming.

## Body

Drumming involves exercise. You might say drumming is a great workout, across multiple dimensions, as is shown in the work of the fitness program, 'Drums Alive'.[6] It promotes coordination, with research showing that rhythm primes the motor system and supports coordination of gait and other muscle activities.[7] That is why we unconsciously tap our feet to the beat. Highlighted in Dr Michael Thaut's book, *Rhythm, Music and the Brain*, is the discovery of neural circuits that connect auditory rhythmic inputs with motor coordination of the feet and arms in a coordinated audio-motor synergy.

Drumming has been shown to reduce blood pressure and benefit cardio-vascular health, particularly when coupled with raised arm lifts.[8] In fact, there are a wide range of stretching and coordination exercises that can be incorporated with simple drumming rhythms. Stimulating music produces increases in cardiovascular measures, whereas relaxing music produces the reverse. These effects are primarily mediated by tempo: slow drumming is associated with a decrease in heart-rate, respiration and blood pressure, and faster play with increases in these measures. Researchers have found that

---

3   Ho, P., Tsao, J.C.I. & Zeltzer, L.K. (2011) 'The impact of group drumming on the social-emotional behavior of low-income children.' *Journal of Evidence-Based Complementary & Alternative Medicine*. https://doi.org/10.1093/ecam/neq072
    Ascenso, S., Perkins, R., Atkins, L., Fancourt, D. & Williamon, A. (2018) 'Promoting well-being through group drumming with mental health service users and their carers.' *International Journal of Qualitative Studies on Health and Well-Being 13*, 1. https://doi.org/10.1080/17482631.2018.1484219
4   Goyal, M., Singh, S., Sibinga, E.M.S. Gould, N.F. et al. (2014) 'Meditation programs for psychological stress and well-being: A systematic review and meta-analysis.' *JAMA Internal Medicine 174*, 3, 357–368.
5   Buckner, R.L., DiNicola, L.M. (2019) 'The brain's default network: Updated anatomy, physiology and evolving insights.' *Nature Reviews Neuroscience 20*, 593–608.
6   www.drums-alive.com.
7   Thaut, M.H. (2005) *Rhythm, Music, and the Brain*. New York: Taylor & Francis.
8   Smith, C., Viljoen, T. & McGeachie, L. (2014) 'African drumming: A holistic approach to reducing stress and improving health.' *Journal of Cardiovascular Medicine 15*, 441–446.

working out to a beat requires 15 per cent less effort, due to the presence of an auditory cue for our movement. It seems that the body loves to be in rhythm and drumming helps, both in listening and playing to the beat.[9]

Additionally, several studies have shown immune system benefits to group drumming.[10] We have all witnessed the devastating impact of poor immune system health with the arrival of the COVID-19 virus, particularly for our elderly citizens. I have personally seen great improvements in clinical cases with non-ambulatory clients who can play the drum in a wheelchair and get the combined benefits of exercise, stress-reduction and joy.

## Spirit

From spiritual uplift to faith-based communities, drumming brings out the transcendent. As ethnomusicologist and Grateful Dead drummer Mickey Hart says, 'when we drum together, we create sacred space'.[11] For thousands of year cultures across the world have used drumming as a way to transcend the everyday and reach alternative states of consciousness. Playing music with others releases the neurotransmitter dopamine in the reward centres of the brain, and alters our brainwaves, inducing states of calm and awareness and providing an alternative approach to accessing a higher power.[12]

Beyond the history of thousands of years of shamans riding on their drums to the upper and lower worlds, there is also strong evidence of the impact of drumming on people's mood. A study by Bittman found that drumming significantly improved the mood states of long-term care workers.[13] Using validated measures, his team found a significant decrease in depression and anxiety even when subjects had no drumming or music experience. More recently, Fancourt and her team of researchers in the United Kingdom tested mental health in consumers using a weekly drum

---

9  Karageorghis, C., Jones, L.,& Stuart, D. (2008) 'Psychological effects of music tempi during exercise.' *International Journal of Sports Medicine 29*, 613–619.
Karageorghis, C., Mouzourides, D., Priest, D-L., Sasso, T., Morrish, D. & Walley, C. (2009) 'Psychophysical and ergogenic effects of synchronous music during treadmill walking.' *Journal of Sport & Exercise Psychology 31*, 18–36.
10  Bittman, B.B., Berk, L.S., Felten D.L., Westengard. J. & Somonton, O.C. (2001) 'Composite effects of group drumming music therapy on modulation of neuroendocrine-immune parameters in normal subjects.' *Alternative Therapy 7*, 38–47.
Fancourt, D., Perkins, R., Ascenso, S., Carvalho, L.A., Steptoe, A. & Williamon, A. (2016) 'Effects of group drumming interventions on anxiety, depression, social resilience and inflammatory immune response among mental health service users.' *PLoS ONE 11*, 3.
11  Personal communication with Mickey Hart, Iraq project (2007).
12  Winkelman, M. (2003) 'Complementary therapy for addiction: "Drumming out drugs".' *American Journal of Public Health 93*, 4, 647–651.
13  Bittman, B., Bruhn, K.T., Stevens, C., Westengard, J. & Umbach, P.O. (2003) 'Recreational music-making: A cost-effective group interdisciplinary strategy for reducing burnout and improving mood states in long-term care workers.' *Advances in Mind-Body Medicine 19*, 3–4, 4–15.

circle. They found a significant decrease in depression and anxiety, and significant improvement in mental wellbeing within just the first six weeks. Furthermore, the results were maintained three months after the study, demonstrating a sustained effect.[14]

Music is used to regulate mood and arousal in everyday life and to promote physical and psychological health. Even just one drum circle may create mood-enhancing results. In a study using a single 45-minute wellness drumming session with university students, researchers found statistically significant mood improvements in all affect variables.[15]

## Community

Science has shown that a sense of belonging is healthy. From teambuilding programs in the workplace to peace-building in war zones, drumming builds relationships across language, race and ethnicity. Research supports the power of synchronized rhythm as a method of building relationships. Synchronized activities such as drumming have long been known to foster feelings of social connection, specifically inter-personal trust and bonding.[16] Dr. Laurel Trainer tested 14-month-old infants at her child development laboratory in Canada to see the effect of bouncing in sync versus out-of-sync with a stranger. Remarkably, when infants bounced to the same song as a stranger, they become more kind and compassionate. In contrast, when out of sync, the infants showed no interest in helping the stranger in a post-test.[17]

In a five-day training program for conflict resolution and peace-making in Northern Iraq, we were able to show a 90 per cent improvement in 'sense of community' with 40 subjects speaking three different languages. Former enemies joined together in rhythm and learned to lead drum circles for peace in their respective communities. The project was highlighted in a United Nations publication on music as a global resource.[18]

---

14 Fancourt, D., Perkins, R., Ascenso, S., Carvalho, L.A., Steptoe, A. & Williamon, A. (2016) 'Effects of group drumming interventions on anxiety, depression, social resilience and inflammatory immune response among mental health service users.' *PLoS ONE 11*, 3.
15 Mungus, R. & Silverman, M.J. (2014) 'Immediate effects of group-based wellness drumming on affective states in university students.' *The Arts in Psychotherapy 41*, 3, 287–292.
16 McNeil, D. (1995) *Keeping Together in Time: Dance and Drill in Human History*. Cambridge, MA: Harvard University Press.
17 Cirelli, L.K., Spinelli, C., Nozaradan, S. & Trainor, L.J. (2016) 'Measuring neural entrainment to beat and meter in infants: Effects of music background.' *Frontiers in Neuroscience 10*, 229.
18 Woodman, C. (2015) 'Recapturing Cultural Identity through Drumming, Drum Making and Documentaries: Drums of Humanity.' In B. Hesser & H.N. Heinemann (eds) *Music as a Global Resource: Solutions for Social & Economic Issues, Compendium, 4th Edition*. New York: United Nations Publications.

## SETTING UP FOR SUCCESS

Wellness programs with drumming include three main steps: setting the space; holding the space; and releasing the space. This common arc includes a beginning, middle and end, always reflecting the intention of health and wellbeing.

## Set up

Before the group arrives, set up the circle to support wellness and healing. This might include a colourful cloth in the centre, drums displayed in an artistic fashion, chairs set in a circle with entry points and music playing. Ensure safety for group sharing by requesting that all participants agree to confidentiality. I have found it useful to keep the drums in a separate location and allow participants to choose one after the opening experiences, such as the statement of purpose and introductions.

## Instruments of transformation

There is a range of sounds used in wellness programs. In Angeles Arian's book, *The Four-Fold Way*,[19] she assigns different timbre groups to the directions of the medicine wheel. The east is represented by rattles and shakers with seeds of new beginning. The south is represented by drums – frame and buffalo drums have a softer and more resonant quality. The west is represented by wood sounds and bones – including clapper sticks and claves. The north is represented by metal sounds of singing bowls, gongs, finger cymbals, and temple bells. Ambient instruments such as ocean drum, rain stick, and melodic percussion like the 'HAPI®' drum or tongue drum add texture. A Native American flute, guitar, pan-drums, and voice are complementary instruments for wellness.

Entrainment can begin by starting a simple beat and inviting group participation, or by teaching the group a prescribed healing rhythm as a spring-board to self-expression and improvisation. These healing rhythms are notated in The Healing Drum Learning Program[20] and include rhythms of life, spirit and the world.

---

19  Arrien, A. (1993) *The Four-Fold Way: Walking the Paths of the Warrior, Teacher, Healer, and Visionary.* New York: Harper Collins.
20  Stevens, C. (2018) The Healing Drum Circle Learning Program. Sounds True.

## Closing
Ending the circle by asking each participant to share one word about their experience gives an opportunity for closure and an insight into how people have received and potentially transformed during the program. Words of joy, love, healing, and freedom are common and have little to do with drumming and everything to do with the heart and their journey of personal growth.

## COMMON CHALLENGES AND HOW TO MINIMIZE THEM
The goal of this work mandates a different approach – I rarely start with a traditional 'Drum Call'[21], especially when the group is not self-selecting. The average person may be afraid of music-making, often bringing a personal history of performance anxiety and negative experiences with music lessons. I recommend beginning by welcoming people, stating the purpose of the group, inviting breathing and grounding, connecting to the inner heartbeat, and taking time for a demonstration of how to hold and play the drum, while reminding the group that it's really not about drumming. The facilitator calls the group's attention to others in the group and the sharing and community present.

I define the drum circle as a collective container for individual expression. It's important to avoid loud drumming that can cause ear damage or give rise to anxiety. You may wish to download a decibel sound level reading 'app' to track the volume in order to ensure healthy sound levels. In wellness programs, you want to hold space for the group's wisdom rather than trying to fix anyone. Entrainment is the goal, rather than fancy facilitation, as less is more. Be careful not to put people on the spot, which can cause stress. Add vocals with chants, play a flute or soothing guitar or other complementary melodic instruments to add beauty. But focus most on a positive rhythmic connection.

## PRACTICAL APPLICATIONS OF THE DRUM CIRCLE
This is a sample template; a progressive series of steps.

## Welcome
Start by stating the intention and goal of the program and putting people at ease with the idea of drumming, not a performance.

---

21  Hull, A. (2007) *Drum Circle Facilitation: Building Community through Rhythm*. Santa Cruz, CA: Village Music Circles, p.68.

## Body

Proceed with a *wellness exercise* such as stretching, breathing, mindfulness or laughter. Even stretching your hands and arms before drumming while breathing to a beat is helpful as a beginning. One example would be to play a heartbeat rhythm at medium tempo using a low-pitched buffalo drum, such as the 'Bahia' buffalo drum. Invite the group: 'If you choose, close your eyes and connect to your heartbeat – the inner drum... Feel the pulse of life beating in you and know that rhythm is your birthright. When you're ready you can close by opening your eyes and coming back into the circle.' Always close by asking if anyone wants to share about their experience. A good question is: 'Does anyone have any comments?'

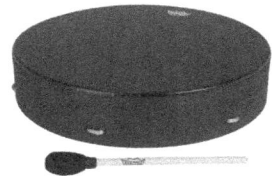

## Community

A good ice-breaker that builds community is playing shakers all together and simply follow the leader. Make sure to explain that you can drop the shaker or make a mistake and no one will notice. With everyone playing shakers, it builds a sense of unity, and equanimity, while continuing to warm up the body within the parameters of what each person is comfortable doing.

Once you pass out the drums, it's important to demonstrate the basics of playing safely. Guiding participants in how to hold their drums, play a sound with hand or mallet, and encouraging them to try out different drums, provides a sense of empowerment. Using 'call and response', the group begins to be comfortable playing.[22]

## Spirit

To create entrainment, you can use a play-along audio track, start a beat yourself or ask someone in the group to begin a rhythm. To connect with emotional expression, I often introduce a healing rhythm (see links below). I recommend starting by setting the intention and letting the group

---

[22] Here is a video tutorial 'How to lead call and response for drum circles': https://youtu.be/p5ZrQZ9-M6w.

contemplate their connection to the meaning of the rhythm. Invite people to put their hands on their hearts and then thank their drums by placing an open sweeping hand on the drum, emulating the air sound. Demonstrate the rhythm and invite the group to join you. Keep the beat going for a minimum of four minutes to create entrainment and playing in unison. Once the entrainment moment has occurred, invite the group to 'add more of yourself to the beat'.

Recommended healing rhythms

- Release – https://youtu.be/UZHM6iWzliM
- Transformation – https://youtu.be/mSJ-FReAYc8
- Laughter – https://youtu.be/3UhCxYbb8vQ

## Guided imagery drumming

Invite the group to close their eyes while quietly tapping on the drum with the facilitator guiding their journey. Add nature sounds by using an 'app' such as 'Relax Melodies' or 'My Noise', which feature ocean waves, crickets at night or a dawn choir of birds.

### Sample script

Begin by taking some slow deep breaths. As the drum beat begins, imagine someone comes to inform you that you have the day off. All work is complete. There are no projects that need completion. All tasks have been taken off your plate. Especially the ones you find more stressful. (pause)

Imagine comfortably walking on a path in nature at a comfortable pace – step by step, while feeling in rhythm with your surroundings. Notice the sounds around you, the sun on your face, the images, welcoming you. It may be a captivating flower or the shimmering light on water? Put that feeling into your drum. (pause)

As the light gradually begins to fade, begin the peaceful journey back, feeling a sense of relaxation and renewal. Know you can always return to this image. Allow the music to come to a natural ending like a setting sun. When you're ready, slowly open your eyes.

## Closing

Close the group with a one-word share, with each participant speaking of, or drumming, what they are taking with them from the experience.

Invite the group to put down their drums or return them to the centre. If someone has a negative experience, check in with them at the end of the program, and ensure that ongoing support is available if required.

## ADDITIONAL ADVICE

This work blends well with chanting and singing. I've recorded a short library of recommended chants, available to listen to at https://ubdrumcircles.com/product/drumming-up-spirit-play-along-cd. The library includes: 'Where I Drum is Holy'; 'Soul of the Drum'; 'Good Where We've Been'; 'Drum Call'; and others.

Finally, this approach integrates metaphors that extend drumming into life. Concepts such as 'finding your groove', 'getting in sync with others', and 'being in tune' are important components. Consider setting a wellness theme for the drum circle and at the end of a rhythm experience such as connecting to the heart, inspiring your dreams, playfulness, releasing grief, etc., always ask, 'How does this experience apply to life?'

## AUTHOR'S BIOGRAPHY
## Christine Stevens, MSW, MA, MT-BC

Christine is the author of the books, *Music Medicine, The Healing Drum Kit* and *The Art and Heart of Drum Circles*. She is the founder of UpBeat Drum Circles, and has appeared on NBC, PBS, KTLA, Discovery Health, Living Better TV, and is a faculty for The Shift Network. Christine has trained facilitators from more than 25 countries including Iraq, China, Hong Kong, Japan and Europe. Christine has worked with Fortune 500 companies, survivors of Katrina, students at Ground Zero and, most recently, led the first drum circle training in a war zone in northern Iraq. She is the host of Global Rhythm Sangha Online and teaches a variety of online training programs, including Awaken Your Rhythm which has served hundreds of people from over 35 countries.

>www.ubdrumcircles.com
>Online facilitation training: https://upbeat.teachable.com/p/healing-drum

## RECOMMENDED READING

Arrien, A. (2013) *The Four-Fold Way: Walking the Paths of the Warrior, Teacher, Healer & Visionary.* New York: Harper Collins.
Some, M. (1997) *Ritual: Power, Healing and Community.* Harmondsworth: Penguin.

# Corporate Groups

## JOHN HAGEDORN

### OVERVIEW

Working as a drum circle facilitator (DCF) for corporate populations can be rewarding, both professionally and financially. Your participants are mostly motivated adults who are looking for novel experiences in professional development, and find drum circles entertaining and enjoyable. Work at the corporate level requires experience and professionalism, however, and a background working in a corporate environment can be very helpful.

Drum circles for corporate populations will generally fall into one of three different settings.

### Corporate entertainment

Companies often have events such as annual dinners, family days, or conferences where drum circles can be brought in as a part of the festivities. The main objective here is for everyone to have a good time, and any experienced DCF can work at this level.

## Teambuilding

Because of the many similarities between bringing a team and bringing a drum circle to performance level, drum circles can be used as an activity (among others) in an extended teambuilding program (e.g., over a weekend) or as a separate short program (2–4 hours). Experienced DCFs can work at this level if they are able to speak to the metaphors and provide participants with takeaways that match the company's teambuilding objectives.

## Organizational development

Drum circles and other rhythm interventions (games) can be used as tools within training programs designed to meet specific corporate learning objectives. Work at this level, however, requires experienced DCFs to have additional skills in training, debriefing, program design, content delivery, proposal writing, etc.

## POSITIVE OUTCOMES

Various positive outcomes in corporate drum circles depend on the setting and the objectives.

## Fun, enjoyment and entertainment

One of the most liberating aspects of running drum circles for corporate populations is that DCFs make no demands and have no expectations. For as long as the drum circle is running, participants are free from meeting their KPIs (Key Performance Indicators) and can express themselves as freely they like.

## Pre-conference synchronizing and post-lunch energizing

Nothing synchronizes a group faster than rhythm. In his book, *Musicophilia*, Oliver Sachs[1] writes:

> Rhythm turns listeners into participants, makes listening active and motoric, and synchronizes the brains and minds (and, since emotion is always intertwined with music, the 'hearts') of all who participate. It is very difficult to remain detached, to resist being drawn into the rhythm of chanting or dancing.

---

1  Sachs, O. (2008) *Musicophilia: Tales of Music and the Brain.* London: Picador.

This is precisely why running a drum circle before a conference or a board meeting can be the perfect activity for developing like-mindedness among participants and beginning their event with their brainwaves aligned.

## Group development

In 1965, American psychological researcher Bruce Tuckman[2] proposed a four-stage model for how groups form, grow and deliver results. These four stages – forming, storming, norming and performing – are correlated with Arthur Hull's four roles for the DCF – dictator, director, facilitator and orchestrator – guiding a group of drum circle participants from individual to orchestrational consciousness. Hull calls this 'running the MAP'.

DCFs and other types of group facilitators can move their groups through the developmental process more quickly if they are aware of the roles they need to assume and the appropriate interventions they need to apply at each stage. This is illustrated in what I have called the *Tuckman/Hull Paradigm* (Figure 27.1).

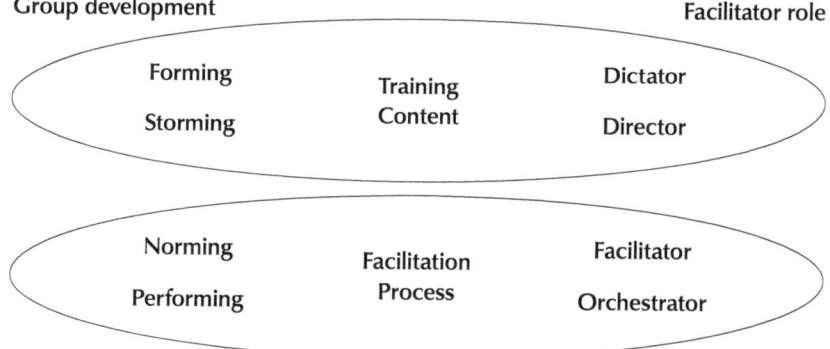

*Figure 27.1: The Tuckman/Hull paradigm*

The group development process and accompanying roles are similar, whether a DCF is leading a drum circle or a team leader is breaking in a new work group. This is why the drum circle *works so very well* as a teambuilding exercise.

During the '*forming*' stage, the DCF assumes the '*dictator*' role. Here, the DCF develops a relationship with the group and helps them to develop relationships with each other. By modelling drum circle body language and

---

2   Tuckman, B.W. (1965) 'Developmental sequence in small groups.' *Psychological Bulletin 63*, 6, 384–399.

helping the participants to *entrain*, they move towards *group consciousness* and begin to develop clarity on the objective.

Participants enter the *'storming'* stage as they learn what it's like to work together as a group. The DCF assumes the *'director'* role and 'directs' their attention to the different parts and sections of the circle. By tasking the group and promoting 'small successes', the DCF develops group bonding more quickly and moves them beyond the feelings of fear, suspicion and anxiety that can potentially arise at this stage.

These first two stages are *training* stages for the DCF as they provide the *content* necessary for participants to perform tasks correctly and maintain group etiquette. However, since the DCF's main objective is to move the group towards performing as quickly as possible, only as little time as necessary should be spent as *dictator* and *director*.

As the group enters the *'norming'* stage, they have grasped what they need to do to progress. The DCF, now a *facilitator*, pays less attention to content and more to *process*. They are there to monitor the group's performance, gently correct any remaining inaccuracies, and continue to task the group at increasingly higher levels. At this stage, the group often realizes that their collective potential is greater than they had thought, and they begin to work as one.

Now that the group has reached the *'performing'* stage, the DCF's role becomes that of an *'orchestrator'*, or conductor. At this stage, the DCF could probably leave the group to progress on their own. The group, however, welcomes the presence of the orchestrator because they provide them with further challenges in 'music-making' that they know they can achieve, behaving in a similar way to a good leader.

Sometimes there may be limitations preventing the group from reaching full orchestration, but that can be expected. The group's playing abilities and motivational levels, the amount of time allowed, and even the physical environment can all have an impact. Keep in mind, however, that the DCF's goal is to bring the group to its fullest potential, and sometimes that may mean never going beyond *director*.

Behind all of this is the fundamental facilitation principle which states that if you know your group, then you will recognize your role and apply the interventions that you need to advance them to the next level. While this is important to know as a DCF in general, it is *critical* for DCFs who wish to work at the corporate level. A DCF's awareness of group development is their foundation for running successful corporate programs.

## Listening and innovation

Musicologist Bruno Nettl[3] defines *beat perception* as 'a fundamental aspect of music cognition, which frequently elicits synchronised rhythmic movement in the form of tapping, swaying, head bobbing, or dancing. Moving rhythmically to a musical beat is observed in every human culture, making it one of the few true universals of human music'. Beat perception in a drum circle is expressed as participants listen, *entrain* and continue to play.

The DCF can encourage participants to be *innovative*. Once they have learned how to continue playing together, they can break away from playing the same beats all the time by adding extra notes, adding accents, and dialoguing with other drummers. Innovation is the catalyst that raises the musicality of the group and moves them closer to full orchestration.

## Stress management and corporate wellness

Research conducted by Daisy Fancourt and colleagues[4] at the Centre for Performance Science, Royal College of Music, in London is just one of many exploring the positive effects of group drumming on stress, anxiety, and depression. Her research demonstrates *again* that regular intervals of group drumming provides numerous psychological benefits and also strengthens the auto-immune system.

Meanwhile, the market for corporate wellness programs is exploding. According to RAND Health,[5] more than 80 per cent of companies in the US (50+ employees) are now offering some kind of wellness benefit. Companies in the United Kingdom are also catching on – almost half are currently offering wellness schemes.

DCFs around the world have introduced group drumming in companies like Apple, Google, Citibank and Siemens. In addition to running wellness circles, they have helped these companies set up their own 'drum clubs', which meet regularly to continue their stress-busting activities. Experienced DCFs can break into the corporate wellness market easily, but knowing the research and being able to explain exactly *how*

---

3  Nettl, B., Wallin, N.L., Merker, B. & Brown, S. (2000) 'An Ethnomusicologist Contemplates Universals in Music. Sound and Musical Culture.' In S. Brown, B. Merker & N.L. Wallin (eds) *The Origins of Music*, pp. 463-472. Cambridge, MA: MIT Press.
4  Fancourt, D., Perkins, R., Ascenso, S., Carvalho, L.A., Steptoe, A. & Williamon, A. (2016) 'Effects of group drumming interventions on anxiety, depression, social resilience and inflammatory immune response among mental health service users.' *PLoS ONE 11*, 3.
5  Mattke, S., Liu, H., Caloyeras, J.P., Huang, C., Van Busum, K., Khodyakov, D. & Shier, V. (2013) *Workplace Wellness Programs Study.* RAND Health. Sponsored by the U.S. Department of Labor and the U.S. Department of Health and Human Services.

group drumming works to relieve stress is a significant benefit. Here is some information you can reference to get you started:

- *Corporate Employee Wellness Impact.* Wachi *et al.* (2017) https://remo.com/experience/post/corporate-employee-wellness-impact
- *The Healing Power of the Drum.* Friedman (n.d.) https://healthy.net/2002/08/12/the-healing-power-of-the-drum-part-i-2
- *Composite Effects of Group Drumming Music Therapy on Modulation of Neuroendocrine-Immune Parameters in Normal Subjects.* Bittman *et al.* (2001) https://www.ncbi.nlm.nih.gov/pubmed/11191041
- *Drum Circles Bring Resilience, Wellness, and Creativity to the Workplace.* Dolle (2015) https://dollecommunicationsblog.wordpress.com/2015/05/06/drum circles-aid-workplace-productivity-employee-engagement-and-inclusion

## Targeted learning objectives

Human resource departments (HR) are always on the lookout for innovative approaches to corporate learning. Their training and development programs run throughout the calendar year, targeting objectives such as inter-personal communications, creative thinking, diversity and inclusion, leadership, and many others that lend themselves nicely to drum circles, drum circle games and other rhythm interventions.

Corporate work at this level, however, requires extensive knowledge in organizational development. Facilitators working at this level are using rhythm activities as one of many different training tools in their repertoire, and these activities are carefully chosen and administered to meet the learning objectives established by HR prior to the program.

## SETTING UP FOR SUCCESS

Work at the corporate level is desirable because that is where the money is. Corporations will pay top dollar for top performers that can deliver a return on their investment and assist them in achieving their objectives. In other words, corporations have high expectations.

Delivering at the corporate level requires a high level of DCF experience. They expect to get what they pay for, and they know quality (or the lack of it) when they see it. It pays to be able to sit down with the people who are hiring you and to speak their language (ROI (Return on Investment)? KPI (Key Performance Indicators)? SOP (Standard Operating Procedure)?).

It looks good to show up with nice equipment and a qualified team with matching T-shirts.

At the corporate level, feedback matters. When your event is finished, participants report back to HR and evaluate their experience. Great feedback will get you another gig and will earn you valuable references (HR departments among various companies are networked like a spider web). Negative feedback, however, will spoil it for you *and* for future DCFs who approach that company with their proposals. ('Oh, drum circles? No, thanks. We've tried that.') See the Appendices for feedback templates.

As Arthur Hull says, 'Don't beta test on your corporate clients.'[6]

## COMMON CHALLENGES AND HOW TO MINIMIZE THEM
### Attitudes and behaviours

If you've ever done a circle for a bunch of 14-year-olds, you know that some of them will look at you funny ('Why do we have to do this?') and others will use your Boomwhackers™ as swords. It's sometimes not a lot different in the corporate world. In some places, drum circles are uncommon and participants may be unfamiliar with what you are attempting to achieve. As a result, they may be reluctant to participate and they will show it. Behaviour can also be a problem. A drum circle at the end of a corporate dinner with a bunch of executives loaded on alcohol will be difficult to control.

Getting everyone engaged and keeping everyone engaged is one solution. When you spot that lady from the finance department tapping on a woodblock with little enthusiasm, offer her a big drum. When a bunch of tipsy engineers start clowning with your Sound-Shapes™ in the back row, sculpt them out and have them do a stand-up performance. As the facilitator in a corporate circle, your relationship with the group *matters*, a lot.

---

6   Personal communication with Arthur Hull, VMC drum circle training (2005).

## Noise

Half of the corporate events you facilitate will be at your client's office; half of them will be in a hotel or a resort. If you're lucky, you may get a gig where the amount of noise you're going to make does not matter. Wherever they plan to have you, warn them in advance that the drum circle will be noisy. Ask if you can be in a room or in a location far from everyone else. Tell the hotel staff *days before* your gig that you may be a disturbance to others in nearby function rooms. I once warned the staff of a downtown hotel how much noise I'd be making with a 50-person circle, and they put us outside on the tennis court. We were far from the hotel function rooms, but we certainly attracted curious looks from the surrounding office buildings.

## Pricing

How much do you charge for a corporate drum circle? Not unlike *any* other drum circle, there are lots of variables. How many participants? How much time allotted? How far out of town? How much advance planning and program design required? How many team members to pay? Set yourself a baseline fee that you will not go below (for corporate work, I never go below US$500.00 for a two-hour program). Before you write your proposal or send your quotation, see if you can find out their budget. If their budget is higher than your baseline, you're in the money. If not, you've got to negotiate or redesign their package ('Well, at that price, I can bring fifty Boomwhackers™ for an hour, but not fifty drums for four hours'). There's a fine balance between not pricing too low, so your work seems cheap and not pricing too high, so your less experienced competition can undercut you.

## PRACTICAL APPLICATIONS OF THE DRUM CIRCLE
### Personality profiling

Corporate trainers use many different platforms for personality profiling (DOVE, DISC, MBTI, etc.) The objective behind each, however, is that if you know your own type and you can recognize the types of others, you will be able to make predictions and adaptations necessary for successful communication and relationship management. While any of these platforms can be used in a corporate rhythm intervention, DISC is the easiest for participants to understand, and the easiest for facilitators to work with.

## A brief history

Personality profiling into four different types has a long history[7] dating back to 400 BC, when Hippocrates defined four temperaments (choleric, sanguine, phlegmatic and melancholic) based on the proportions of a person's bodily 'humours', or fluids, and their influence on a person's behaviour and emotions. Centuries later, in 1921, Carl Jung re-examined the 'four temperaments' and modernized them, based on how people think and process information. His four styles were: thinking, feeling, sensation and intuition, which were later adapted into the Myers-Briggs Type Indicator (MBTI) in 1944.

With the foundation for personality profiling firmly laid, in 1928 William Moulton Marston (PhD, American University) published *Emotions of Normal People*,[8] in which he defined four predictable personality traits (Dominance, Influence, Steadiness, and Compliance) that people act out in their everyday lives. DISC profiling finally reached its present state in 1940 when industrial psychologist Walter Clarke took Marston's theory and developed the DISC personality profile that is still in use today.

Under the DISC profiling platform, people display these four different traits based on their outlook on their environment and the amount of control they have over it:[9]

- *Dominance*: To the point, decisive, and bottom-line oriented. These people tend to be independent and results driven. They are strong-willed people who enjoy challenges, taking action and achieving immediate results.

- *Influence*: Optimistic and outgoing. These people tend to be highly social and outgoing. They prefer participating in teams, sharing thoughts, and entertaining and energizing others.

- *Steadiness*: Empathetic and cooperative. These people tend to be team players and are supportive and helpful to others. They prefer being behind the scene, while working in consistent and predictable ways. They are often good listeners and avoid change and conflict.

- *Conscientiousness*: Concerned, cautious and correct. These people are often focused on details and quality. They plan ahead, constantly check for accuracy, and want to know 'how' and 'why'.

---

7   People Keys, Inc. (2020) *DISC History – Where Did DICS Come From?* https://discinsights.com/disc-history (accessed 8 August 2020).
8   Marston, W.M. (1928) *Emotions of Normal People*. New York: Taylor & Francis.
9   Center for Internal Change (2019) *DISC Begins with a Theory…* https://internalchange.com/what-is-disc (accessed 8 August 2020).

The community drum circle offers many metaphors for teaching and reinforcing learning in a corporate program that includes DISC profiling (or any other profiling platform). Here are two activities.

DRUM SELECTION
After the facilitator has taught the DISC profile and everyone has determined their type (without telling anyone else!), participants are invited to sit in a pre-set drum circle with one chair for each participant and a specific instrument on each chair. A pre-set drum circle usually has half drums and half percussion, usually placed on alternating chairs with the largest bass drums evenly spaced around the centre of the circle.

It would not be unusual to expect that the Dominant/Influencing types would gravitate towards the larger, more 'dominant' bass drums and larger hand drums while the Steady/Conscientious types would go for the smaller hand drums and percussion.

The DCF runs the circle according to the MAP (as explained on page 234) until everyone is synchronized. At this point, an interesting debrief can be run to help reinforce the DISC concepts. Examples of debriefing questions are:

Discussion with the group:

- What did you notice about who selected which instrument? Could there be a relationship between their personality type and their selection? Explain.
- What did you notice about individual playing styles? Is there a possible relationship between their playing style and personality type as well? Explain.

To the individual players:

- Why did you choose that particular instrument? Is there a relationship between your personality type and your choice? Explain.
- What did you notice about X-individual's playing style? Based on your observation of their playing style and their instrument choice, which personality type would you guess for them? Explain.

PLAY THE TYPE
Again, the DCF runs the circle according to the MAP (as explained on page 234) until everyone is synchronized. Using 'stop cuts' and 'calls to groove',

the facilitator calls out a personality type and the group is expected to play their instruments according to how they interpret that type's behaviour.

For example, during the groove, the DCF indicates an attention call (finger in the air) then stop cuts the group and says, 'Play like a DOMINANT! One-two-let's-all-play!' The group then changes their playing style to how they imagine a Dominant type would drum. This can continue for each type. The DCF can then begin playing around with this using drum circle techniques (e.g., half the group plays Influencing, half plays Conscientious; individuals or small sections sculpted out to 'solo'; switchbacks from Conscientious to Steady, etc.).

It would not be unusual to expect, for example, that:

- *Dominants* would play loudly and perhaps attempt to change the tempo
- *Influencers* would also play loudly and throw in crazy fills to draw attention to themselves
- *Steadies* would do their best to ensure that everyone played together without disrupting the group
- *Conscientious* would pay attention to their own playing and ensure precision in timing.

To debrief this activity, ask the group:

- When I asked for Dominant/etc., how did you play? Why do you associate that style of playing with the Dominant/etc. personality type?
- What did you notice about the music the group produced when everyone was Dominant/etc.? Did it sound better when everyone was playing the same style, or when everyone played according to their own style? Explain why.

Regardless of the activities you use, two very important concepts that can come out of using the drum circle to teach personality profiling are these:

- It takes all types to make up a successful organization.
- Success can be maximized when an organization leverages its diversity.

## Change management

This energy-charged intervention can be used as a metaphor in the midst of a change management exercise within the organization. Here, participants shift their positions around the circle and pick up the next drum the previous person left behind. This activity lends itself well to training in corporate change management, which every company goes through periodically.

The DCF plays along with the group and gets a groove going and without notice counts off '1, 2, 3, 4, Change!' The group now has eight beats to get up, leave their instrument behind, and move on to the next chair while the facilitator counts, '2, 3, 4, 1, 2, Ready, Play!' Sometimes the change happens immediately; sometimes the players have enough time to adapt to their new instrument and get another groove going. After a number of changes (at least ten), the facilitator does a stop cut and debriefs the group with a simple question: 'What can you tell me about change?' Responses are sometimes brilliant:

- 'Change happens when you least expect it.'
- 'Everybody has to flow with the change.'
- 'Sometimes even after a change, we end up playing the same beat.'
- 'Just when you get comfortable with something new, change happens again.'

All of these responses are written down on flip charts and reviewed after the debrief. These are all great takeaways on how to manage and deal with change as it happens on the job.

## Leadership

The drum circle lends itself nicely to examining leadership when the DCF stands out of the way and encourages participants to jump in. A simple activity would be to run a 45-minute circle, demonstrate simple body language, and allow participants to jump in and try. After five or six have had a chance to lead, debrief them on their feelings and responses.

A more complex leadership activity for groups of 20 or more, *Alpha Leaders*, inspires participants to express what they admire most about leaders from various professions and callings, and to emulate those qualities in their own leadership roles.

Play begins by hanging eight sheets of flip-chart paper along the walls with the name of a recognizable leader written across the top of each.

These could be from various fields such as sports (e.g., Lionel Messi), politics (Angela Merkel), business (Bill Gates), humanists (Mother Theresa), etc. Give each participant a marker, and have them stand nearby the sheets.

Have participants write responses (reasons for their choices) on the sheets to three questions that you ask:

- Which leader inspires you the most?
- Which leader would you trust the most in a crisis?
- Which leader would want for your own boss/teacher/parent?

And finally, for the last question:

- Which leader is the most like you?

Have participants line up in front of the sheet representing their last choice. This will form your performance groups. Each group must now put together a piece (drama, song, dance, etc.) using the information written on the sheet in honour of the leader they have chosen. Allow 20 minutes to put the piece together and run the performances as a talent show.

## ADDITIONAL ADVICE

- Corporate gigs are professional gigs. Your clients need to see that what you provide gives value for money (ROI – Return on Investment). Take your time. Get your DCF chops together before moving into the corporate world.

- Bring a team. You are the facilitator and you've got a job to do. Your job will be a lot easier if you have people to help you set up, manage the circle and pack things away while you schmooze with the clients. *Pay your team members.* Unless you are working pro bono, there is no reason why they should have to.

- As Arthur Hull says, 'Work with what they give you.'[10] Corporate people like dealing with contractors that are easy to work with. You always want to give them the impression that you are flexible and adaptable. Getting it done *their* way is more important than doing it *your* way.

---

10  Personal communication with Arthur Hull, VMC drum circle training (2005).

## AUTHOR'S BIOGRAPHY
### John J. Hagedorn, BEd., MAT (Linguistics)

John has been a corporate trainer since 1991. In 2004, he introduced drum circles into his teambuilding programs and had a blast. His training with Arthur Hull began in 2005 and since then he has attended 25 Village Music Circle training programs around the world, finally graduating as a certified drum circle facilitator trainer. Arthur Hull's drum circle facilitation process also applies to facilitating learning, and following his philosophy has changed the way John now works with all his different groups.

Better Training Solutions Sdn Bhd

> Email: jhagedorn@bts-my.com
> www.bts-my.com
> Facebook: https://www.facebook.com/BTSMY

MYbeat Drum Circles

> Email: MYbeat@bts-my.com
> www.MYbeat.com.my
> Facebook: www.facebook.com/mybeat.my

## RECOMMENDED READING

Boneau, J. (2020) *The Rumble Zone: leadership strategies in the rough & tumble of change*. Fresno, CA: Ignite Press.

Faulkner, S. (2020) *Workplace Development Manual: Rhythm based exercises for promoting a healthier, happier & more productive workplace*. https://rhythm2recovery.com/products

For understanding corporate training and learning the language:

Cameron, E. (2005) *Facilitation Made Easy*. London: Kogan Page.

# EVALUATION MEASURES

All pages marked with ★ can be photocopied and downloaded at www.jkp.com/catalogue/book/9781787755246

# Appendix 1: Post Session Questionnaire: Participants

Date of event . . . . . . . . . . . . . . . . . . .        Location. . . . . . . . . . . . . . . . . . . . . . . . .

Name. . . . . . . . . . . . . . . . . . . . . . . . . . .        Position . . . . . . . . . . . . . . . . . . . . . . . .
Leave blank if you prefer

Please circle the answer that most resembles your opinion

1. Have you enjoyed your time in the drum circle?

   Yes             Partly            No
   (If not please detail in section 10)

2. Did you feel safe and respected with the facilitator?

   Yes             Partly            No

3. Did your mood improve when you were playing music in the circle?

   Yes             Partly            No

4. Was the facilitator warm and inviting?

   Yes             Partly            No

5. Did you feel a connection with others in the circle?

   Yes             Partly            No

6. Were the sessions the right length for you?

   Yes             Partly            No

7. Was the venue and seating comfortable for you?

   Yes             Partly            No

8. Did you feel uplifted and empowered by the sessions?

   Yes             Partly            No

9. Would you recommend attending a drum circle to others?

   Yes             Partly            No

10. In what ways could we have made this a better experience for you?

   ............................................................
   ............................................................
   ............................................................
   ............................................................
   ............................................................

11. Please write a brief statement describing your experience of the event below:

   ............................................................
   ............................................................
   ............................................................
   ............................................................
   ............................................................

Rate your overall experience below
(Circle your preference)

| Very high | Above average | Average | Below expectations | Poor |
|---|---|---|---|---|

............................................................

# Appendix 2: Post Session Questionnaire: Managers

Date of event . . . . . . . . . . . . . . . . . . .      Location. . . . . . . . . . . . . . . . . . . . . . . . .

Name. . . . . . . . . . . . . . . . . . . . . . . . . .      Position . . . . . . . . . . . . . . . . . . . . . . . . .

1. Did the event meet your expectations?

   Yes          Partly          No
   (If not please detail in section 10)

2. Was the facilitator professional in their conduct?

   Yes          Partly          No

3. Did the participants benefit from their attendance?

   Yes          Partly          No

4. Was the facilitator warm and inviting?

   Yes          Partly          No

5. Did the facilitator have a clear understanding of the participants' needs?

   Yes          Partly          No

6. Were the participants empowered by this session?

   Yes          Partly          No

7. Were the participants uplifted by this session?

   Yes          Partly          No

8. Was communication by the facilitator in the lead up to the session clear and prompt?

   Yes          Partly          No

9. Would you recommend our work to others

   Yes          Partly          No

Copyright © Simon Faulkner – *Drum Circles for Specific Population Groups* – 2021

10. Were there areas in which we could improve our work? If so, please detail below

...............................................................
...............................................................
...............................................................
...............................................................
...............................................................

11. Please write a brief statement describing your experience of the event.

...............................................................
...............................................................
...............................................................
...............................................................
...............................................................

Rate your overall experience below
(Circle your preference)

| Very high | Above average | Average | Below expectations | Poor |
|---|---|---|---|---|

# Appendix 3: Feedback from Third Parties

## (TEACHERS, CLINICIANS, PARENTS, ETC.)

Date........................    Name ........................

Please rate your assessment of the following participants on a scale of 1 to 10 with 5 being no change, 1 being significant detrimental change and 10 being significant positive change

1   2   3   4   5   6   7   8   9   10

| Participant name | General mood | Level of self-control | Level of self-esteem | Level of attention & focus | Level of social comfort | Level of social interaction | Level of collaboration with others |
|---|---|---|---|---|---|---|---|
|  |  |  |  |  |  |  |  |
|  |  |  |  |  |  |  |  |
|  |  |  |  |  |  |  |  |
|  |  |  |  |  |  |  |  |
|  |  |  |  |  |  |  |  |
|  |  |  |  |  |  |  |  |
|  |  |  |  |  |  |  |  |
|  |  |  |  |  |  |  |  |
|  |  |  |  |  |  |  |  |
|  |  |  |  |  |  |  |  |

Participants' names will be de-identified after research

# Appendix 4: How Are We Doing?

Date.......................... Name............................

Circle the image that fits.
(Program coordinator may read the questions and instructions out loud.)

1. Do you think the drum circle is helping you?
   ☹   😐   ☺

2. Do you feel safe and respected in the drum circle?
   ☹   😐   ☺

3. Do you think we are working well together as a group?
   ☹   😐   ☺

4. How are you doing generally? Do you feel as if you are moving forward, standing still or going backwards?
   ☹   😐   ☺

5. How are your relationships with other people? Do you feel these are improving, standing still or getting weaker?
   ☹   😐   ☺

6. How are you doing emotionally? Do you feel more stable, just the same or more vulnerable?
   ☹   😐   ☺

7. Would you like to continue doing drum circle work?
   ☹   😐   ☺

Copyright © Simon Faulkner – *Drum Circles for Specific Population Groups* – 2021

# Recommended Reading

At the conclusion of each section we have asked participants to nominate books that have been important to them in their work with the population group they specialize in. Many of these books are not drum circle related, but more about the issues of working with these populations generally. This section details drum circle related literature only.

Balfour, M., Bartleet, M.L., Davey, L., Rynne, J. & Schippers, H. (eds) (2019) *Performing Arts in Prisons*. Bristol: Intellect.

Clottey, K. (2003) *Mindful Drumming*. Oakland, CA: Sankofa Publishing.

Das, K. (2004) *Together in Rhythm: A Facilitator's Guide to Drum Circle Music*. Van Nuys, CA: Alfred Music.

Das, K. (2005) *The Amazing Jamnasium: A Playful Companion to Together in Rhythm*. Van Nuys, CA: Alfred Music.

Drake, M. (2014) *Shamanic Drumming Circles Guide*. USA: Talking Drum Publications.

Faulkner, S.C. (2016) *Rhythm to Recovery – A Practical Guide to Using Rhythmic Music, Voice and Movement for Social and Emotional Development*. London: Jessica Kingsley Publishers.

Faulkner, S.C. (2018) 'Therapeutic applications for integrating rhythm and reflection in support of people with co-occurring drug and alcohol, and mental health issues.' *Dual Diagnosis Open Access 3*, 2, 4.

Hill, N. & Hull, A. (2011) *Drum circle Facilitator's Hand Book*. Santa Cruz, CA: Village Music Circles.

Holland, D. (2007) *Drumimagination: A Rhythmic Play Book for Music Teachers, Music Therapists and Drum Circle Facilitators*. USA: Dave Holland & Beating Path. www.interactiverhythm.com.

Holland, D. (2011) *Interactive Rhythm: Games, Songs and Interactions for the Music Educator, Music Therapist and Drum Circle Facilitator*. USA: Dave Holland & Beating Path. www.interactiverhythm.com.

Holland, D. (2015) *Body Jammin' – A Rhythm Facilitator's Guide to Portable Percussion*. USA: Dave Holland & Beating Path. www.interactiverhythm.com.

Hull, A. (2007) *Drum Circle Facilitation – Building Community through Rhythm*. Santa Cruz, CA: Village Music Circles.

Knysh, M, (2017) *Innovative Drum circles: Beyond Beat into Harmony*. Millville, PA: Rhythmic Connections Publications.

Knysh, M. & Leathley, L. (2017) *1, 2, Let's All Play: Music Activities for Pre-School and Primary Grades*. Vancouver, BC: LuluJam.

MacTavish, H. & Balsara, Z. (2011) *Songs, Science and Spirit: Musical Keys to Open Special Doors of Ability*. USA: Provident Publishing.

Matney, B.B. (2007) *Tataku – The Use of Percussion in Music Therapy*. Winchester: Sarsen Publishing.

Perkins, R., Ascenso, S., Atkins, L., Fancourt, D. & Williamon, A. (2016) 'Making music for mental health: How group drumming mediates recovery.' *Psych Well-Being* 6, 11. https://doi.org/10.1186/s13612-016-0048-0.

Ratigan, S.L. (2009) *A Practical Guide to Hand Drumming and Drum circles*. Available on Amazon Kindle & Barnes & Noble Nook.

Stevens, C. (2003) *The Art and Heart of Drum Circles*. Milwaukee, WI: Hal Leonard.

Stevens, C. (2012) *Music Medicine – The Science and Spirit of Healing Yourself with Sound*. Louisville, CO: Sounds True.

Wolf, Z. (2015) *Whole Person Drumming: Your Journey into Rhythm*. USA: Publishing-Partners.

For additional research on the benefits of the drum circle, visit www.rhythmresearchresources.net.